Suzanne Kirschner traces the origins of contemporary psychoanalysis back to the foundations of Judaeo-Christian culture, and challenges the prevailing view that modern theories of the self mark a radical break with religious and cultural tradition. She argues instead that they offer an account of human development which has its beginnings in Biblical theology and Neoplatonic mysticism. Drawing on a wide range of religious, literary, philosophical, and anthropological sources, Dr. Kirschner demonstrates that current American psychoanalytic theories are but the latest version of a narrative that has been progressively secularized over the course of nearly two millennia. She displays a deep understanding of psychoanalytic theories, while at the same time raising provocative questions about their status as knowledge and as science.

The religious and romantic origins of psychoanalysis

Cambridge Cultural Social Studies

General editors: JEFFREY C. ALEXANDER, *Department of Sociology, University of California, Los Angeles, and* STEVEN SEIDMAN, *Department of Sociology, State University of New York, Albany*

Editorial Board
JEAN COMAROFF, *Department of Anthropology, University of Chicago*
DONNA HARAWAY, *Department of the History of Consciousness, University of California, Santa Cruz*
MICHELE LAMONT, *Department of Sociology, Princeton University*
THOMAS LAQUEUR, *Department of History, University of California, Berkeley*

Cambridge Cultural Social Studies is a forum for the most original and thoughtful work in cultural social studies. This includes theoretical works focusing on conceptual strategies, empirical studies covering specific topics such as gender, sexuality, politics, economics, social movements, and crime, and studies that address broad themes such as the culture of modernity. While the perspectives of the individual studies will vary, they will all share the same innovative reach and scholarly quality.

The religious and romantic origins of psychoanalysis

Individuation and integration in post-Freudian theory

Suzanne R. Kirschner
Harvard University

CAMBRIDGE
UNIVERSITY PRESS

Published by the Press Syndicate of the University of Cambridge
The Pitt Building, Trumpington Street, Cambridge CB2 1RP
40 West 20th Street, New York, NY 10011-4211, USA
10 Stamford Road, Oakleigh, Melbourne 3166, Australia

First published 1996

Printed in Great Britain at the University Press, Cambridge

A catalogue record for this book is available from the British Library

Library of Congress cataloguing in publication data

Kirschner, Suzanne R.
   The religious and romantic origins of psychoanalysis:
individuation and integration in post-Freudian theory/Suzanne R.
Kirschner.
      p.   cm. – (Cambridge cultural social studies)
Includes bibliographical references and index.
ISBN 0 521 44401 2 (hc)
     0 521 55560 4 (pbk)
1. Psychoanalysis – History. 2. Psychoanalysis and religion.
3. Psychoanalysis and culture.   4. Individuation (Psychology)
I. Title. II. Series.
BF173.K437 1996
150.19′5′09–dc20 – 95-16490 CIP

ISBN 0 521 44401 2 hardback

ISBN 0 521 55560 4 paperback

For Helen Kirschner Berke
and
Leonard N. Evenchik

... we still live in what is essentially, although in derivative rather than direct manifestations, a Biblical culture, and readily mistake our hereditary ways of organizing experience for the conditions of reality and the universal forms of thought.

M.H. Abrams,
Natural Supernaturalism

Weber was so intent upon establishing the unique predominance in the West of the penetration and remaking of the world to innerworldly asceticism that he failed to give enough weight to another fact that he no less than Troeltsch implicitly recognized. Weber does not ... in his work sufficiently stress the significance of *innerworldly mysticism* as contrasted with otherworldly mysticisms.

Benjamin Nelson,
"Max Weber, Ernst Troeltsch,
Georg Jellinek as Comparative
Historical Sociologists"

Contents

Acknowledgements

I owe a great debt to many of my teachers. In the classrooms of the late Lucy Swallow, Ruthe Spinninger, Sandra Shaw, and the late Ellen Silberblatt Edwards, I first learned to appreciate many of the literary, religious, and psychological writings that are explored in this study. Ellen Edwards was a particularly important teacher and friend; with this book I hope I honor her memory. At Swarthmore College, I was fortunate to be taught about psychological theory by Kenneth Gergen, Dean Peabody, Jeanne Marecek, and Barry Schwartz, and about Romanticism by Harold Pagliaro and the late Eugene Weber. At Harvard, Robert LeVine was a wonderful model of multidisciplinary erudition and breadth; it was he who first encouraged me to explore both Romanticism and Protestantism as sources of contemporary American ideas about childhood and child development. Also at Harvard, Carol Gilligan inspired me with her visionary work and style of thought, and offered gracious encouragement of my ideas. Others who have provided helpful feedback and/or various forms of support include Jamie Walkup, Bernard Kaplan, Sheldon White, the anonymous reviewer who read the manuscript for Cambridge University Press, Donald Spence, Robert Paul, Gananath Obeyesekere, Louis Sass, John Christopher, Philip Cushman, David Spain, Jeannette Mageo, Suzanne Golden, Merry White, Lewis Wurgaft, Andrea Walsh, Terry Aladjem, Pratap Bhanu Mehta, and my colleagues in the Committee on Degrees in Social Studies at Harvard. I especially wish to thank Stanley Kurtz, a trusted friend and valued colleague, for his most useful suggestions. A Larsen Doctoral Research Fellowship, awarded by the Harvard Graduate School of Education, helped to fund this project during its earliest stages. Needless to say, not all of the scholars named above would fully concur with all of the arguments made in this book, and the usual disclaimers apply.

I also thank Julia Hough (who did not know that she and I had once been classmates in Pagliaro's Romantic poetry class), Emily Loose, and Jeffrey Alexander, who first saw merit in the manuscript; Steven Seidman for his endorsement of this project, his patience, and his extremely useful comments; Catherine Max for her perceptive editorial guidance; Sandy Anthony for her thoughtful and erudite copyediting; and Rachel Bundang for her assistance with the proofs.

A slightly different version of Chapter 2 was published under the same title in *Social Research*, vol. 1, no. 4, Winter 1990; this version appears here with the permission of *Social Research*. Portions of Chapters 4 and 8 appear as "Sources of Redemption in Psychoanalytic Developmental Psychology," in Kenneth J. Gergen and Carl F. Graumann (eds.), *Historical Dimensions of Psychological Discourse* (Cambridge: Cambridge University Press, 1996); they are reprinted with the permission of Cambridge University Press.

Kenneth Gergen, more than anyone else, inspired me to take my interest in theoretical and philosophical psychology to the graduate level and to make it my "calling." For that, and for his generosity and enduring faith in me, I am deeply grateful. I am grateful, too, to Leonard Evenchik, who has been a constant, loving source of help and encouragement. Finally, I am indebted beyond words to my parents, Helen Kirschner Berke and the late Ludwig Kirschner, for the examples they have set and for their unfailing support.

Introduction

In contemporary society, many of us look to psychoanalysis to tell us the truth about ourselves. Even with the current ascendance of biological models in psychiatry, both Freudian and post-Freudian approaches remain powerfully attractive to many clinicians, scholars and laypersons; they continue to exert a strong hold on our cultural and scientific imaginations. What accounts for these theories' resonance and appeal? In this book I suggest that much of the compelling quality of contemporary psychoanalysis derives from the fact that it is deeply rooted in Western religious and cultural values.

Received wisdom has long held that psychoanalytic conceptions of the self and its development embody a radical break with our Judaeo-Christian spiritual heritage. A broader perspective on the history of ideas, however, reveals that these psychological theories tell the story of human development in terms of a distinctive narrative pattern, a pattern that is derived from Biblical history and Greek mysticism. In the pages that follow I demonstrate how, over the course of nearly two thousand years, an originally religious story about the soul's fall away from God and reunion with him was transformed into a modern secular theory about the life and growth of the self.

At first glance it is not obvious that our ancient religious doctrines and our modern psychoanalytic pronouncements belong to the same cultural family. However, their genealogical connection becomes clearer and easier to grasp when we consider that the transmutation of spiritual narrative into psychological theory did not happen all at once. It took place over many hundreds of years, in a series of steps that coincided with the secularization of our culture. A key transitional period in the history of that secularization was the Romantic era. Romanticism was the great pivot-point in Western spiritual history. In the years immediately following the American and French revolutions, numerous artists and thinkers, disillusioned by what they perceived to be the broken promises and failed utopias of the Enlightenment and the emerging modern world, translated key religious themes and values into non-theological terms. The "soul" was refigured as the "mind" or the "self," and God receded from view. The traditional religious quest for redemption also was re-envisioned by these Romantic poets and philosophers. They asserted that salvation was not something we would find in heaven; rather, they claimed, we must seek our saving graces in this world: in our art, in our loves, in our selves. It was the Romantics, then, who took the old stories of heaven and hell, of paradises lost and apocalypses to come, and refashioned them into a new (but still recognizably Judaeo-Christian) cultural language.

To the degree that we continue to seek some measure of salvation in our everyday lives and emotional attachments – to the degree that we earnestly and attentively scan our selves and our relationships for the worldly redemptions they might yield – we are all heirs to the Romantics' quest. During the past century, psychoanalytic approaches, particularly those that have flourished in the Unitd States, have further extended and promoted the Romantic imperative of self-development and worldly fulfillment. Thus they too articulate the dilemmas of human existence, along with the prospects for their mitigation, in terms of an inherited Biblical template. To a far greater degree than is generally recognized, psychoanalysis is a product of those same religious and spiritual traditions whose authority it has helped to undermine.

It is tempting to seek a moral in this story of psychoanalytic theories' cultural and spiritual entanglements. Some readers may scan this history hoping to find support for the view that psychoanalysis is invalid because the lens through which it examines the self is clouded by cultural prejudice and ideological bias. Others, by contrast, may try to use the genealogical documentation I provide to unequivocally endorse psychoanalysis's legitimacy and value. But as the reader of this book will discover, there are good reasons to resist both of these easy conclusions.

1

Towards a cultural genealogy of psychoanalytic developmental psychology

Theories of human development are fascinating objects of cultural history because they possess a dual nature. One side of this duality is readily apparent: contemporary developmentalist models[1] are predicated on a disenchanted, naturalistic view of the world and thus display a distinctively modern character. These theories, like their late nineteenth-century predecessors,[2] were conceived with the confident expectation that psychologists would substitute science for folk knowledge, rational-empirical understanding for cultural canon and religious belief. Where tradition and faith were, there would social science be.

Yet at the same time as the new science of child psychology resulted from, and was intended to further advance, a radical break with older

[1] The phrase "contemporary developmentalist models" is used here to denote three psychological paradigms: cognitive-developmental theories that trace the development of reasoning about the physical and social worlds (such theories are built on the work of Jean Piaget; those who have worked within this framework include Lawrence Kohlberg, Carol Gilligan, Robert Selman, William Damon, and others); the organismic theory of Heinz Werner; and psychoanalytic theories, particularly those aspects and branches of psychoanalysis that trace the development of the ego or self and its modes of relating to others.

It can be argued that the most basic developmentalist assumptions pervade not only these models, but virtually all other psychological theories as well. Thus the child psychologist William Kessen has argued that even learning theories evince developmentalist assumptions (see Chapter 4). However, the intricacies of the narrative I highlight here are peculiar to those theories that are more strictly termed developmental; more specifically still, my focus is on the structure and genealogy of the psychoanalytic developmental narrative.

[2] The proto-developmentalists included G. Stanley Hall, the founder of the child study movement (Hall, then President of Clark University, was the man who invited Freud and members of his circle to visit America in 1909), James Mark Baldwin, George Romanes, and Ivan Sechnov. See, e.g., Sheldon White, "The Idea of Development in Developmental Psychology," in Richard Lerner (ed.), *Developmental Psychology: Historical and Philosophical Perspectives* (Hillsdale, NJ: Lawrence Erlbaum Associates, 1983).

understandings of the person and the human condition, in fact that break was by no means a complete or absolute one. The history of the idea of development has not been just a history of rupture with the past, but also a history of continuity. Contemporary developmentalist models are structured in terms of an inherited vocabulary drawn from much older – in some respects ancient – cultural reservoirs.

In this book I focus on this second aspect of developmental psychology's nature: its continuity with older cultural forms. I explore how a particular group of developmentalist models, psychoanalytic theories of the development of the self, are structured in terms of a culturally constituted, centuries-old spiritual narrative. The narrative pattern in question appears to have originated in the Christian mystical story of the movement of the soul towards salvation. Over the course of nearly two millennia, this template has undergone several successive waves of transmutation. It has become increasingly secularized and interiorized (i.e., seen as pertaining to the history of the individual soul, mind, or self, rather than to the history of an entire group or the human race), yet to this day it retains certain characteristic features.

Chief among those features is a distinctive plot structure. I explicate that structure and trace its cultural genealogy. In other words, I demonstrate the linkage of themes and patterns found in current psychoanalytic theories to older sources within the culture, delineating the various transformations and branchings that the original theological narrative has undergone over the centuries. In its earliest form, that narrative chronicles man's[3] creation, fall out of unity with God, and redemption via reunion with God. It has been transformed or assimilated into newer doctrines, and those doctrines into still newer ones.

Four successive versions of the doctrine – four historical "moments" – are examined in order to chart the narrative's transmutations over time. The earliest version is the Christian mystical doctrine of mankind's fall and ultimate redemption. This narrative resulted from the intermingling of two different theological traditions: the Biblical story of human history and destiny, and the speculative theodicy of the third century pagan philosopher Plotinus (Neoplatonism). During the early modern period, a significantly modified version of the narrative emerged. Neoplatonized Biblical history took on a more worldly and interiorized cast, as can be seen in the writings of radical Protestant mystics. An important figure

---

[3] Most of the theologians, theorists, and artists I discuss in this book were writing when it was the unquestioned convention to use the terms "man" or "mankind" to denote the "generic human" or "all human beings." For that reason, I retain those terms in my explications of these thinkers' doctrines, theories, or systems.

during this transitional era was Jacob Boehme, a seventeenth century Silesian who is widely considered to be the father of Protestant mysticism. Boehme's teachings are used to exemplify the second moment in the history I trace. The definitive secularization of the narrative was effected during the early nineteenth century by English and German Romantic philosophers and men of letters. Selections from Romantic texts are used to illustrate this third, very striking moment in the history of the narrative's diachronic transformations.

Finally, a fourth link is added to this genealogical chain, that link being the story of development as told by contemporary Anglo-American psychoanalytic theorists (ego psychologists, object-relations theorists and self psychologists). I explore the ways in which these theoretical models partake of this same narrative pattern, while they take even farther the secularizing and interiorizing trends evinced by their cultural forebears. Thus, by a sort of principle of transitivity, I argue that in spite of the very tangible social, economic, and cultural transformations that European–American civilization has undergone during the past two millennia, these modern theories of human development are heir to much older spiritual and cultural structures and themes.

Long-standing cultural themes persist not only in the plot structure of psychoanalytic developmental theories, but also in the ends or goals of development as depicted in those theories. In this book, those goals – self-reliance, authenticity and intimacy – also are shown to be intertwined with cultural images and values. Self-reliance and self-direction (authenticity) are revealed as Anglo-American ideals, explicitly prescribed patterns of self-reflection and social interaction. These visions of ideal personhood are diffused throughout American (and to a lesser degree and with some variation, English) culture. They are "commonsense" for many in Anglo-American culture areas, but they are by no means universal in their reach or desirability. And, as in the case of the developmental narrative itself, these contemporary ideals also are drawn, albeit only in part, from older religious motifs. The ideals of self-reliance, self-direction, and even intimacy are articulated in terms that recapitulate several Judaeo-Christian images of salvation. Specifically, these images of the ideal self are secularized versions of Protestant ascetic and mystical visions of the soul's election by God or reunion with him.

Thus both the plot structure and the substantive goals of the psychological narrative bear the imprint of a Judaeo-Christian (and, in particular, radical Protestant) template. But psychoanalytic developmental theory's linkage to its theological past goes beyond the fact that it is shaped in terms of received images and preexisting narrative forms. For the psychoanalytic narrative also is kin to its spiritual forebears in that, like them, it offers a powerful vision of the human condition. Both types of narrative – psychological theory as much as theological doctrine – embody attempts to delineate and address the deepest and most difficult existential issues that human beings face: suffering, loss, frustration, and various forms of moral "evil." Both can be seen as forms of what Max Weber (referring to explicitly religious doctrines) called "theodicy,"[4] i.e., systematic doctrines through which the existence of all forms of human suffering and the imperfections of human life are addressed and imbued with meaning. A theodicy constructs the dilemmas of human existence along certain lines and offers the possibility of their resolution (e.g., salvation) or mitigation along similarly structured lines. In this study, then, I emphasize the persistence of a culturally distinctive version of theodicy in contemporary psychoanalytic theory, and thereby highlight the latter's status as a secular theodicy, a way of constructing issues of ultimate concern.[5]

Challenges to the objectivist view of psychological theory

To underscore these theories' continuity with a premodern cultural past – in structure, in thematic substance, and even in function – is to call into question the conventional (if often tacit) self-image of psychoanalytic developmental psychology. According to that conventional image, these models of human development depict empirical realities that have been discovered through the observation of behavior or the reconstruction of individuals' biographical histories. In other words, we tend to assume an objectivist and naturalist view of psychological knowledge, including psychoanalytic knowledge. Objectivism (here defined by philosopher Richard Bernstein) holds that "knowledge is achieved when a subject [the

---

[4] "The Social Psychology of the World Religions," p. 274 and "Religious Rejections of the World and Their Directions," pp. 358–9, in Hans Gerth and C. Wright Mills (eds.), *From Max Weber: Essays in Sociology* (New York: Oxford University Press, 1976). For additional discussion of the theodicy concept, see Chapter 4.

[5] Sociologists and anthropologists of religion, as well as theologians, have offered a variety of interpretations of the "meanings" and "functions" of religious discourse. Certainly there are many ways of studying the social and cultural meanings of formal religious rhetoric and its deployment in practice. I am not suggesting that theodicy is the only meaning of religious discourse (any more than it is the only meaning or use of psychology). But I am one with Weber in deeming it a deep and consequential one. When we try to analyze religious or psychological models and classification schemes only as enactments of social order or power, or solely in terms of the pragmatics of their deployment in concrete social or historical situations, we risk losing sight of this other crucial dimension of their meaning, persistence, and subjective salience.

knower] correctly mirrors or represents objective reality."[6] Closely allied with objectivism is naturalism; as stated by the psychologist and historian Kurt Danziger, the naturalist position is that "psychological events have fixed natural forms, which a few lucky philosophers and an army of systematic investigators have found and labeled. Thus, to each label there corresponds a fixed natural form."[7] The objectivist-naturalist model is not the only available perspective on the nature of knowledge or even of science, but most of us – psychologists and non-psychologists alike – tend to speak, write, and work as if it were. Thus when we grant legitimacy and authority to a particular model of human nature and social life, we tend to assume that that model mirrors an essential reality found in the world or in the mind.

By contrast, the genealogical perspective offered in this book suggests that the contours of the psychoanalytic developmental trajectory are derived less from empirical observation than from the redeployment of a preexisting cultural template to a new context, the recently delineated domain of the psychological. It suggests that current psychoanalytic depictions of the self's development explicate a pattern that has been reassigned rather than discovered. A corollary of this is that the theories' language is better understood as structuring analog than as reflecting mirror.

In making this claim about these psychoanalytic theories, I do not mean to single them out as unique in this respect. The adequacy of objectivism as a theory of knowledge increasingly has come to be challenged for all forms of psychological and social theory, and arguably for knowledge in other domains as well. The problematizing of objectivism has been a central project of many influential philosophers during the twentieth century.[8] This concern has been shared by theorists associated with a variety of philosophical and theoretical movements, including ordinary language philosophy,[9] postempiricist philosophy of science,[10] ontological

---

[6] Richard Bernstein, *Beyond Objectivism and Relativism* (Philadelphia: University of Pennsylvania Press, 1983), p. 9.

[7] Kurt Danziger, "Generative Metaphor in the History of Psychology," in David E. Leary (ed.), *Metaphors in the History of Psychology* (Cambridge: Cambridge University Press, 1990), pp. 334–5.

[8] For overviews of the history of challenges to objectivism, see Bernstein, *Beyond Objectivism and Relativism* and Richard Rorty, *Philosophy and the Mirror of Nature* (Princeton: Princeton University Press, 1979). See also George Lakoff, *Women, Fire and Dangerous Things* (Chicago: University of Chicago Press, 1987).

[9] Ludwig Wittgenstein, *Philosophical Investigations*, trans. G. Anscombe (Oxford: Basil Blackwell, 1953).

[10] Thomas Kuhn, *The Structure of Scientific Revolutions* (2nd edn. enl., Chicago: University of Chicago Press, 1970); Mary Hesse, *Revolutions and Reconstructions in the Philosophy of Science* (Brighton, England: Harvester Press, 1980); Paul Feyerabend, *Against Method: Outline of an Anarchistic Theory of Knowledge* (London: NLB, 1975).

hermeneutics,[11] social constructionism,[12] poststructuralism,[13] postmodernism,[14] and neopragmatism.[15] These movements, like the philosophers from whom they claim descent (chiefly Nietszche, Wittgenstein, Heidegger and Dewey) diverge from one another on significant points. "Even taken together," write the editors of *The Rhetoric of the Human Sciences*, "these writers are nothing like a school – unless common enemies make a school."[16] But they do share in the endeavor to undermine naturalistic epistemology (in Danziger's sense that "to each label there corresponds a fixed natural form"). And, in one way or another, they all aim to replace such naturalism with an emphasis on language, social life, culture and history as generative sources of our knowledge, particularly our social knowledge.[17]

The metaphorical character of psychological knowledge

The increasing prominence and influence of these anti-objectivist accounts has prompted an intensified celebration of an old insight – the central role of metaphor in the constitution of knowledge. The historian

[11] Martin Heidegger, *Being and Time*, trans. J. Macquarrie and E. Robinson (New York: Harper and Row, 1962); Hans-Georg Gadamer, *Truth and Method*, trans. G. Burden and J. Cumming (New York: Seabury Press, 1975); Charles Taylor, "Interpretation and the Sciences of Man," in Paul Rabinow and William M. Sullivan, *Interpretive Social Science: A Reader* (Berkeley, CA: University of California Press, 1979), pp. 25–71. See also Stanley B. Messer, Louis A. Sass and Robert L. Woolfolk (eds.), *Hermeneutics and Psychological Theory: Interpretive Perspectives on Personality, Psychotherapy, and Psychopathology* (New Brunswick: Rutgers University Press, 1988).

[12] Kenneth J. Gergen, "The Social Constructionist Movement in Modern Psychology," *American Psychologist*, vol. 40, 1985, pp. 266–75 and "Introduction: Towards Metapsychology," in Henderikus J. Stam, Timothy B. Rogers, and Kenneth J. Gergen (eds.), *The Analysis of Psychological Theory: Metapsychological Perspectives* (Washington: Hemisphere Publishing Co., 1987), pp. 1–21; Edward E. Sampson, "The Deconstruction of the Self," in John Shotter and Kenneth J. Gergen (eds.), *Texts of Identity* (London: Sage, 1989), pp. 1–19; John Shotter, *Social Accountability and Selfhood* (Oxford: Basil Blackwell, 1984).

[13] Michel Foucault, *The Order of Things* (New York: Vintage Books, 1970) and "What is an Author?" in *Language, Counter-Memory, Practice*, ed. Donald F. Buchard (Ithaca: Cornell University Press, 1977), pp. 113–38; Jacques Derrida, *Of Grammatology*, trans. G. Spivak (Baltimore: Johns Hopkins University Press, 1976).

[14] Jean-Francois Lyotard, *The Postmodern Condition: A Report on Knowledge*, trans. Geoff Bennington and Brian Massouri (Minneapolis: University of Minnesota Press, 1984).

[15] Richard Rorty, *Philosophy and the Mirror of Nature* (Princeton: Princeton University Press, 1979).

[16] John S. Nelson, Allan Megill and Donald N. McCloskey (eds.), *The Rhetoric of the Human Sciences: Language and Argument in Scholarship and Public Affairs* (Madison: University of Wisconsin Press, 1987), p. 11.

[17] For a brief discussion of how several of these anti-objectivist perspectives might consider the implications of this genealogical approach to the psychoanalytic narrative, see Chapter 9.

of psychology David Leary offers this definition: "Metaphor consists in giving to one thing a name or description that belongs by convention to something else, on the grounds of some similarity between the two."[18] Invoking a long line of thinkers (beginning with Aristotle), as well as current understandings of the nature of language, Leary argues that the allegedly hard distinction between literal and metaphorical language is an inaccurate one. Literalness and metaphoricity are matters of degree more than kind, and there is "continual commerce between these two poles."[19] In everyday language as in theoretical knowledge, today's literal terms were yesterday's metaphors.

Comparison and analogy thus play a central role in all thought, psychological theories being no exception. Such an appreciation of psychology's metaphoricity contributes to the anti-naturalist critique, particularly when it is recognized that metaphors have what Danziger calls a "generative" function.[20] For when we look more closely at how metaphors are used to delineate psychological entities or processes, we see that the process is not simply a matter of static comparison. Rather, once a "root" metaphor[21] has been set in place, it continues to be elaborated and thereby to structure subsequent investigations and the findings they yield. Metaphors, Danziger reminds us, bring together not two "specific words describing specific features of the world," but rather "two *systems* of implications":

What is involved is not simply a comparison of two units, which could be reduced to a literal statement, but an application to the one subject of a whole set of implications previously linked with the other subject: ... [T]he notion of generative metaphor ... suggests that we treat the objects of psychological discourse not as things that were lying around waiting to be discovered, but as the product of generative schemata applied across various domains.[22]

---

[18] Leary, Introduction, *Metaphors*, pp. 1–78, p. 4. In this book, I follow what Leary terms his "broad definition" of metaphor, which, he writes, "encompasses a variety of other figures of speech. Indeed, according to the above definition, metaphor can hardly be distinguished from trope (figure of speech) in general. Furthermore, a consequence of this definition is that such things as fables, parables, allegories, myths, and models, including scientific models, can be seen, by implication, as 'extended and sustained metaphors' [Turbayne, 1970, pp. 1–20]." (Leary, *Metaphors*, p. 5).

[19] Ibid., p. 6. See also George Lakoff and Mark Johnson, *Metaphors We Live By* (Chicago: University of Chicago Press, 1980).

[20] Danziger, "Generative Metaphor in the History of Psychology," in Leary, *Metaphors*; he follows Stephen Pepper, *World Hypotheses: A Study in Evidence* (Berkeley: University of California Press, 1942), and Max Black, *Models and Metaphors* (Ithaca, NY: Cornell University Press, 1962) and "More about Metaphor," in A. Ortony (ed.), *Metaphor and Thought* (Cambridge: Cambridge University Press, 1979), pp. 19–43.

[21] The term is Stephen Pepper's; Danziger uses it in "Generative Metaphor," p. 334.

[22] Danziger, "Generative Metaphor," pp. 334–5.

Once a root metaphor is invoked and "naturalized," "a whole complex of knowledge and belief," associated with the first domain, is brought to bear on the psychological domain that is likened to it.[23]

Thus, in the case of psychoanalytic developmental psychology, we will see that the development of the self implicitly has been likened to the Judaeo-Christian mystical theodicy. The developmental trajectory is compared, step by step, to the episodes of the soul's necessary fall and progression, while the ends of development are framed in terms derived from depictions of salvation. The movement of the self through the life course (a phrase that already contains a few metaphors) is construed to resemble the soul's fall away from paradise and its movement back towards greater moral and spiritual proximity to God. Actually, as will be shown, this is too crude a way of describing the analogy at work here. For there are at least two generations of the root narrative that can be detected in the psychoanalytic theories: not only the Christian mystical story, but also its secularized variant, the Romantic spiral or *Bildung*. In the Romantic spiral, the religious terms are recast into natural and secular ones, and some features of the narrative pattern are significantly modified. Instead of being a story about the soul, it is a tale of the mind's estrangement from nature and gradual development towards reintegration with nature at a higher level. Most of the time, the psychoanalytic narrative is depicted in terms that implicitly portray it as being similar to this Romantic spiral, which is explicated in Chapter 7. As will be explained, Romanticism provided the accessible and acceptable vocabulary from which analytic theorists drew and from which they continue to draw, often without apparent awareness.

To underscore the crucial role of generative metaphor in the growth and elaboration of psychological theory is not to deny the existence of reality, of a world that is "external" to human perception. The anti-naturalist perspective discussed here is, in fact, compatible with a commitment to a non-objectivist form of what linguist George Lakoff calls "basic realism."[24] But it does hold that we engage with much of that

---

[23] Ibid., p. 334.

[24] Lakoff asserts that "[b]asic realism [of which objectivism is an increasingly discredited form, but not the only form] involves at least the following:
- a commitment to the existence of a real world, both external to human beings and including the reality of human experience
- a link of some sort between human conceptual systems and other aspects of reality
- a conception of truth that is not merely based on internal coherence
- a commitment to the existence of stable knowledge of the external world
- a rejection of the view that 'anything goes' – that any conceptual system is as good as any other."

Lakoff notes that "objectivism...is one version of basic realism," but not the only sort. He advocates an alternative version called "experientialism." (*Women, Fire, and Dangerous Things*, p. 158).

reality only and always through the use of metaphor and related imaginative devices.[25] It also should be noted that the focus on rhetoric, in this book, is not to be taken as an assertion that the study of (articulated or implicit) metaphors alone can provide a complete account of the circumstances and influences surrounding the production and deployment of scientific, social, or psychological knowledge. In addition to scrutinizing the rhetoric of psychology, scholars also need to attend to psychology's and psychiatry's pragmatics – to the practical circumstances, institutional dynamics, and various forms of micro- and macrosocial relations that influence psychological theories' construction, deployment in clinical practice and everyday talk, and revision.[26] Nonetheless, it remains important to attend specifically to the rhetoric as well, because when a particular generative metaphor is invoked and routinized, it does structure and limit researchers' and practitioners' engagement with social and psychological reality in highly significant and consequential ways.

The generative metaphors utilized by natural and social scientists are derived from a multiplicity of sources. There are many different types of factors, including historical and social influences, that affect why a particular analog is put into play to delineate an entity or a process. Neither the selection nor the persistence of a given generative framework, in the social sciences at least, can be explained solely or fully in terms of the metaphor's "robustness," its instrumental consequences or its pragmatic utility. Hence, as is explained in Chapter 4, psychologists' invocation of the Judaeo-Christian narrative of the soul's fall and progress (and of its secular variants) to initiate the scientific study of mental and emotional growth is not attributable simply to some pragmatic goodness-of-fit between the metaphor and the reality. Rather, the selection of this generative metaphor[27] owes much to the moral and existential concerns and hopes that psychologists and others brought, and continue to bring, to the study of development. For at the close of the nineteenth century, and arguably still today, many in our society were feeling the lingering aftershocks of secularization and disenchantment. The social sciences in general, and the emerging fields of child development and the study of the "psyche" in particular, were coming to be invested with the visions, the functions and the aspirations that heretofore had been the province of theology.

[25] See Lakoff, Ibid., pp. 302–3.
[26] See Leary, *Metaphors,* pp. 358–9.
[27] Psychologists and analysts often construe their generative metaphor as a Darwinian-evolutionary one. In fact, however, as is explained in Chapter 4, the narrative of development has teleological features that Darwin never endorsed and that derive from the design of Biblical history.

Consequences of reification

Some of our greatest psychological theorists, including Sigmund Freud and William James, recognized (much of the time, at least) the metaphorical nature of the frameworks they created.[28] But with the rise and dominance of positivism (another variant of objectivism) in American psychology during the better part of the twentieth century, the analogical foundations of psychological theory apparently were forgotten or denied.[29] The quasi-medicalization of psychoanalysis has promoted essentially the same effect. During the past decade, the psychoanalyst Donald Spence has been an eloquent and influential voice reminding us about the metaphoricity, and the limitations, of some central Freudian constructs.[30] Spence's work has gained wide attention; yet his and other theorists'[31] related insights have not been assmilated on a broad scale into the self-understanding of psychoanalytic psychologists, or indeed into what philosophers Richard Bernstein and Charles Taylor call "mainstream social science."[32] We continue to reify our psychological

---

[28] See Leary, *Metaphors* (pp. 18–21 and 41–50), for a discussion of Freud's use of metaphors and his awareness of the metaphorical nature of his theories. Leary depicts Freud as something of a pragmatist in his orientation to both the aims of knowledge and the goals of therapy (albeit one who believed the metaphors used in scientific language could advance towards increasingly closer "approximations" of reality). He quotes Freud: "What is our work aiming at? We want something that is sought for in all scientific work – to understand the phenomena, to establish a correlation between them and, in the latter end, if it is possible, to enlarge our power over them." ("Introductory Lectures on Psychoanalysis," vols. 15 and 16, in J. Strachey [ed. and trans.], *The Standard Edition of the Complete Works of Sigmund Freud* (London: Hogarth Press, 1963/1917), p. 100. Leary notes that "Freud's criterion of psychological health was similarly pragmatic: It is 'a practical question and is decided by the outcome – by whether the subject is left with a sufficient amount of capacity for enjoyment and of efficiency' ("Introductory Lectures," Ibid., p. 457). Of course, he related this outcome to a metaphorical premise regarding 'the relative sizes of the quota of energy that remains free.' (p. 457)." Ultimately, Freud believed, psychological facts would be formulated in physiological or chemical terms that also use "figurative language" but "one with which we have long been familiar and which is perhaps a simpler one as well" ("Beyond the Pleasure Principle," in J. Strachey [ed. and trans.], Ibid., vol. 18, pp. 1-64, p. 60; quoted in Leary, *Metaphors*, p. 43).

Spence is somewhat less sanguine than Leary regarding Freud's orientation to his metaphors. He points out that Freud "was perhaps less sensitive to the underside of metaphorical usage – less concerned about the fact that the concept which sensitizes us to one part of the domain will blind us to another" (Donald Spence, *The Freudian Metaphor: Toward Paradigm Change in Psychoanalysis* [New York: W.W. Norton, 1987], p. 9).

[29] Leary, *Metaphors*, e.g. p. 21.

[30] See, e.g., *Narrative Truth and Historical Truth: Meaning and Interpretation in Psychoanalysis* (New York: W.W. Norton, 1982); *The Freudian Metaphor; The Rhetorical Voice of Psychoanalysis* (Cambridge, MA: Harvard University Press, 1994); "The Hermeneutic Turn: Soft Science or Loyal Opposition?" *Psychoanalytic Dialogues* vol. 3, no. 1, 1993, pp. 1–10.

[31] See Leary, *Metaphors*, (p. 44 fn 40) for a listing of writings on Freud's use of metaphor.

[32] Bernstein, *Beyond Objectivism and Relativism* and *The Restructuring of Social and Political Theory* (New York: Harcourt, Brace and Jovanovich, 1976); Taylor,

metaphors, to treat the entities and processes that they delineate as essential and, often, universal realities.

The consequences of this reification are notable in the case of psychoanalytic theories of the development of the self. These theories take a template derived from Judaeo-Christian civilization's oldest and most influential story about the path to moral goodness and spiritual fulfillment and make of it a story about the everyday life of the secular self. When this particular metaphor is literalized, it is easy to lose sight of the fact that these ostensibly naturalistic and universal theories of emotional and personality development and psychopathology draw heavily upon a cultural tradition that does nothing less than to proclaim what is at stake, morally and existentially, in human life. In other words, when we take this developmental metaphor literally, it is easy to obscure its cultural and value-laden character.

The particular ideals of personhood promoted in these theories (self-reliance, self-direction, and the capacity for intimacy for which the first two characteristics are considered prerequisite) frequently are viewed simply as being the psychological traits that, for better and for worse, are corollaries to modern social and political arrangements.[33] Yet when we treat these ideals as wholly modern actualities, and regard them as radically severed from cultural tradition and religious doctrine, we miss two of their important characteristics. First, we miss their cultural specificity: as is explained in Chapter 2, self-reliance and self-direction (both as rhetorical ideals and as actual sets of behaviors and practices[34]) have been

[33] The linkage of individuation (a characteristic or tendency of the self) and individualism (an ideology or set of prescriptions and ideals regarding the self) to modernization is one of the most ubiquitous truisms found in sociological theory and social history. Yet even Durkheim, architect of one of the most influential developmentalist depictions of the linkage between the ascendance of individuation/individualism and the evolution of social structure, noted that "it is...a singular error to present the individualist ethic as the antagonist of Christian morality. Quite the contrary – the former is derived from the latter." (Emile Durkheim, "Individualism and the Intellectuals," in *On Morality and Society: Selected Writings,* Robert Bellah ed., Chicago: University of Chicago Press, 1973). See also Louis Dumont, "The Christian Beginnings: From the Outworldly Individual to the Individual-in-the-World," in *Essays on Individualism: Modern Ideology in Anthropological Perspective* (Chicago: University of Chicago Press, 1986), pp. 23–59.

[34] I make this distinction (and repeat it in various places throughout the text) in order to make clear that it seems to me imprudent to assume that our formally stated ideals and theoretical rhetoric are perfectly isomorphic with the broader array of shared but unstated values and codes (many of them intertwined with macro- and microsocial processes and power relations) by which we – psychologists and laypersons alike – also live. To assert that the fit is not a perfect one between our explicit ideals and formal theories on the one hand, and broader largely unarticulated "forms of life" on the other, is to leave open the possibility (indeed, the likelihood) that terms such as "self-direction" and "autonomy" derive some of their meaning from the particular situations and contexts in which such terms are deployed, and therefore that there is more to understanding the cultural values and social processes of Anglo-American society, than can be gleaned solely by relying on what is written in formal texts or even spoken in words.

most strongly elaborated and celebrated in Northern European Protestant culture areas, particularly in the United States. Second, we miss their theological overtones: these two ideals (as well as a third, the capacity for intimacy) bear the imprint of an inherited religious problematic and vision of redemption.

In the United States – a nation built on several strata of radical Protestant foundations – the rhetoric of individuation and individuality has enjoyed a long and intimate association with both sacred and secular ideas about salvation. When psychoanalytic theory was introduced into the medium of Anglo-American culture, certain aspects of the psychoanalytic corpus resonated especially well with these "hypercognized"[35] prescriptions for selfhood. If American cultural ideals valorize individuation, the psychoanalytic narrative of preoedipal development – present in, but not the central focus of, Freudian theory – highlights individuation's vicissitudes. Transplanted to America and Britain, psychoanalysis came more and more to prioritize and elaborate upon that preoedipal narrative. In these culture areas, psychoanalysts have focused almost entirely on the difficult developmental path to autonomy's attainment, and on individuation's never-ending dialectical interplay with wishes for dependency and oneness. (Chapter 2 deals with this cultural borrowing of psychoanalytic theory by the United States and Britain.) This complementarity and mutual reinforcement between Anglo-American ideals of the self and the psychoanalytic narrative of individuation is not surprising. Both American ethnopsychology[36] and psychoanalytic develop-

---

[35] The term is Robert Levy's; see *Tahitians: Mind and Self in the Society Islands* (Chicago: University of Chicago Press, 1973), and "Emotion, Knowing and Culture," in Richard A. Shweder and Robert A. LeVine (eds.), *Culture Theory: Essays on Mind, Self and Emotion* (Cambridge: Cambridge University Press, 1984).

[36] Here I use the term as Richard Shweder does, to denote "indigenous representations of mind, body, self and emotion." See Richard A. Shweder, "Cultural Psychology: What is it?" in James W. Stigler, Richard A. Shweder and Gilbert Herdt (eds.), *Cultural Psychology: Essays on Comparative Human Development* (Cambridge: Cambridge University Press, 1990), pp. 1–43, p. 16. Shweder makes a distinction between ethnopsychology (which he calls "cultural psychology without a psyche at all") and cultural psychology (which he glosses as the shared culturally constituted conceptions of self and world, interdependent upon one another, that direct our actions and constitute our "forms of life"). As I read him, ethnopsychology overlaps with cultural psychology, and perhaps is subsumed by it, but does not encompass the entirety of the intentional worlds we live in or metaphors we live by.
  More recently, Geoffrey White has challenged this definition, proposing a broader meaning of the term "ethnopsychology," one that emphasizes the "discourse processes through which social and emotional realities are constituted in ordinary talk and interaction." See Geoffrey White, "Ethnopsychology," in Theodore Schwartz, Geoffrey M. White and Catherine A. Lutz (eds.), *New Directions in Psychological Anthropology* (Cambridge: Cambridge University Press, 1992), pp. 21–46, p. 39. Since in this study I am mainly concerned with texts and rhetoric, I use "ethnopsychology" here in the narrower sense proposed by Shweder.

mental psychology share a common cultural gene pool: both are legatees of radical Protestant beliefs and hopes regarding the self and its redemption. American (and to a lesser degree, British) culture has come by this legacy through its Puritan and nonconforming Protestant foundations. Psychoanalysis received it through the derivation of some of its discourses from Northern European Romanticism.

Of course, our modern-day rhetoric of individualism, and the behaviors it is used to describe and legitimize, look quite different, in many ways, from the theological doctrines and traditional forms of life to which, in some respects, they are heir. But as symbolic depictions of the self's pain and progress, both American ideals of the self, and the psychoanalytic developmental narrative that has further canonized them, retain the shapes and the hopes of a distinctive Christian and Romantic heritage.

Thus, when we reify these images of the self and its development, we blind ourselves to their cultural specificity, historical roots, and entanglement with spiritual tradition. There is another dimension, too, that eludes us when we treat these metaphors as invariant structures of nature, rather than as a theodicy-turned-poetics that delineates the meaning and goals of life. We risk a certain ingenuousness and complacency regarding these theories' social roles. For, as it turns out, these psychological metaphors are "generative" not only in the schematizing sense discussed previously. They also are generative in two other, more directly social, senses. First, to some degree we "live by" our theories' metaphors. They structure our self-understanding and guide the ways in which we engage with each other and with the world.[37] Hence it behooves us to attend to the consequences of our psychological metaphors – what sort of persons,

[37] I follow Lakoff and Johnson, *Metaphors We Live By,* and Leary, *Metaphors* (e.g., pp. 22–3 and pp. 351–2), in asserting that many of our activities are guided by the metaphors we choose or that are bequeathed to us. However, it is also important to note that the rhetoric itself is not always perfectly transparent. In other words, not all of the meanings and values, or even all of the symbolic structures and metaphors, that people live by are articulated in the rhetoric of theory or everyday talk. Thus, for example, the rhetoric of equality can be use to rationalize constraint and inequality. Similarly, the rhetoric of self-direction and authenticity (and its salvationist moral undertone) can be invoked to endorse actions that might just as plausibly be interpreted as "conformist." A corollary of this is that changing the language alone will not necessarily alter the way in which people interact with one another, because broader forms of life and power relations are involved. The point here is that in at least some cases, neither the full intentional world (the implicit cultural meanings and values), nor the social arrangements and power relations that are enacted in particular situations, are revealed through examination of the articulated metaphor alone. Additional ethnographic study should be able to contribute to a fuller understanding of the degree to which we live by such metaphors in particular types of situations, and of the ways in which such a formulation is overly simple, shallow, or incomplete.

what type of practices, and what kind of social world, do they help to shape? There is a second sense, too, in which psychological metaphors generate social consequences. Psychologists', psychiatrists', and psycho-analysts' professional interpretations – the meanings and labels they attribute to situations, relationships and persons – are themselves social actions, with powerful social consequences. When we naturalize and universalize such categories of analysis, there is an obfuscation of the social processes and power relations that inhere in, or are enacted with the use of, psychologists' discourse.[38]

In literalizing our metaphors, then, we risk losing sight of both their cultural contingency and their socially generative dimensions. We are deprived of the opportunity to reflect on the relative merits and limita-tions of applying specific theoretical lenses in particular contexts or to various groups. Moreover, we are less likely to detect and analyze the social arrangements and processes with which particular metaphors are intertwined. Finally, we give ourselves little leeway to seriously explore supplementary or alternative ways of conceptualizing human nature, "growth," "health," and social life. As is discussed below, recent investi-gations by cultural anthropologists, critical psychologists, and other social theorists have brought such concerns to the foreground.

During the past two decades, social scientists have been exploring the potentially distorting and harmful effects of unreflectively using Western psychological yardsticks (and in particular their valorization of various forms of individualism) to appraise the development of selves and minds in non-Western cultural settings. When our theories and assumptions about personality and its development have been utilized as metadis-courses with which to understand and evaluate persons in other cultures, such persons almost invariably have been represented as underdeveloped and deficient. Among cultural anthropologists, there has been an increas-ing appreciation of the fact that such formal psychological constructions embody relatively "local" ("American" or "Western") ethnopsychologi-cal beliefs and ideals[39] regarding the nature of the self, its development

---

[38] The classic exposition of how psychological attributions (to self and others) function as "accounting schemes" (i.e., are used to endorse, justify, or delegitimize behavior) is C. Wright Mills' "Situated Actions and Vocabularies of Motive," in *Power, Politics and People: The Collected Essays of C. Wright Mills* (New York: Oxford University Press, 1979).

[39] See, e.g., Clifford Geertz, "'From the Native's Point of View': On the Nature of Anthropological Understanding," in Shweder and LeVine (eds.), *Culture Theory*, pp. 123–36; Michelle Z. Rosaldo, "Toward an Anthropology of Self and Feeling," in Shweder and LeVine, *Culture Theory*, pp. 137–57; Catherine A. Lutz, *Unnatural Emotions: Everyday Sentiments on a Micronesian Atoll and Their Challenge to Western Theory* (Chicago: University of Chicago Press, 1988); Dorinne K. Kondo, *Crafting*

and its connection to others. In essence, what has been called into question is the assumption that Western psychological categories, both everyday and academic or clinical, are the most veridical rendering of psychological reality or that they provide a universally superior interpretive language. The recognition that our categories may embody local values, assumptions, and prescriptions does not inevitably necessitate that we discard or delegitimize them. But such enhanced self-consciousness does (or at any rate should) engender greater attentiveness to our theories' own sources and continuing situatedness, as well as to the ways in which our frameworks and categories may at times mitigate against the very understanding and illumination they are intended to promote. As the anthropologist Stanley Kurtz has so trenchantly put it, "while it may be [that our own culture's assumptions and beliefs capture reality and 'are conveniently perched on top' of the developmental and epistemological scales ...], the coincidence of this scheme with our self-regard constitutes grounds for suspicion."[40]

Among psychoanalytically oriented researchers and clinicians, there have been a few noteworthy attempts to rectify this theoretical ethnocentrism. Some of these scholars have argued that psychoanalytic theory lacks an appreciation for the diversity of sociocultural contexts in which development may take place.[41] Hence, they suggest, such theory remains an inadequate framework for interpreting and evaluating persons in or from other cultures. In place of it they have proposed alternative psychodynamic models of the development of the self. These models retain many psychoanalytic premises, including the idea of development itself, while they propose more flexible depictions of the developmental

Selves: Power, Gender and Discourses of Identity in a Japanese Workplace (Chicago: University of Chicago Press, 1990); Nancy Scheper-Hughes, *Death Without Weeping: The Violence of Everyday Life in Brazil* (Berkeley, CA: University of California Press, 1993); Geoffrey White, "What is Ethnopsychology?" For many anthropologists, the labels "American" and "Western" have become problematized terms: intensified attention has been focused on the transnational and multicultural character of contemporary societies as well as on the reified nature of the culture concept (see footnote 54, this chapter). This sort of deconstruction can be taken to counterproductive extremes, however: I would argue that so long as we remain self-conscious about the limitations and potential abuses of the culture concept (and the notion of "American" culture in particular), and about our tendency to essentialize it, it remains a useful construct to employ in certain contexts.

[40] Stanley Kurtz, *All the Mothers Are One* (New York: Columbia University Press, 1992), p. 242.

[41] See, e.g., L. Takeo Doi, *The Anatomy of Dependence,* trans. John Bester (New York: Kodansha International, 1973); Levy, *Tahitians*; Alan Roland, *In Search of Self in India and Japan: Toward a Cross-Cultural Psychology* (Princeton: Princeton University Press, 1988); Robert A. LeVine, "Infant Environments in Psychoanalysis: A Cross-Cultural View," in James W. Stigler, Richard A. Shweder and Gilbert Herdt (eds.), *Cultural Psychology*, pp. 454–74; Kurtz, *All the Mothers Are One.*

trajectory and its ends. Such writings are important and highly valuable contributions to clinical practice and cross-cultural understanding. However, the present work diverges from such approaches in two ways. First, those psychoanalytic models still naturalize the metaphor of development and related psychoanalytic premises, whereas the aim of this book is to promote greater self-consciousness regarding those very constructions. Second, most of those revisionist models utilize (in practice if not explicitly) a functionalist or adaptationalist framework wherein the ends of development endorsed within a given sociocultural milieu tend to be viewed as, while not unproblematic, then at least, on balance, appropriate and therefore not in need of detailed critical scrutiny or problematization. The legitimacy of a culture's manifest vision of the "good" person is seen to hinge upon the fact that such successfully developed persons "fit" with, and are well adapted to, their particular sociocultural system. By contrast, in this book I make a deliberate attempt not to assume such a functionalist stance.

In problematizing such functionalism, this study draws upon the work of another group of social researchers. That group consists of psychologists whose chief concern has been to cast a critical gaze on their own society's systems and practices of self-understanding. For it is not only in their application to cultural others that Western psychological models have come under scrutiny. Particularly since the 1970s, critical and feminist psychologists have sought to study how the authority wielded by their discipline affects members of their own society and culture. They have focused attention on how social and political situations have influenced both the construction and the deployment of psychological theories.[42] As was noted above, it has become increasingly clear that many of the categories and explanations used by psychologists – in social

---

[42] Such critical and feminist psychologists include Edward E. Sampson, Kenneth Gergen, Philip Cushman, John Broughton, Carol Gilligan, Jeanne Marecek, Jill Morawski, and the Changing the Subject collective. See, e.g., Edward E. Sampson, "Psychology and the American Ideal," *Journal of Personality and Social Psychology,* vol. 35, no. 1, 1977, pp. 767–82; "The Decentralization of Identity: Toward a Revised Concept of Personal and Social Order," *American Psychologist,* vol. 40, no. 11, Nov. 1985, pp. 1203–11, "The Debate on Individualism: Indigenous Psychologies of the Individual and their Role in Personal and Societal Functioning," *American Psychologist,* vol. 43, 1988, pp. 15–22; Philip Cushman, "Why the Self is Empty: Toward a Historically Situated Psychology," *American Psychologist,* vol. 45, 1990, pp. 599–611; Julian Henriques et al., *Changing the Subject: Psychology, Social Regulation and Subjectivity* (New York: Methuen, 1984); John M. Broughton (ed.), *Critical Theories of Psychological Development* (New York: Plenum Press, 1987); David Ingleby, *Critical Psychiatry: The Politics of Mental Health* (New York: Pantheon, 1980); Allan R. Buss, *Psychology in Social Context* (New York: Irvington Press, 1979); Philip Wexler, *Critical Social Psychology* (Boston: Routledge and Kegan Paul, 1983); Ian Parker and John Shotter (eds.), *Deconstructing Social Psychology* (New York: Routledge, 1990).

psychology, personality theories, psychodynamic theories, and even in the "harder" subdisciplines – reproduce some variation of "Western" cultural common sense. Critical and feminist psychologists have alerted us to the fact that the common sense that becomes canonized as theory tends to embody those values and assumptions that are commonsensical not to all, but rather to those groups that are given voice and status in our society. In other words, our theories formalize and authorize certain cultural norms (often, they canonize those norms that are favored by and favor persons with high status and power), and they tend to marginalize that which, and those who, don't fit or resist them.

Carol Gilligan's critique of theories that trace the development of moral reasoning[43] is perhaps the most vivid and far-reaching demonstration of the extent to which psychological theories have reflexively treated difference as deficiency. Gilligan brought to light the unwitting and pervasive androcentric bias of Lawrence Kohlberg's and Jean Piaget's theories of moral development. The work of Gilligan[44] and others[45] has underscored the degree to which the yardsticks psychologists have used to measure minds and selves, even when employed in the service of educating and helping, all too often function as blunt instruments. That is, our frameworks and measures have tended to be insensitive to many types of difference save in a pathologizing or devaluing way, and in some instances have served to reinforce and extend relations of social inequality.

With the dissemination of Foucaultian and poststructuralist theories as tools of cultural critique, we also have become sensitized to the ways in which power is at work in situations that do not entail the direct repression or domination of one group by another. In poststructuralist forms of analysis, modern state power is revealed as decentralized and ubiquitous, and power itself is understood to be constitutive and constructive

---

[43] See Carol Gilligan, *In a Different Voice* (Cambridge, MA: Harvard University Press, 1982).

[44] Gilligan and her associates have extended her critique beyond the domain of moral developmental theory, to include other forms and aspects of developmental theory and issues in girls' development: see, e.g., Lyn Mikel Brown and Carol Gilligan, *Meeting at the Crossroads* (Cambridge, MA: Harvard University Press, 1992).

[45] On gender bias and ethnocentrism in abnormal psychology and psychiatry, see, e.g., Jeanne Marecek and Rachel T. Hare-Mustin, "A Social History of the Future: Feminism and Clinical Psychology," *Psychology of Women Quarterly*, vol. 15, no. 4, December 1991, pp. 521–36; Atwood D. Gaines, "From DSM I to III–R; Voices of Self, Mastery and the Other: A Cultural Constructivist Reading of U.S. Psychiatric Classification," *Social Science and Medicine*, vol. 35, no. 1, 1992, pp. 3–24, and "Ethnopsychiatry: The Cultural Construction of Psychiatries," in A.D. Gaines (ed.), *Ethnopsychiatry: The Cultural Construction of Folk and Professional Psychiatries* (Albany: State University of New York Press, 1992), pp. 3–49.

as well as inescapably constraining. We might say, then, that Foucaultian analysis highlights the degree to which our psychological theories are metaphors (and practices) we are subjected to, or subjugated by. On this view, it hardly matters which metaphors we choose, or are chosen by – all psychological discourse imprisons our bodies and governs our souls. It is the enterprise of classifying, surveying, and disciplining the inner self that is emphasized here. The human sciences, as well as psychotherapeutic and "helping" practices such as psychoanalysis, all function to create persons and selves as objects and subjects, and thereby to extend state power into (indeed, via the construction of) the most intimate reaches of human behavior and experience. In the words of Foucault-indebted psychologist Nikolas Rose, "[o]ur personalities, subjectivities, and 'relationships' are not private matters, if this implies that they are not the objects of power. On the contrary, they are intensely governed."[46]

For all its ambiguities and disturbing aspects,[47] the Foucaultian vision of the role played by human science in modern life is profoundly illuminating.[48] However, it seems to me that if we accept that vision as encompassing the totality of what social science and psychoanalysis are and do, then we lose an appreciation of the theodicy dimension of social and psychological theory. We need to include, in any understanding of the role of psychology in contemporary life, not only analyses of how it is implicated in power relations and enacts social order, but also a recognition of how psychological discourse has emerged, and continues to be used, as a way of making sense of the human condition.

Thus far I have described how psychological discourses, theories, and metaphors have drawn criticism for their hegemonic and constraining character. There is yet another, related, sense in which psychological theories have been perceived to generate pernicious social effects. Such theories have been accused of celebrating forms of individualism that are not merely partial, ideological, or subjugating, but also inherently distorted and socially deleterious. Constructionist and communitarian social and psychological theorists[49] (with some significant variations among them)

[46] *Governing the Soul: The Shaping of the Private Self* (London: Routledge, 1990), p. 1.
[47] See, e.g., Nancy Fraser, *Unruly Practices: Power, Discourse and Gender in Contemporary Social Theory* (Minneapolis: University of Minnesota Press, 1989), chs. 1–3, for a lucid and incisive discussion of some of the tensions inherent in, and unsatisfying aspects of, Foucault's work. See also Jane Flax, *Thinking Fragments: Psychoanalysis, Feminism, and Postmodernism in the Contemporary West* (Berkeley, CA: University of California Press, 1990).
[48] See Chapter 9 for further discussion of this understanding of the role of psychology and psychiatry in modern social life.
[49] Prominent constructionist psychologists include Edward Sampson, Kenneth Gergen, and Philip Cushman. Social theorists who can be termed "communitarian" include Robert Bellah, Alasdair MacIntyre, Michael Sandel, and Charles Taylor.

argue that the individualistic assumptions and values that are at the core of most psychological theory evince an erroneous grasp of human nature and social life. They further hold that such visions of the human situation have had profoundly negative effects on society. The idea here is that the forms of selfhood that are both assumed and prized in psychological theories (and in the practices associated with them, e.g. psychotherapy) are in fact evidence of an ethos and a social system gone wrong. As psychologist Henderikus Stam has put it, these theorists view psychology's hyperindividualism as reflecting and worsening a more fundamental "cultural error,"[50] an error that has led us to (or past) the brink of moral and societal degeneration. Such critiques encompass a complicated set of themes; it is not possible to do justice to them within the confines of this book. It is not my aim within these pages to summarily reject or condemn self-reliance, self-direction, or any other variations of individualism, or to ascribe to their alleged overgrowth the source of our social ills. Nor, certainly, is my purpose to celebrate them as the only high and moral forms of life. My point is simply this: what these critiques, and the others I have discussed, make clear is that our psychological theories, and the models of the person that they celebrate, are indeed culturally constituted, value laden, and implicated in power and status relations in several different (until recently, largely hidden or unrecognized) ways. The developmental trajectories that buttress psychology's ideals are similarly enmeshed in cultural webs and implicated in social operations.

Thus the evidence mounts. Not only do we live, in some measure, by our metaphors; we also may not live in the best of all possible metaphorical worlds. For all sorts of reasons – epistemological, social, political, moral – it seems prudent to continue to acknowledge and explore the metaphorical and cultural sources, as well as the social consequences, of psychological theories. The primary aim of this genealogy is simply to underscore these theories' metaphoricity, and thereby to further undermine their naturalistic pretensions. It is hoped that this underlining of their contingent and imaginative character will contribute to an enhanced understanding of the multiple roles such theories play in social life.

Another consequence of a study such as this one is that it can lend support to attempts to invoke supplementary or alternative metaphors. There is clearly much of worth in these psychodynamic theories and the values they express and enact. But it also grows increasingly evident that

---

[50] Henderikus Stam, "Is There Anything Beyond the Ideological Critique of Individualism?" in Henderikus J. Stam, Warren Thorngate, Leendert P. Mos, and Bernie Kaplan (eds.), *Recent Trends in Theoretical Psychology*. Vol. III (New York: Springer-Verlag, 1993), pp. 143–51.

our reigning paradigms of development by no means fully articulate the range of valuable human actions, motives, and experiences. Thus it may be possible and even desirable to consider metaphors that embody additional ways of construing what is meaningful and moral in individual and communal life.[51] This is not to suggest that we have infinite choice in how we may construct our selves or the world. The limitations of physical life, of the various forms of suffering in which humans are immersed, and of the need for social order (an exigency that in great measure is met, in contemporary life, by the human sciences and helping professions), all pose powerful constraints on the sorts of alternative theories or values we might viably conceive. And of course, as the hermeneuticists tell us, we can never fully stand outside our own tradition or set of traditions, or what Richard Shweder has called our own intentional worlds. There is no Archimedean point, no view from nowhere. But surely there are relative degrees of freedom; there are stances of relative critical thoughtfulness that we can take towards the beliefs we hold and the activities in which we participate.

Finally, then, examination of the metaphors and cultural values that shape our psychological practices can help us achieve a clearer and fuller understanding of what we – as researchers, as clinicians, as educators – are doing. In particular, such analysis can contribute to the ongoing (but still largely marginal) project of sharpening our awareness of the contradictions and tensions that inhere in human science research and therapeutic practices. Chief among those contradictions – one that I am hardly the first to note – is this: on the one hand, the models that guide our intellectual and professional activities enjoy the epistemological privilege and authority that we accord to positive science and medical practice. Yet on the other hand they are profoundly moral and cultural "sciences." That psychology and psychiatry traffic in values is not inherently a bad thing, and in any case it is inescapable. But at the very least, it behooves us to recognize this state of affairs, and to reflect on it more openly and thoughtfully than the prevailing scientistic self-understanding of developmental psychoanalysis (and of most other psychological models) comfortably accommodates.

One final point again must be emphasized: To highlight that distinctive cultural visions and values inhabit these psychoanalytic theories, and that such theories are implicated in processes of hegemony and social order, is not to assert that these theories are solely vehicles of social

---

[51] Feminists (e.g., Gilligan), constructionists (e.g., Gergen), and communitarian-interpretivists (e.g., Bellah), among others, already are engaged in such attempts to broaden and modify our repertoire of available psychological metaphors.

regulation and control. For it is just as vital to appreciate that they are also compelling ways of construing life's vicissitudes. Human suffering – in both its inevitable and its contingent forms – is no less real because our representation of it and of its sources is inescapably culture-bound. A theory that proposes a particular understanding of the nature of life's tragedy is no less profound for that theory's distinctive metaphorical casting. Thus, with this genealogy I intend to honor these narratives as well as to situate, ironize, and challenge them.

Psychoanalytic theories of the development of the self: The primary "data" of this study

By "contemporary Anglo-American psychoanalytic theories," I refer to three interrelated psychoanalytic schools or loosely affiliated groups of theorists under the broader umbrella of "psychoanalysis." These are ego psychology, object-relations theory, and self psychology. Ego psychology was initiated by Freud himself and initially developed by Heinz Hartmann and Anna Freud in the 1930s; in this project I am concerned with the "later" ego psychology of Rene Spitz, Edith Jacobson, Margaret Mahler, and Otto Kernberg. Object-relations theory has been mainly a British movement; it was initiated by Melanie Klein, but subsequently was developed along rather different lines in the work of analysts including W.R.D. Fairbairn, D.W. Winnicott, Harry Guntrip, and others. Heinz Kohut was the founder and leading proponent of self psychology, which has been very influential in American psychoanalysis since the 1970s. I call these three schools "Anglo-American" because, as I explain in Chapter 2, all these versions of psychoanalytic theory have undergone their fullest elaboration in the United States and Great Britain during the post-Freudian era (rather than in classical Freudian psychoanalysis or in France, South America, or other areas where psychoanalysis has undergone elaboration during the past fifty years).

Each of these theorists offers a distinctive, and in some respects unique, vision of human personality and development. Even theorists considered to be of the same school (e.g., Fairbairn and Winnicott, or Mahler and Kernberg) may vary with respect both to their interpretations of particular phenomena and to the specific topics that interest them. Nevertheless, virtually all of their theories have certain features in common. The most important shared characteristic, for our purposes, is that they all chronicle the story of individual personality and emotional development in terms of a distinctive narrative pattern, a pattern that I explore in detail in Chapters 2 and 3.[52] In order to draw parallels between this generic psychoanalytic narrative and older forms of the pattern, I focus mainly on the theories of three psychoanalytic theorists: ego psychologist Margaret S. Mahler, object-relations theorist D.W. Winnicott and self psychologist Heinz Kohut.

A note on method: The idea of a cultural genealogy[53]

This work, then, constitutes an attempt to trace the historical transformations undergone by some broad, culturally constituted narrative patterns. Precisely because these patterns are shared by a variety of theoretical systems spanning several domains and disciplines (religion, philosophy, social theory, psychology, literature), we are all the more likely to mistake them for what literary critic M.H. Abrams called "the conditions of reality" and "the universal forms of thought." The aim of this work is to highlight some of the narratives' culture-specific features.

[52] The psychoanalyst and developmentalist Daniel Stern has advanced an influential challenge to some of the assumptions inherent in the psychoanalytic developmental narrative that I trace in this book. In *The Interpersonal World of the Infant: A View from Psychoanalysis and Developmental Psychology* (New York: Basic Books, 1985), he spells out what is in some respects an alternative model of the development of the infant's sense of self and relatedness. Specifically, Stern takes issue with Mahler's assertion of a "symbiotic" phase of development (i.e., a phase during which the infant is said not yet to have developed a differentiated sense of self-versus-other). Stern's infant, by contrast, is seen to possess a rudimentary sense of self, as well as the capacity to differentiate itself from others, from the beginning; it only develops the capacity for a sense of union later on. It is beyond the scope of the present study to probe in detail the ways in which Stern's theory – which is based on recent observational research but also involves a considerable amount of inference about the infant's "subjective world" – both diverges from and adheres to the developmentalist assumptions, design, and values that characterize the psychoanalytic theories I examine here. However, at the very least, it is clear that it, too, is susceptible to analysis of its cultural and social dimensions. (For a critique of some of its ideological aspects, see Philip Cushman, "Ideology Obscured: Political Uses of Self in Daniel Stern's Infant," *American Psychologist*, vol. 46, no. 3, March 1991.)

[53] By "genealogy" I mean an attempt to trace themes and patterns found in current theories to older sources within the culture; the psychologist Louis Sass uses the term in a similar way (see "The Self and Its Vicissitudes: An 'Archaeological' Study of the Psychoanalytic Avant-Garde," in *Social Research*, vol. 55, no. 4, Winter 1988, pp. 551–608). This usage differs from a second sense of "genealogy," in which it denotes a Nietzschean-Foucaultian orientation to the history of ideas and practices. This poststructuralist sense of "genealogy" emphasizes discontinuities and breaks, over time, in the discourses through which the world and the person are articulated; it highlights, as well, the ways in which social order and relations of power are enacted through such discourses. This second meaning of "genealogy," which is discussed briefly in Chapter 9, has been explicated by political theorist William Connolly in "Where the Word Breaks Off," in *Politics and Ambiguity* (Baltimore: Johns Hopkins University Press, 1985).

This "cultural"[54] perspective furnishes the rationale for ranging so freely and generally over such a vast array of complex systems of meaning-making.

This is a study of the psychoanalytic developmental narrative as cultural discourse. It is not a study of how these patterns were transmitted to particular psychoanalytic theorists. I have not undertaken to trace the channels through which specific psychoanalysts had contact with Romantic (or religious) texts. I have no doubt that such specific channels could, and should, be traced for virtually all these theorists. Indeed, there are so many possibilities for such contact and influence that one scarcely knows where to begin. For example: if one were to attempt to trace, via conventional historical methods, the means by which ego psychologists, object-relations theorists and self psychologists gained awareness of the generic Romantic narrative, one might begin simply by examining the curricula of primary schools, gymnasia and secondary schools, and universities in Austria-Hungary, Germany and England during the late nineteenth and early twentieth centuries. Among the figures studied were various Romantic poets and essayists. The generic Romantic narrative also is present in many "post-Romantic" poems and writings that were widely studied during that period. As for particular analysts' intellectual biographies, any of the following cases promises to yield information about a psychoanalytic theorist's exposure to Romanticism:[55] Otto Rank (whose work in many ways foreshadowed and influenced that of the Anglo-American the-

---

54 Robert LeVine defines culture as "a shared organization of ideas that includes the intellectual, moral and aesthetic standards prevalent in a community and the meanings of communicative actions" ("Properties of Culture: An Ethnographic View," in Shweder and LeVine [eds.], *Culture Theory*, p. 67). During the past two decades, the concept of culture has been problematized in two distinct but overlapping ways. First, attention has been drawn to the fact that "culture" itself is a construct and a reification (a metaphor, in fact), one that has incited anthropologists to impose a false uniformity, a specious holism, on phenomena that are in fact less than perfectly ordered, shared, or static. For a recent discussion of these concerns and their political dimensions, see Lila Abu-Lughod, "Writing Against Culture," in Richard G. Fox (ed.), *Recapturing Anthropology: Working in the Present* (Santa Fe: School of American Research Press, 1991), pp. 137–62. A second, more recent line of critique challenges the "assumed isomorphism of space, place and culture" (Akhil Gupta and James Ferguson, "Beyond Culture: Space, Identity and the Politics of Difference," *Cultural Anthropology*, vol. 7, no. 1, 1992, pp. 6–23, p. 7). Both of these are valuable critiques: they remind us that "culture" is as liable to counterproductive reification as is any other social scientific construct, and highlight the changing nature of our increasingly transnational world. But these insights, valid as they are, can be taken too far. As Geoffrey White recently wrote of both the constructs "culture" and "self," they are at once "intractable and indispensable" ("The Self: A Brief Commentary," *Anthropology and Humanism Quarterly*, vol. 16, no. 1, March 1991, p. 33). Clearly groups of humans do communicate and interact on the basis of shared patterns of meaning, dynamic and "frayed around the edges" as those patterns are.

55 These are offered merely as suggestions of avenues to pursue in future research; no doubt there were many other such points of contact with Romanticism for these and other theorists including Kohut, Kernberg and Balint.

orists) took a doctorate at the University of Vienna in literature and mythology.[56] Margaret Mahler studied philosophy at university before going into medicine.[57] D.W. Winnicott was clearly familiar with much English poetry including that of Wordsworth, in addition to being the son of a Methodist minister.[58] Edith Jacobson and Otto Fenichel, as intellectual Marxists or socialists in Europe, were acquainted with and congenial to both dialectical and developmentalist visions of the human condition.[59] But I have not intended this to be an intellectual biography of Mahler, Winnicott, or any other analysts, because to conceive it in that way would be to risk trivializing the broader point that I emphasize here. To focus on documenting direct transmission of the pattern to one or a few specific analysts, or on analysts' personal motives and experiences, would detract attention from my main argument, which is that this discourse – its structure, its persistence, its transformations – transcends the specific lives and inventiveness of single individuals. This is why I call it a "template," or "cultural narrative." I deliberately emphasize this perspective on psychoanalytic theory as a counter-weight to the "individualistic fallacy" dictated by certain conventions of intellectual history; when we dismiss investigations of commonalities and contexts in favor of attention to individual differences, it can sometimes cloud our view of the larger picture.

The psychoanalytic narrative of the development of the ego or self is closer to the Romantic version of the narrative than it is to earlier, explicitly theological forms of Christian (or Jewish) mysticism. For this reason, and because most psychoanalysts seem to have had stronger exposure to Romantic literary and philosophical themes than to Christian mystical ones, it seems likely that for the most part[60] it was the Romantic version of the narrative that was absorbed directly into psychoanalysis.

In fact, there is a scholar who argued that Freudian psychoanalysis contained various images, patterns, and themes directly taken from mysticism, in this case Jewish mysticism. This is David Bakan, who asserted this linkage in his controversial *Sigmund Freud and the Jewish Mystical Tradition*.[61] In a sense, his study is of limited relevance to this book

[56] See Paul Roazen, *Freud and his Followers* (New York: New American Library, 1974), and Dennis Klein, *Jewish Origins of the Psychoanalytic Movement* (New York: Praeger, 1981).

[57] See *The Memoirs of Margaret S. Mahler*, ed. Paul Stepansky (New York: The Free Press, 1988).

[58] See Adam Phillips, *Winnicott* (Cambridge, MA: Harvard University Press, 1988).

[59] See Russell Jacoby, *The Repression of Psychoanalysis: Otto Fenichel and the Political Freudians* (New York: Basic Books, 1983).

[60] This is not true in every single case: Balint speaks quite directly of adult love as involving a *unio mystica*. See Chapter 8.

[61] David Bakan, *Sigmund Freud and the Jewish Mystical Tradition* (London: Free Association Books, 1990).

because he cites different mystical themes and patterns than the ones with which I am concerned, and because he analyzes Freud's own writings only. Moreover, his thesis is that Freud purposely included Kabbalist doctrines and motifs in his theories, albeit in a deliberately hidden form. It is difficult to accept this interpretation, particularly given Freud's manifest vehemence about the anti-religious and anti-mystical content and aims of psychoanalysis. Peter Gay, among others, scoffs at Bakan's thesis. Gay insists, as he always does, that Freud was above all a Jew who "wholly identified with the values of the European Enlightenment."[62] Even granted that this was Freud's self-image, Gay seems astonishingly short-sighted when he plays down the connection between psychoanalytic discourse (or certain aspects of it) and non-Enlightenment doctrines, be they secular (i.e. Romantic) or literally theological. There is, after all, an alternative interpretation to that proposed by Bakan to account for the apparently mystical patterns and themes in Freud's theories. Harry Trosman,[63] speaking of Bakan's thesis, suggests that while the latter was probably wrong about the direct source of these mystical motifs in psychoanalysis, he need not have been wrong in detecting the presence of such motifs. Trosman astutely pursues a line of reasoning apparently overlooked by Gay: he points out that Jewish mysticism shared some significant features with Romantic thought and art. Gay, among others, has underlined Freud's rich literary background.[64] Why has he not recognized in literature a source of the infusion of erstwhile religious ideas into Freudian theory? One can only surmise that this is due to a rigid insistence on keeping religion and psychoanalysis separate; in this Gay seems intent upon not challenging Freud's own vision of psychoanalysis as being at the opposite end of the cultural and intellectual spectrum from any form of religious belief. Of course it is important to acknowledge that Freud viewed himself as an "Enlightenment" man, but this should not blind Gay to myriad other cultural discourses – some of them even counter-Enlightenment – which also were absorbed by and built into psychoanalytic theory, whether wittingly or not. In this book I focus on only one – the mystical-turned-Romantic discourse – but this is not to deny that there are numerous other cultural traditions that are "inscribed" in both classical and post-Freudian analytic theories. These include not only Enlightenment rationalism and German Romanticism, but also Classicism, evolutionary theory (both Darwinian and other,

---

[62] *A Godless Jew: Freud, Atheism and the Making of Psychoanalysis.* (New Haven: Yale University Press, 1987), pp. 130–2, p. 130.

[63] "Freud's Cultural Background."

[64] Peter Gay, *Freud, Jews and Other Germans* (New York: Oxford University Press, 1978).

now-outmoded versions), nineteenth-century neurology and psycho-physics, and other discourses.[65]

Confronted with a demonstration of the strong parallels between psychoanalytic developmental psychology and older theological and literary narratives, many psychoanalytic theorists and practitioners would respond that psychoanalytic theory embodies a more refined, systematic, and scientific version of what was intimated in a cruder and more primitive fashion in Romantic and (cruder still) religious texts.[66] They might suggest that psychoanalytic theory embodies the definitive transposition of spiritual and artistic systems into "scientific" language, that it is an articulation of the deep structure of psychic reality – a truth of which there had been only glimmerings in the myths and artistic and philosophical systems of the past.

The implication of such an argument is that "God" and the "soul" are symbolic substitutes, while "self" and "object" are ontological essences. Yet, as was discussed earlier in this chapter, the idea of there being such a deep structure of "fixed natural" psychic forms has been seriously undermined by the various anti-objectivist critiques of social and psychological knowledge. A strong form of the anti-objectivist stance – implied by Marcel Mauss[67] and voiced more recently by his provocative intellectual descendant Michel Foucault[68] – is that contemporary secular humanist categories such as "psyche," "self," "ego," and "object" or "other," as discursive formations, are no more "natural" than are their theological predecessors. Thus, according to this humbling perspective, we have no way of knowing whether these particular current conceptualizations will endure or precisely what will take their place.

But even if we assume a less radical position, and grant privileged ontological status to natural and human (as opposed to supernatural) phenomena – as surely many if not most of us late modern intellectuals do – the psychologistic reduction of religious doctrines and experiences to erotic, familial, and (for neo- and post-Freudians) self-and-relational experiences and situations turns out to be inadequate and in need of

---

[65] See Chapter 2, footnote 4.

[66] This view is implied in the title of Henri Ellenberger's *The Discovery of the Unconscious: The History and Evolution of Dynamic Psychiatry* (New York: Basic Books, 1970). At some points in the text, however, Ellenberger is more ambiguous regarding the linearity of this "evolution."

[67] "A Category of the Human Mind: The Notion of Person; the Notion of Self," (trans. W.D. Halls), in Michael Carrithers, Steven Collins and Steven Lukes (eds.), *The Category of the Person: Anthropology, Philosophy, History* (Cambridge: Cambridge University Press, 1985), pp. 1–25.

[68] *The Order of Things: An Archaeology of the Human Sciences* (New York: Vintage Books, 1971).

refinement. In order to understand why, let us consider the widely accepted proposition that religious dogma and experience are essentially projections, drawn from the most primal and intense (and universal) human feelings, fantasies, and forms of relationship. Such an argument is lent support when it is recognized that the mystics themselves used metaphors too, to help convey the experience of both the fall away from, and (especially) the soul's mystical reunion with, the divine. And what metaphors did they use? As we shall see in Chapter 4, they used images of sexual ecstasy, of marital union, of falling away from and then reuniting with the parent of the opposite sex (Plotinus speaks of salvation as being analogous to a wayward daughter's return to the father), and even of coming to know who and what one truly is; such metaphors figure prominently in Neoplatonic and Judaeo-Christian mystical accounts. Thus, the standard interpretation goes, it is these all-too-human situations and wishes that are the prototypes of, and disclose the true meaning(s) of, all lapsarian and redemptive projections and emotions – indeed, of all spiritual experiences regardless of the particular culture or tradition in which they are situated.

What is missing from such an account is a recognition that, in their contemporary articulations, these erotic, familial, and other "personal" images still carry with them traces and connotations derived from the distinctive theological doctrines that were once fleshed out with the use of such human analogs. Psychological reductionist analyses do not give sufficient weight to the fact that Judaeo-Christian and Neoplatonist theodicies, and their blendings, are systems of meaning and expectation that envision the nature and course of cosmic and human destiny. As narratives of history and ultimate concern, they possess certain structural features and evaluative stances that are not ubiquitous or universal. The human and earthly pictures and experiences that were invoked by theologians to lend vividness and comprehensibility to these Judaeo-Christian and Plotinian accounts thus were linked, in their original association with these theological doctrines, to particular ways of schematizing broad existential issues and the prospects for their resolution or mitigation. These personal images – of losing and regaining a parent–child connection, or yearning for and ultimately attaining sexual and marital union with one's beloved, or achieving a sense of "what one truly is" (which in the Plotinian system means coming to recognize one's source in the One) – came to be associated with a broader spiritual problematic that formulated and attempted to resolve the whys and wherefores of human finitude and suffering. That problematic assumed a particular form in the Judaeo-Christian theodicy, certain aspects of which are not universally found in all visions of cosmic history and human fate. What is distinctive about the Judaeo-Christian scheme, in both its mystical and non-mystical variants, is the structure of its narrative design (i.e., it has a particular linear or spiral shape and set of episodes, and is prospectivist), as well as certain values that inhere in that structure (i.e., in contrast to "non-Western" mysticisms, Judaeo-Christian systems evince an activistic orientation, stressing the necessity of individuation and valorizing earthly life and individuality). Thus, images of the loss and refinding of true self and intimate union, in being invoked to illustrate episodes in the Judeao-Christian mystical theodicy, came to personify lapsarian and redemptive moments which were situated in a narrative design, and evinced values, that in some respects are culture-specific. (This Judaeo-Christian narrative structure and set of values are explored throughout this book, particularly in Chapters 4 and 5.)

Over the course of secularization, this association between images of human experience and relationship on the one hand, and spiritual meanings and values on the other, has become tighter and more literalized. As the theological discourse has been cast aside, the structure, values, and significance of that discourse have become absorbed into the personal and interpersonal images that had been used by the religious mystics to illustrate spiritual experiences and themes. As disenchantment has proceeded, personal and interpersonal images (of self, family, relationship, even work) have become subtly "divinized." That is, our secular understandings of self, relationship, and certain types of experiences (including sexual union, creativity, falling-in-love, and the mother–infant relation) have taken on salvationist connotations and importance, especially in culture areas and in high cultural discourses that bear the strong influence of Protestant mysticism. They have come to assume a spiritual and moral significance and intensity that are the legacy of their earlier coupling with the Judaeo-Christian mystical theodicy.

Hence it is a mistake to construe the secularization process simply as a "boiling down" of religious illusions to their deep natural and ultimately psychological essences. A more adequate understanding of that process would take account of how, over the course of disenchantment, the human and earthly analogs invoked by the mystics to help render palpable the experience of salvation have absorbed into themselves key meanings, values, and (above all) redemptive connotations that heretofore they did not possess. As David Walsh has written of the early modern period, "the [historical] picture that emerges ... is not of a world increasingly separating itself from God, but of a world progressively absorbing the divine substance into itself."[69] A consequence of this is that much more is now crystallized and literalized in our psychological images of self, mothering, and marital and sexual relations than was the case when those images were invoked simply to give more immediacy to depictions of salvation. We now imbue these personal experiences, attributes, and interpersonal forms, with a significance and an ultimacy that heretofore they had been associated with in a much looser and more figurative way. We now see in these worldly images and human situations, and ask of them, far more than the mystics ever did.

In short, the human forms and ostensibly natural imperatives that populate psychoanalytic discourse still are tied to their supernatural forebears, and continue to evince culturally distinctive ways of formulating the human situation and the potentials for its renovation. The displacement of the root metaphor of Christian mystical theodicy onto the realm of the self and relationships is concomitant to the shift from a primarily religious view of the world to our contemporary secularized and "disenchanted"[70] vision of existence. Issues of ultimate concern, and considerations of the meaning of evil and suffering, are no longer constructed in terms of otherworldly concerns and anticipations. Rather, our spiritual interest has shifted to earthly existence, including what the philosopher Charles Taylor calls "ordinary life." It is in this context that we may understand how the locus of ultimate meaning and value, for many of us, has come to be situated in the self, the lifecourse, and human relationships. Thus does our theodicy now wear a human face.

The plan of the book is as follows: Chapter 2 contains a discussion of cultural sources of the emergence of self- and object-relations themes in Anglo-American psychoanalytic theory. Chapter 3 deals with the developmental narrative that was elaborated in tandem with this intensified focus on the self. In Chapter 4, theological sources of the idea of development are discussed, and a particular cultural genealogy for psychoanalytic developmental psychology is suggested. In Chapters 5, 6, and 7, that genealogy is traced; I follow its transformations from Neoplatonized Christian mysticism, through the more worldly narrative of Protestant mystic Jacob Boehme, and into the subsequent secularization of that narrative by English and German Romantics of the early nineteenth century. In Chapter 8 I return to the psychoanalytic developmental narrative and demonstrate its continuation of the lineage traced in

[69] David Walsh, *The Mysticism of Innerworldly Fulfillment: A Study of Jacob Boehme* (Gainesville: University Presses of Florida, 1983), p. 9.
[70] Weber, "Science as a Vocation," in Gerth and Mills, *From Max Weber*.

Chapters 5, 6, and 7. In Chapter 9, I consider some broader implications of this understanding of psychoanalytic developmental psychology as a secularized spiritual narrative.

2

The assenting echo:
Anglo-American values in
contemporary psycho-analytic
development psychology

It was only in America, and only owing to the tremendous professional encouragement I received in America, that I no longer felt I was
laboring under the shadow of titans. If I had not come to America,
where I felt free to formulate insights at which I had empathically
arrived, I would have accomplished very little. I would never have
begun to publish, to teach, to undertake research. Because if one does
not find an assenting echo to one's ideas, if one is passed over, as I was
in Vienna, then one cannot create. To create, after all, is to believe that
what one says will count.
        Margaret S. Mahler, *The Memoirs of Margaret S. Mahler*, 1988

[C]ulturally congruent phenomena unearthed or constructed by modern
theories of human development come to be canonized as desirable realities if they conform to values already independently in being within the
culture ... [T]heories of human development become classic ... when
they unearth or discern a previously undiscovered grouping of processes that extend or elaborate a cultural value that was previously implicit and is now made explicit.
        Jerome S. Bruner, "Value Presuppositions of
        Developmental Theory," 1986

As Jerome Bruner suggests in the passage cited above, there is a powerful relationship between formal psychological theories and the cultural
environments in which they are conceived and elaborated. Theories of
human development that attract the greatest interest, and exert the
strongest influence, are those that rationalize and extend a culture's most
deeply rooted and dearly held traditions of belief, value, and social interaction. A theory becomes "classic" because it resonates with, and further
elaborates and promotes, heretofore implicit culturally constituted views

regarding desirable attributes and capacities of the person.[1]

This perspective on the relationship between culture and psychological theory is particularly illuminating when used to examine the dynamics of the "cultural borrowing" of a psychological theory. By this phrase I mean that process by which a theory is transplanted from one culture to another and gradually comes to assume a form congruent with the host culture's ideologies, concerns, and values. In this chapter I explore one such case, that of the "borrowing" of psychoanalytic theory by the cultures of the United States and Great Britain. In so doing, I suggest a reason why the Christian mystical/Romantic narrative has become more prominent in Anglo-American psychoanalytic theories than it was in Freudian texts. Over the course of the past five decades, psychoanalytic theory has absorbed several central themes and concerns of American (and some strains of British) culture – above all, "autonomy" and "individuality." This in turn has promoted a selective elaboration (and in some instances modification and amendment) of Freudian theory along the lines of certain discourses that were not as prominent, and in some cases not found at all, in classical psychoanalysis. Chief among those discourses is the "preoedipal" developmental narrative (explicated in Chapter 3), which in turn is a descendant of the high Romantic narrative and its cultural ancestor, Neoplatonized Biblical history.

As a great many commentators have noted, Freud continually revised and added to his theories such that, taken overall, his writings contain many points of ambiguity and even self-contradiction. Another way of saying this is that Freudian texts are shot through with myriad cultural discourses, both esoteric and ethnopsychological.[2] Thus, subsequent

---

[1] I recognize that this statement of the relationship between theory and socio-cultural context accords to theory an entirely "conservative" function: it is viewed as a discourse that articulates and preserves the status quo, or at least *a* status quo. One might ask, what of theory intended (or "read") as resistance and subversion of some cultural and/or political situation (e.g., critical theory, feminist theory)? I argue only that in this particular case – the elaboration and diffusion of post-Freudian psychoanalytic clinical discourse and practice in the United States – the discourse has taken on a predominantly conservative cast (i.e., it articulates and rationalizes a "Protestant" and "liberal" ethnopsychology), in spite of its also possessing aspects that embody resistance to or loosening of hegemonic cultural values. See pp. 00–00 of this chapter for a review of some commentary on psychoanalytic "conservatism" in the United States.

[2] See, e.g., Robert R. Holt, "Ideological and Thematic Conflicts in the Structure of Freud's Thought," in S. Smith (ed.), *The Human Mind Revisited: Essays in Honor of Karl A. Menninger.* (New York: International Universities Press, 1978), pp. 51–98, "Ego Autonomy and the Problem of Human Freedom," in *Freud Reappraised: A Fresh Look at Psychoanalytic Theory* (New York: Guilford Press, 1989), pp. 220–1; William J. McGrath, *Freud's Discovery of Psychoanalysis* (Ithaca: Cornell University Press, 1986); Harry Trosman, "Freud's Cultural Background," in *The Annual of Psychoanalysis* 1 (New York: Quadrangle, 1973); and Madeleine and Henri Vermorel, "Was Freud a Romantic?" *International Review of Psychoanalysis*, vol. 13, 1986, pp. 15–37.

psychoanalytic theorists have had a rich collection of discourses from which to (tacitly) select and upon which to expand. This situation has helped to facilitate the mutation and development of "psychoanalysis" into multiple "psychoanalyses," ostensible continuations of Freudianism which actually have diverged radically from one another. As Edith Kurzweil recently noted, "the Freudians primarily are united by their profession rather than by their ideas."[3]

Psychoanalytic theorists working in the United States and Great Britain have participated in this selective reading and interpretation of earlier psychoanalytic texts. They have emphasized and extended certain aspects of "classical"[4] psychoanalytic theory, and deemphasized or discarded other aspects. Specifically, those versions of psychoanalysis that have been emphasized and elaborated in Anglo-American culture areas, particularly during the past twenty-five to thirty years (and arguably since the 1930s), have come more and more to focus on the development of the "ego" and/or the "self" and its modes of relating to objects, principally other persons. Increasingly, in these post-Freudian theories, the primary imperative of reality is no longer considered to be instinctual renunciation, but rather separation and individuation. Correspondingly, a person's degree of pathology or maturity has come to be assessed not in terms of his present-day relationship to the vicissitudes of the instincts and the Oedipus complex, but rather in terms of how successfully he or she has negotiated the separation-individuation process.

In this chapter I highlight the influence of Anglo-American culture on this "reshaping [of] the psychoanalytic domain" (to borrow Judith Hughes' phrase). I explore how the intensified emphasis on and elaboration of "self and object-relations" (so-called "preoedipal") issues and motifs evinces a commingling of classical psychoanalytic themes with some characteristically Anglo-American concerns and anxieties about the self's autonomy and individuality. In Bruner's terms, those psycho-

---

[3] E. Kurzweil, *The Freudians: A Comparative Perspective* (New Haven: Yale University Press, 1989), p. 283.

[4] I use this term to refer to what is written in Freudian texts, recognizing that "classical psychoanalysis" itself is a problematic and ambiguous term and cannot be used to refer to a unitary body of theory: As I have noted, Freud's psychoanalytic writings taken as a whole are replete with revisions, internal inconsistencies, and even contradictions. Hence these writings are constituted by myriad sometimes-conflicting cultural discourses (including Enlightenment rationalism, evolutionary theory, nineteenth-century neurology and psychophysics, German Classicism, and Romanticism, among others). My principal argument is that in the United States and the United Kingdom, some of these discourses and themes – many of which were not as prominent, or scarcely to be found at all, in the Freudian corpus – have been "selected," elaborated, and in some cases extended or altered beyond their original meaning.

analytic theories that have achieved hegemony in America and Britain have done so because they emphasized and expanded elements in psychoanalysis that are congruent with certain pervasive Anglo-American cultural values and ideals. Simultaneously, these formal theories have served to "canonize" such ethnopsychological discourses on the self, and implicit rules of behavioral display, as "desirable realities."

First I discuss the ascendance, in the United States and Great Britain, of those psychoanalytic theories – "later" ego psychology, object-relations theory, and self psychology – which highlight the development of the ego and/or the self. Then I identify three specific attributes of selfhood that Americans (and, with some qualification, the British) deem desirable and important – self-reliance, self-direction and verbal expression – and explore some ways in which these dimensions have become highlighted in psychoanalytic ideas. At the same time I connect these contemporary values to some older cultural traditions – nearly all of them what the historian and sociologist of religion Benjamin Nelson called "Protestant variants of conscience, character, and culture."[5] Of particular import are two different types of Protestantism which have had their fullest and most enduring influence on the culture of the United States but which also have influenced intellectual and cultural life in Great Britain: Puritanism and Nonconformism. The persistence of key elements of these spiritual models, and, especially, of their secular derivatives, has helped to promote the transformation of Anglo-American psychoanalysis into a more explicit and unambiguous discourse on the development of self-reliance and self-direction than can be found in Freudian psychoanalytic texts or in more recent continental versions of psychoanalysis such as that of Lacan.

So as not to collapse the differences between American and English ethnopsychologies,[6] I considered restricting this analysis to the cultural borrowing of psychoanalysis by the United States only. However,

[5] B. Nelson, "Self-Images and Systems of Spiritual Direction in the History of European Civilization," in S. Z. Klausner (ed.), *The Quest for Self-Control* (New York: The Free Press, 1965).

[6] Seymour Martin Lipset considers the United States, Canada, the United Kingdom, and Australia to be part of the same culture area, although the United States is deemed the most "individualistic" of the four for both religious and historical reasons ("Anglo-American Society," in *International Encyclopedia of the Social Sciences* [New York: Macmillan Co./The Free Press, 1968], pp. 289–301). The historian David Hackett Fischer also emphasizes the influence of certain aspects of British culture on the different regional cultures of the United States (*Albion's Seed: Four British Folkways in America* [New York: Oxford University Press, 1989]). For more detailed attention to differences between American and British cultural values, see Geoffrey Gorer, *The American People: A Study in National Character* (New York: Norton, 1948) and *Exploring English Character* (New York: Criterion, 1955).

although psychoanalysis never attracted as widespread an interest or as great a popularity in Great Britain as in the United States, it is nonetheless clear that there are strong similarities in the theoretical directions taken in both American and British theories. In both nations psychoanalytic theory has come to emphasize "self" and "preoedipal" issues, and to posit a developmental trajectory in which the self moves from a sense of undifferentiatedness towards autonomy and separate-selfhood as well as the capacity for mature relatedness. In both Britain and America, these formulations bear the strong imprint of nonconforming Protestant doctrines and their secular derivatives, as well as of a more general emphasis on self-sufficiency, emotional restraint and verbal fluency that pervades both cultures.

The preoedipal turn in Anglo-American psychoanalysis

Numerous commentators[7] have observed that most of the elaborations and innovations in psychoanalytic theory that have come to prominence in the United States and Great Britain during the past several decades have accorded central attention and importance to the development of the "self" (viewed at times as a representation within the ego,[8] at other times as a separate structure coexisting with the ego,[9] and at still other times as a structure which, whether called "ego" or "self," essentially replaces the classical ego[10]). Not only has the development of the self been of special interest, but also the development of the self's modes of relating to "objects," by which is usually meant other persons. Theorists

---

[7] See Harry Guntrip, *Psychoanalytic Theory, Therapy, and the Self* (New York: Basic Books, 1973); Jay Greenberg and Stephen Mitchell, *Object Relations in Psychoanalytic Theory* (Cambridge, MA: Harvard University Press, 1983); Morris N. Eagle, *Recent Developments in Psychoanalysis* (New York: McGraw Hill, 1984); Fred Pine, *Developmental Theory and Clinical Process* (New Haven: Yale University Press, 1985); Gregorio Kohon, *The British School of Psychoanalysis: The Independent Tradition* (New Haven: Yale University Press, 1986); Judith M. Hughes, *Reshaping the Psychoanalytic Domain* (Berkeley: University of California Press, 1989).

[8] This usage of "self" is found in the writings of Heinz Hartmann, the father of ego psychology and originator of the concept of "self" as a representation within the ego. Another analytic theorist who used "self" in this way was Edith Jacobson: see Jacobson, *The Self and the Object World* (New York: International Universities Press, 1964).

[9] In her memoirs (*The Memoirs of Margaret S. Mahler*, ed. Paul Stepansky [New York: Free Press, 1988]), Margaret Mahler speaks of the development of self and ego as parallel trajectories, one not reducible to the other. Kohut adopts a similar stance in his two major works, *The Analysis of the Self: A Systematic Approach to the Psychoanalytic Treatment of Narcissistic Personality Disorders* (New York: International Universities Press, 1971), and *The Restoration of the Self* (New York: International Universities Press, 1977).

[10] This path has been taken in the writings of British object-relations theorists such as Fairbairn, Winnicott, and Guntrip.

and clinicians have come to focus upon the self and its patterns of relating to objects, as these patterns are expressed in interpersonal interaction as well as intrapsychic fantasy. The three best-known contemporary schools which exemplify these trends are ego psychology (particularly the "later" ego psychology of Edith Jacobson, Rene Spitz, Margaret Mahler, and Otto Kernberg, whose theories have achieved strong popularity among American clinicians, intellectuals, and educated laypersons since the 1960s and 1970s), object-relations theory (a central concern in the work of many British analysts, including W.R.D. Fairbairn, D.W. Winnicott, Michael Balint, Joseph Sandler, and others) and self psychology (the brainchild of Heinz Kohut).

Although they vary in some of their particulars, virtually all of these theories chronicle a developmental sequence in which the individual's sense of distinctiveness and separate identity develops out of an original subjective state of "undifferentiation." At this earliest stage the infant is inferred to experience himself not only as essentially in union with the rest of the world, but also as omnipotent (even as his actual situation is one of extreme dependence). By the age of 3, the individual is supposed to have arrived at a provisional appreciation and acceptance[11] of his own separateness, and of the limitations of his powers, as well as of the separateness and limitations of other human beings. The attainment of a sense of one's separateness and individuality, and of the capacity for relationship, is seen to be effected mainly in the context of the development of the infant's relatedness to its mother (the patterns developed by the child in this one central relationship are seen to be extended to his mode of relating to the rest of the world). Emotional and personality disturbances are attributed to arrests, failures, or distortions of this developmental process.

The increasing prominence of these "preoedipal" themes and issues in psychoanalytic theory has not gone unnoticed by analysts themselves. The eminent analyst Hans Loewald, in a 1978 address given in plenary session at the Annual Meeting of the American Psychoanalytic Association – an address entitled "The Waning of the Oedipus Complex" – noted "the contemporary decline of psychoanalytic interest in the oedipal phase and oedipal conflicts and the predominance of interest and research in preoedipal development, in the mother–infant dyad and in

---

[11] Of course, the process of psychological development, including the consolidation of the sense of individual identity and capacity for relationship, is not considered to be completed by the age of 3. Rather, according to these theories, it is the essential groundwork that must be laid by this time.

[12] Hans Loewald, "The Waning of the Oedipus Complex," in *Papers on Psychoanalysis* (New Haven: Yale University Press, 1980), p. 386. In a similar vein, another prominent

issues of separation-individuation and of the self and narcissism."[12]

This declining interest in instinctual and Oedipal issues, and its replacement by the elaboration of "self" and "object-relational" themes, is not really new to psychodynamic theory: these themes were also prominent in the theories of the NeoFreudians. The NeoFreudians were a loosely affiliated group of theorist-clinicians, most of whom had been psychoanalytically trained, who broke away or were expelled from orthodox analytic circles in the United States during the 1930s and 1940s. Included among them were Harry Stack Sullivan, Karen Horney, Erich Fromm, Frieda Fromm-Reichmann, and Clara Thompson. During their lifetimes their theories were extremely popular in the United States, not only utilized by (non-orthodox) analysts but also widely read by intellectuals and the educated lay public.[13] In particular, Sullivan's theories, and his ideas about clinical practice, have been and continue to be extremely (albeit often covertly) influential in American psychoanalysis.

However, the psychoanalysts with whom I am concerned in this study – ego psychologists, most adherents of the "British" schools, and Kohutians – have taken pains to distinguish themselves from these "revisionists." Most of these theorists have never explicitly broken from the "classical" analytic tradition. Instead, each has tried (albeit at times ambiguously or ambivalently) to present his or her theory as a continuation or elaboration of, or a supplement to, Freud's ideas, rather than as an outright contradiction of them.[14] Probably the most common means of evading the charge of "revisionism" has been to suggest that the issues raised by these theorists are applicable to a different type of patient than

analyst, John Gedo, has written that "the most recent period in the history of psychoanalysis has been characterized by a gradual shift in focus from a view of ... archaic phenomena ['fixation behaviors, solutions to the psychological vicissitudes of still earlier phases of development'] as part of the background of nuclear oedipal transactions toward more complex conceptualizations that accord these phenomena degrees of pathogenicity in their own right....Almost everyone [no matter what their specific school or orientation within the psychoanalytic community] seems to agree that the research agenda of our time is the exploration of the deepest layers of the unconscious mind." (John Gedo, *Psychoanalysis and its Discontents* [New York: The Guilford Press, 1984], pp. 6–7).

[13] Karen Horney's bestselling books include The *Neurotic Personality of Our Time* (New York: W.W. Norton, 1937) and *New Ways in Psychoanalysis* (New York: W.W. Norton, 1939); a recent biography is Susan Quinn, *A Mind of Her Own* (New York: Summit, 1987). Fromm's widely read works include *Escape from Freedom* (New York: Avon Books, 1989). See also H. Stuart Hughes, *The Sea Change* (Middletown, CT: Wesleyan University Press, 1987) and Paul Roazen, *Freud and His Followers* (New York: New American Library, 1976). On Harry Stack Sullivan, see Helen Swick Perry, *Psychiatrist of America* (Cambridge, MA: Harvard University Press, 1983).

[14] Greenberg and Mitchell, *Object Relations*, have extensively explored the strategies employed by post-Freudian Anglo-American analysts to preserve this appearance of theoretical continuity with classical analysis.

those treated by Freud. The idea here is that while the neurotic conditions investigated by Freud involve the vicissitudes of the instincts and the Oedipal conflict (and thus classical psychoanalytic theory and technique can account for and treat them), the more serious disorders (narcissistic disturbance, "borderline" conditions and psychoses) derive from disturbances in the sense of identity and the capacity for relationship. While neurotics are seen to have floundered on Oedipal issues (which emerge between the ages of 3 and 5), these more severely disturbed patients are seen to have been derailed at an earlier stage of development. It is during this earlier era (before the age of 3, in the context of the mother–infant relationship) that the seeds are sown for the sense of bounded, cohesive, realistic "self" and "identity," as well as for the ability to form enduring relationships based on the capacity to integrate "good" (gratifying) and "bad" (frustrating and disappointing) images of both the other and the self.[15] In other words, the rationale for this apparent digression from classical theory is that in order to understand and treat these more "basic" emotional and personality disturbances, more detailed attention to the emergence of the sense of "self and objects" is required.

This might be a viable way of shifting focus while still asserting fundamental agreement with Freudian writings, but for the fact that many of these theorists have not left it at this. In apparent contradiction of the preoedipal/Oedipal distinction, some of these same theorists also elaborate upon classical theory in a way that at least implicitly challenges the primacy of instinctual and Oedipal themes in *all* emotional disturbance, not only in borderline and narcissistic personalities. In late-career writings by Mahler (one of the most lucid and influential of the later ego psychologists),[16] for example, there are suggestions that *all* pathology, including "Oedipal" pathology, is conditioned by developmental distortions originating during the preoedipal period, for example during what she calls the "separation-individuation" phase.[17] In 1975, Mahler wrote:

[15] There are differences in the particulars formulated by these various theorists, but this general depiction of the developmental narrative holds for all.

[16] Margaret S. Mahler, "On the Current Status of the Infantile Neurosis," in *The Selected Papers of Margaret S. Mahler*, vol. 2 (New York: Jason Aronson, 1975); see also "Epilogue," in Mahler, *Memoirs*. Kohut, *Restoration*, argues a similar point.

[17] In two major books, *On Human Symbiosis and the Vicissitudes of Separation-Individuation* ([with Fred Pine and Anni Bergman] New York: International Universities Press, 1968) and *The Psychological Birth of the Human Infant* (New York: Basic Books 1975), Margaret S. Mahler and her associates chronicle an allegedly necessary and universal developmental sequence by which the initially unself-conscious infant comes to achieve a sense of his own separateness and distinctiveness as well as the separateness and limitations of others. Mahler calls the initial states of psychic "undifferentiation" *autism* and *symbiosis*. This is followed by the *separation-individuation* phase, during

It seems inherent in the human condition that not even the most normally endowed child, with the most optimally accessible mother, is able to weather the separation-individuation process without crises, come out unscathed by the rapprochement struggle, and enter the oedipal phase without developmental difficulty.[18]

And one of Mahler's chief research collaborators, Fred Pine, spoke for many psychoanalytically oriented clinicians and thinkers when he asserted, in 1985, that "[i]t is not that oedipal level dynamics and pathology are inconsequential but I doubt that a child gets stuck on issues of that level ... if things have proceeded in a satisfactory way until that point."[19]

One might protest that it is possible to reconcile these two seemingly contradictory points of view: i.e., (1) that preoedipal pathology is characteristic of more seriously disturbed individuals and (2) that individuals who exhibit Oedipal pathology tend also (upon closer or more theoretically refined scrutiny) to exhibit that of the preoedipal type. To effect such a reconciliation one could invoke the commonly voiced assertion that psychoanalysts today encounter many more of these "lower-level" personalities than in past years – that many if not most of the patients nowadays are "borderlines" or narcissistically disordered, as opposed to the higher-level, better individuated neurotics (hysterics and obsessionals) who consulted Freud and about whom he wrote his theories.

Further weight has been lent to this argument in the writings of Kohut and of the social historian and critic Christopher Lasch, both of whom argued that changed social and childrearing conditions have given rise to a different (and perhaps more developmentally primitive) modal abnormal personality structure.[20] In other words, preoedipal pathology is pandemic to our contemporary situation. A greater proportion of personalities exhibit disorders of the self at this point in history than during Freud's era.

which the infant is propelled (by virtue of both innate tendencies and environmental exigencies) in the direction of awareness of himself as a separate and rather helpless being whose interests do not always coincide with mother's. This period has three subphases: *differentiation*, *practicing*, and *rapprochement*. This last subphase – *rapprochement* – includes a crisis, during which the toddler (aged 18–24 months) must confront and begin to come to terms with his separateness from mother and the limitations of his own and mother's powers. Only as the *rapprochement* crisis begins to subside (by age 3) is the child considered to be on the road to "identity" and "object constancy."

[18] Mahler, "Current Status of the Infantile Neurosis," p. 190; see also the epilogue of her *Memoirs*.

[19] Fred Pine, *Developmental Theory and Clinical Process* (New Haven: Yale University Press, 1985), p. 4.

[20] Kohut, *Analysis*, and Kohut, "Summarizing Reflections," in A. Goldberg (ed.), *Advances in Self Psychology* (New York: International Universities Press, 1980); Christopher Lasch, *The Culture of Narcissism: American Life in an Age of Diminishing Expectations* (New York: W.W. Norton, 1979).

42 The religious and romantic origins of psychoanalysis

Let us pause at this point to review, and attempt to integrate, the rationales that have been offered to explain the shift from an "Oedipal" to "preoedipal" emphasis in psychoanalytic theory: "preoedipal" and "self" theories have been elaborated to help us understand and treat those patients whose pathology is developmentally and dynamically more "primitive" than that of neurotics. Freud's theory is applicable to neurotics, but not adequate for these more disturbed patients. A potential contradiction of this rationale surfaces in writings that assert that preoedipal dynamics and problems are also detectable in most so-called neurotics – that it seems as if virtually all contemporary patients evince not only oedipal but also preoedipal pathology. But this might not be a contradiction after all: it could be due to the fact that, as many have suggested, there are more borderline and narcissistic personalities, and hence patients, these days. It would appear, then, that changed sociocultural conditions have had an impact on childrearing and personality formation such that borderline and narcissistic characters have become the modal abnormal (or, in a more diffuse way, simply the modal) personalities of our time. No wonder, then, that virtually all patients (even those who at first glance appear, for whatever reason, to be simply neurotic) seem to manifest these disturbances if we look long or closely enough. It is precisely this sociohistorical situation, in fact, which has brought to our attention these more "archaic" aspects of human character and its development, fostering the growth of our knowledge in an area that analysts didn't have need or opportunity to study before. But ultimately this is not a contradiction of classical analytic theory, only an elaboration of some aspects of it that had not been well explored.

This would be a plausible argument, provided that one condition were fulfilled: there still would have to be, or at least to have been (even if only in the past), a population of Oedipal neurotics somewhere. And this categorical discrimination between "neurotics" and "borderlines" would still have to be based on the "Oedipal" versus "preoedipal" criterion. Otherwise the foundations of classical analysis – to which, as I have noted, these analysts are intent upon pledging theoretical allegiance – are very seriously undermined, and these later ego psychologists, object relations theorists and self psychologists, are open to the dreaded charge of revisionism. That is, they may be seen as deviating from Freudian metapsychology in their devaluation of the primacy of instinctual and Oedipal vicissitudes in favor of self and relational ones.[21] I repeat: in

[21] Greenberg and Mitchell, *Object Relations,* make just this point in their book. They do not, however, relate the emergence of what they call "relational" psychoanalysis to a broader cultural context.

order for these contemporary models of psychoanalytic explanation to assert successfully their fundamental continuity with classical theory, the classification, "oedipal neurotic," and the Freudian account of the etiology of neurosis, would still have to be applicable to a real patient population somewhere – at the very least, to that population from which the theory was derived.

In fact, however, it is not only *today's* analysands who increasingly are being scrutinized in terms of preoedipal issues and found wanting. Gertrude and Rubin Blanck, authors of the texts *Ego Psychology* and *Ego Psychology 2* assert in their more recent volume, *Beyond Ego Psychology*, that

[t]he many reconsiderations in the literature of Freud's five cases raise questions about whether those patients were truly structured. Schreber was clearly psychotic, which Freud knew. It appears that the Wolf Man was certainly understructured, which Freud overlooked because his investigations were not directed toward borderline phenomena. Whether the Rat Man suffered from a true obsessional neurosis is also in doubt. Similar doubts apply to Dora and Little Hans. Today, the three latter cases would probably be regarded as possessing both neurotic and borderline features.[22]

And Harold P. Blum hints of Freud's own borderline or narcissistic features when he suggests that "contemporary evaluation" of aspects of Freud's personality "would include consideration(s) ... of conflicts related to symbiosis and separation-individuation."[23]

Thus the population of true neurotics is shrinking dangerously, not only in today's degenerate world but also within the roster of Freud's own clinical cases. In the face of this problematic logic, it is difficult to escape the conclusion that this shift from Oedipal to preoedipal, this "waning of the Oedipus complex," does not result only from a difference in those whom we are observing. Rather, it also is linked, at least as strongly, to a change in the lens through which we are looking. And if, indeed, these recent developments in psychoanalytic discourse are related more to a change of vision than to a clear-cut diagnostic difference in what is being seen, then the question is raised as to what the source is of this new psychoanalytic way of seeing.

Kohut[24] used the phrase "experience-near" to emphasize the fact that recent psychoanalytic theoretical concepts have moved closer to

---

[22] Rubin Blanck and Gertrude Blanck, *Beyond Ego Psychology* (New York: Columbia University Press, 1986), p. 122.

[23] Harold P. Blum, "The Prototype of Preoedipal Reconstruction," in Mark Kanzer and Jules Glenn (eds.), *Freud and his Self-Analysis* (New York: Jason Aronson, 1979), p. 157. See also Kohut, "Summarizing Reflections."

[24] *Restoration.*

phenomenology, utilizing everyday language. Kohut was more explicit and emphatic than some other theorists in his predilection for such language and in his insistence on deriving it from patients' self-reports. However, in a more general sense, *all* of these theories have become increasingly "experience-near," if this phrase is used to signify the fact that psychoanalytic terms such as "self," "identity," and "separation-individuation" correspond closely to their usage and connotations in the language of the wider culture.[25]

Of course, everyday language is not "everyday" everywhere: In making increasing use of more "experiential" or "accessible" terms and concepts, psychoanalytic theorists have introduced into their theories (and strengthened already existing psychoanalytic tendencies that are in accord with) intuitively plausible formulations and commonsense connections that are in fact derived from a cultural "logic," a set of assumptions and premises deeply embedded in Anglo-American cultural values and by no means universal.

In other words, to note that these theories have come to utilize words and concepts nearer to our "everyday" ones is really to say that they have become more congruent with Anglo-American ethnopsychology.[26] And indeed, in emphasizing and augmenting psychoanalytic discourse about the development of autonomy and individuality, the theories of Mahler, Erikson, Winnicott, and others would seem to have absorbed, and to have rendered still more explicit, some characteristically Anglo-American beliefs and values concerning what a person should be like and how he or she should behave. These cultural beliefs and values are manifest both at the level of formal ideology and in (often unstated or implicit) rules of behavioral display and social interaction.[27] Prominent among these desirable characteristics are *self-reliance* (self-sufficiency, self-confidence, and the avoidance of displays of dependency and of nonverbal displays of strong emotion), *self-direction* (the capacity to know what is in one's heart and mind and to act in accord with these inner beliefs and feelings), and *verbal expression.*

---

[25] Even American theorists who retain more "classical" psychoanalytic terminology, e.g. the late Edith Jacobson and Otto Kernberg, have moved such concepts into the realm of the phenomenological, thereby providing a point of entry for ethnopsychological beliefs and cultural values. (See Greenberg and Mitchell's commentary on these theorists' "phenomenologizing," in *Object Relations,* pp. 304–48.)

[26] I use the word ethnopsychology here in Shweder's "narrower" sense (see Chapter 1, footnote 36), referring to explicitly articulated values, but still leaving open the precise degree to which it is congruent with the broader "cultural psychology" or "cultural psychologies" by which Americans live.

[27] Once again: I am not suggesting that there is perfect congruence between stated ideals and values, and the often unstated or implicit values that even these theories do not completely articulate.

As numerous cross-cultural researchers have pointed out, these assumptions concerning the self, and prescriptions regarding behavioral display, are hardly ubiquitous; they are not even to be found in Southern European cultures let alone in non-Western ones.[28] Nor is there a simple causal linkage (in either direction) between these values and a high degree of industrialization and its attendant social institutions.[29] It is mainly in Northern European[30] culture areas that these values and norms are dominant. These Northern European cultural values have their sources both in cultural traditions that have existed for many centuries[31] and in the basic tenets of Protestantism.[32] As Steven Lukes[33] points out, Protestantism exemplifies "religious individualism" with its doctrines of the priesthood of all believers (highlighting the individual's personal unmediated relationship with God, and the inner life in general) and the respect for individual conscience (emphasizing the individual's right to his own spiritual practice and responsibility for his own spiritual condition).

Although these values are embedded in most versions of Protestantism, they are most strongly elaborated in two branches of radical Protestantism which originated during the sixteenth and seventeenth

[28] For basic contrasts between the Northern European (Protestant) "referential" self and the Latin-Mediterranean (Catholic) "indexical" self, see Atwood D. Gaines, "Cultural Definitions, Behavior, and the Person in American Psychiatry," in A.J. Marsella and G.M. White (eds.), *Cultural Conceptions of Mental Health and Therapy* (Dordrecht, Holland: D. Reidel, 1982).

[29] For example: in Japan, a highly industrialized society, "dependency" wishes and behaviors (at all stages of life) are sanctioned to a far greater degree than in the United States and Northern Europe. And qualities such as "independent" thought and its expression, which Americans value highly and consider to be important ends of development, are not similarly promoted in Japan. The primacy we accord to verbal expression also is absent in Japanese culture: Many writers point out that in Japanese relationships, verbalization is rarely the means by which one communicates anything considered really important, and that, correspondingly, Japanese tend to possess a more highly developed empathic sensitivity than do, e.g., Americans. See L. Takeo Doi, *The Anatomy of Dependence,* trans. John Bester (New York: Kodansha International, 1973); Takie Lebra, *Japanese Patterns of Behavior* (Honolulu: University of Hawaii Press, 1976); Alan Roland, *In Search of Self in India and Japan: Towards a Cross-Cultural Psychology* (Princeton: Princeton University Press, 1988).

[30] By "Northern European" I refer to all Western European nations north of the Alps, as well as Switzerland and the Anglo-American culture areas (United Kingdom, Scotland, United States, Canada, Australia).

[31] A. Macfarlane, *The Origins of English Individualism* (Oxford: Basil Blackwell, 1978); David Hackett Fischer, *Albion's Seed: British Folkways in America* (New York: Oxford University Press, 1989).

[32] Ernst Troeltsch, *The Social Teaching of the Christian Churches.* Vol. I (New York: Macmillan, 1931); Troeltsch, *Protestantism and Progress: A Historical Study of the Relation of Protestantism to the Modern World* (Boston: Beacon Press, 1958); Steven Lukes, *Individualism* (Oxford: Basil Blackwell, 1973); Lawrence Stone, *The Family, Sex and Marriage in England 1500–1800* (New York: Harper, 1979); Nelson, "Self-Images."

[33] Lukes, *Individualism*, p. 94.

centuries in Germany and England. The first branch included dissenting sects (I refer to them all as "nonconformists") such as the Pietists in Germany and the Netherlands, and the Methodists and Quakers in England. These groups emphasized Luther's doctrines of the priesthood of all believers and respect for individual conscience in a manner which was more radical and often more mystical than in Lutheran or Calvinist versions of these principles. The second branch encompassed the Puritans, a radical Calvinist group. Both branches – nonconformists and Puritans – stressed various aspects of autonomy and the inner life. They were among the first settlers of the United States, and their influence on our cultural values and folkways persists to this day, probably more strongly than anywhere else in the world.[34] Hence the United States may be considered the radical Protestant culture *par excellence*. However, these values are also detectable in certain strands within English (whence came the Puritans and other dissenters such as the Quakers and Methodists) and Scottish (Presbyterian, i.e. Calvinist) culture. In the following section I discuss how secular transformations of these Puritan and nonconforming doctrines persist in contemporary Anglo-American folk psychological and psychoanalytic ideas.

Of course, social theorists have proposed a variety of economic, political and social forces to account for the emergence of the ideals of autonomy and individuality in modern times. My purpose here is neither to review nor to dismiss the various explanations that have been offered. Nor is it to dismiss the suggestion that there were other, non-Protestant cultural sources of some of the conventions and ideals subsumed under Anglo-American self-reliance. Rather, I wish only to emphasize that any understanding of the sources and contemporary salience of the ideals of self-reliance and self-direction must include an appreciation of the fact that the moral coherence and authority they carry, and their emotionally persuasive character, derive at least in part from their genealogical connection to, and continuing expression of, salvationist images and themes.

Three Anglo-American values and their expression in contemporary psychoanalytic developmental psychology

Scholars who have examined the influence of American society and culture on psychoanalytic theory (usually focusing on the NeoFreudians and/or ego psychologists such as Hartmann and Erikson) have tended to

[34] Fischer, *Albion's Seed.* See also Ralph Barton Perry, *Puritanism and Democracy* (New York: Vanguard Press, 1944).

highlight the influence upon psychoanalytic theory and practice of a few central "American" themes and situations. The first of these is American "meliorism" or "optimism" regarding the perfectability, or at least the malleability, of human beings and the human condition itself. This is contrasted to the rather more pessimistic and sober estimation of man and his fate voiced in Freud's writings.[35] Related to this meliorist strain is an "environmentalist" one – a belief in the malleability of human nature and of individuals which far exceeded Freud's own views. Hence American psychoanalysis – beginning perhaps with the NeoFreudians but continuing to the present day – has been shown to place more emphasis than Freud did on the influence, both positive and adverse, of the environment (particularly the human environment, i.e., the quality of parenting) on personality development. Some commentators have given a more pejorative cast to such observations of Americanized analysts' stronger optimism and environmentalism, suggesting that in absorbing these tendencies into their theories, NeoFreudians and ego psychologists also assimilated American shallowness and conformity, and a "drift toward social and political conservatism."[36] A few commentators have noted Puritan elements in American culture which have contributed to the strength of psychoanalysis's reception here. Benjamin Nelson, for example, suggested that the "instrumental activism" (emphasis on worldly activity and excellence of performance as evidence of one's salvation) of our Puritan culture promoted Americans' zealous adoption of psychoanalytic therapy as a regime of self-improvement.[37] And Philip Rieff made a related point when he wrote that "there was something about Protestantism itself that made it ready, upon decline, for psychoanalysis ... For Protestant culture, it was Calvin, with his doctrine of predestination, who first turned all action into symptom. Only the most careful scrutiny of the outer actions could give even a hint of the inner condition, whether that be of grace or damnation."[38] This imperative of self-

---

[35] See Hendrik Ruitenbeek, *Freud and America* (New York: Macmillan, 1966); H. Stuart Hughes, *The Sea Change* (Middletown, CT: Wesleyan University Press, 1987), p. 175; and Paul Roazen, "Ego Psychology," in *Encountering Freud: The Politics and Histories of Psychoanalysis* (New Brunswick: Transaction Publishers, 1990), pp. 139–61.

[36] Hughes, *Sea Change*, p. 195. See also Russell Jacoby, *The Repression of Psychoanalysis: Otto Fenichel and the Political Freudians* (New York: Basic Books, 1983). On the related vicissitudes of the medicalization of psychoanalysis in America, see Nathan G. Hale, Jr., "Berggasse XIX to Central Park West: The Americanization of Psychoanalysis, 1919–1940," *Journal of the History of the Behavioral Sciences*, vol. 14 (1978), pp. 299–315; see also Nathan G. Hale, Jr., *The Rise and Crisis of Psychoanalysis in the United States: Freud and the Americans 1917–1985* (New York: Oxford University Press, 1995).

[37] Nelson, "Self-Images."

[38] Philip Rieff, "The American Transference: From Calvin to Freud," in *The Feeling Intellect* (Chicago: University of Chicago Press, 1990), pp. 12–13.

scrutiny in Puritan thought is seen by Rieff to have made America fertile soil for the introspective orientation of psychoanalysis.

Yet for all that has been written about the "Americanization" of psychoanalysis, there has been surprisingly little attention paid to the relationship between Anglo-American hyperindividualism (and its radical Protestant ancestry) and the ascendance of self and ego issues in psychoanalytic theory. One can only speculate that the cultural derivation of themes such as self-reliance and self-direction has been overlooked because these values are so pervasive and strong that we tend to take them for granted. They are so much a part of our cultural fabric that even as social scientists we have tended not to subject them to analytic or critical scrutiny.[39] In recent years, however, interest on the part of cultural anthropologists in the comparative study of ethnopsychologies has brought to greater prominence the culturally distinctive (and probably rather atypical) nature of these and other "individualistic" assumptions inherent in "Western," and specifically Anglo-American, folk psychology.[40] Exposed to models of the person and the lifecourse that are different from our own, we see our own culture and its belief-systems (both ethnopsychologies and formal theories) in a more self-conscious light.

Below I consider three attributes of the self that Americans deem desirable and valuable, and offer some examples of how these beliefs and values have entered into or been strengthened in recent psychoanalytic discourse. First, however, I wish to make one prefatory remark regarding this cultural borrowing process that I have been describing. Thus far, this chapter has been framed in terms of how psychoanalytic theory has been altered to "fit in" with Americans' values and their world view. In fact, however, one cannot consider how our concerns about autonomy have intensified this emphasis within psychoanalysis without acknowledging that in this commingling the American folk psychological ideas

---

[39] Robert Bellah et al., *Habits of the Heart* (Berkeley: University of California Press, 1985) constitutes an exception to this generalization. See also T.C. Heller, M. Sosna and D.E. Wellbery (eds.), *Reconstructing Individualism: Autonomy, Individuality and Self in Western Thought* (Stanford: Stanford University Press, 1986) and Lukes, *Individualism*.

[40] See, e.g. Clifford Geertz, "From the Native's Point of View: On the Nature of Anthropological Understanding," in Richard Shweder and Robert LeVine (eds.), *Culture Theory: Essays on Mind, Self and Emotion* (Cambridge: Cambridge University Press, 1984); Michelle Z. Rosaldo, *Knowledge and Passion: Ilongot Notions of Self and Social Life* (Cambridge: Cambridge University Press, 1980); P. Heelas and A. Lock, *Indigenous Psychologies: The Anthropology of the Self* (New York: Academic Press, 1981); Robert A. LeVine and Merry I. White, *Human Conditions: The Cultural Basis of Educational Development* (New York: Routledge and Kegan Paul, 1986); and Catherine Lutz, *Unnatural Emotions: Everyday Sentiments on a Micronesian Atoll and their Challenge to Western Theory* (Chicago: University of Chicago Press, 1988).

have also been modified, at least as they are manifest in the psychoanalytic discourse. Anglo-American psychoanalytic theory has indeed absorbed, and even serves to rationalize, the imperative of autonomous behavior and thought. But at the same time it also brings to our attention, and cautions us about, the stresses and hazards of too-great an independence, suggesting that this style of selfhood, too, bespeaks an incomplete development.

To be more specific: the story of development as told by these theorists is not only conceived as a movement out of "symbiosis" (Mahler) or "hallucinatory omnipotence" (Winnicott) or "absolute dependence" (Fairbairn) towards autonomy and self-reliance. These theories also include the postulate that, on some level, all of us always are struggling with the longing for reunion, and that even if one has developed to a higher, more securely individuated level, one still seeks out relationships where this desire for some sort of "oneness" can be integrated with the imperative of separateness. If we are able to negotiate the painful and difficult but necessary process of separation and individuation, to achieve true identity and the capacity for relationship, then we may be "granted" (or rather, we will have "earned") the capacity to engage in limited and partial experiences of reunion with our objects, but without losing the sense of separate and distinctive identity which we have struggled to achieve. Such reunion-in-separateness is of two basic types: (1) "regression in the service of the ego" (present in falling-in-love, artistic and other types of creativity, orgasm and some aspects of the mother–infant relationship) and (2) a more limited and partial type of reunion with the object which is a part of any intimate relationship. For, in any such relationship, if one does not have the capacity to display some dependency, "regression," and permeability of "ego boundaries," then one also is not considered fully healthy and mature.

The inclusion of this dimension alongside the dominant emphasis on independence and individuation, then, preserves a non-folk psychological element in these psychoanalytic theories, an element in which we see the persistence of a distinctively "psychoanalytic" way of looking at things. For surely one meaning of the term "dynamic" as it pertains to psychoanalysis is the postulate that, "underneath" what is normal, healthy, and mature, there always lurk opposing tendencies and longings, and that maturity and sanity actually consist of a delicate balance of tensions, conflicts, and desires. Introduced into a culture which upholds strong conventions and values concerning separate-selfhood and autonomy, the psychodynamic system – which exposes and articulates points of tension and contradiction – has come to fixate on the tension between oneness and separateness, fusion and individuation. These are now viewed as the vital issues for making sense of, and helping to heal, the limitations and dilemmas of human existence.

All this is not to suggest that this "dynamic" vision stands outside the flux of culture: in it, too, we can detect older cultural discourses, albeit "high" rather than "folk psychological" ones. In Anglo-American post-Freudian theories, this view of development and maturity as a perennial balance between, and integration of, conflicting forces (now conceived less in terms of instinctual tensions than in terms of simultaneous longings for oneness and separateness) closely resembles a generic high Romantic narrative pattern. Indeed, this narrative, along with its cultural genealogy, is the main subject of this book; I begin to explore it in greater detail in Chapter 3, once I have discussed (in this chapter) the cultural sources of the shift to "ego" and "self" themes and concerns.

The three values discussed below are self-reliance, self-direction, and verbal expression. I have chosen to highlight them here because they are very central and pervasive, both in American cultural values and in contemporary Anglo-American psychoanalytic theories. Needless to say, this list is by no means exhaustive either as a set of desirable attributes of the American self or as a set of American values that have become highlighted in contemporary psychoanalytic thought.

Self-reliance

To be self-reliant is to not depend upon another for care or for the regulation of one's self-esteem. The opposite of self-reliance is overdependence upon others: one is overdependent if one requires or demands the assistance or support of others in order to function or to be comfortable. To help one's child become independent in a variety of ways is probably the single most important goal of the American parent.

Takeo Doi, Alan Roland, and others[41] have pointed out that Americans tend to evince much more extreme discomfort with displays of dependency, or of what we interpret as dependent behaviors, than do

---

[41] L. Takeo Doi, "Some Thoughts on Helplessness and the Desire to be Loved," *Psychiatry*, vol. 26, no. 3, August 1963, pp. 266–72, and *Anatomy of Dependence*; Roland, *In Search of Self*; H. Morsbach and W.J. Tyler, "A Japanese Emotion: *Amae*," in Rom Harre (ed.), *The Social Construction of Emotion* (Oxford: Basil Blackwell, 1986). Atwood Gaines ("Cultural Definitions," p. 183) has observed that in Mediterranean cultures, complaining (which Anglo-Americans tend to perceive as evidence of moral weakness and psychological immaturity) may be perceived as communication of the self's ennoblement, because to complain is to describe the extent to which one has suffered, and suffering is seen to enhance one's moral dignity.

those in at least some Asian or Mediterranean cultures. This discomfort is apparent in many aspects of American psychoanalysis. Concerning the therapeutic relationship itself, Takeo Doi has pointed to "a cultural assumption which many psychotherapists in this country seem to share unwittingly that they can help the patient only insofar as he helps himself."[42] Robert Bellah and his collaborators, in *Habits of the Heart* (an ethnographic study of contemporary American life), quote their prototypical therapist as saying of her profession, "If you've done a really good job, they don't think you've helped them at all, and they think they've done it themselves – and in a sense they have."[43] Not only must all help for the patient ultimately come from within himself, but the more that a patient is able to express a self-reliant attitude (provided it is not defensive) the better is deemed his progress. In Ernst Kris's famous paper on the "good hour,"[44] the patient's improvement and movement in the direction of termination is gauged in terms of indications that he has begun to perform for himself the functions of the analyst, most notably the interpretive function.

It is testimony to the centrality of the themes of independence and separate-selfhood in American ethnopsychology that American psychoanalysis has come to view all severe psychopathology (and, for some theorists, *all* psychopathology) as related to failed individuation and failed independence. On one hand, the more extremely "dependent" a patient is seen to be, the more severely disturbed he or she is deemed. But on the other hand, it is not only overtly overdependent behaviors that are explained in these terms, but also certain types of more "withdrawn" and "distant" personalities (e.g., "schizoid" and some narcissistic types). In such cases, the outward appearance of self-sufficiency or detachment is considered to belie an inner world of impaired autonomy,[45] and greatly feared wishes for merger with the object.[46]

As has been noted, virtually all Northern European cultures encourage self-sufficiency and discourage displays of dependency and

---

[42] Doi, "Some Thoughts."

[43] Robert Bellah et al., *Habits*, p. 70.

[44] Ernst Kris, "On Some Vicissitudes of Insight in Psychoanalysis," *International Journal of Psycho-Analysis*, vol. 37, 1956, pp. 445–55.

[45] David Shapiro, *Autonomy and Rigid Character* (New York: Basic Books, 1981).

[46] William Meissner, *The Borderline Spectrum: Differential Diagnosis and Developmental Issues* (New York: Jason Aronson, 1984), pp. 206–8. Another commonsense linkage which psychoanalytic thinkers tend to take for granted is that between extremely dependent behaviors and poor discrimination between self and others. This seemingly intuitive association of "inappropriately" dependent behaviors with an inference of weak "ego boundaries" and lack of "self-cohesion" bears further philosophical and anthropological scrutiny.

emotion.[47] These conventions are strengthened and rationalized by the generic Protestant emphasis on individual responsibility. One finds these or similar values in Freud's writings, too. The Kantian ideal of rational autonomy[48] is deemed by Freud an index of maturity and civilization, and scattered throughout his theories there are references to infantile "passivity" versus more mature "activity," as well as to the developmental movement towards greater "detachment" from one's parents. "From the first," wrote Benjamin Nelson, "Freud emphasized that the goal of treatment was the achievement of autonomy on the part of the patient, the ability to regulate his own life by norms of his own devising." This, as Nelson also noted, is already a "Protestant" element within psychoanalysis,[49] and thus a preexisting source of congruence between Freudian psychoanalysis and Anglo-American cultural values.

However, "self-reliance" has taken on an even stronger and more central importance, as well as additional meaning, in recent American and British psychoanalytic theories. As was noted above, pathological dependence (whether observed or inferred) has become *the* central diagnostic criterion for discriminating between "normal neurotics" (as they often are called) and lower-level characters. Following Max Weber,[50] I would suggest that this extreme preoccupation with and valorization of self-reliance (and the intrapsychic sense of "separateness" which is considered its concomitant), and of related qualities such as self-confidence and self-control, is linked to the Puritan strain in Anglo-American culture, with its distinctive version of the Protestant vision of autonomy. Weber and other scholars[51] have pointed out that it was in Calvinist doctrines that Protestant ideas about self-reliance and individual responsibility attained their most extreme form, due to the intimate connection in Calvinism between self-reliance and salvation. Weber argued that, in response to the doctrine of predestination, there developed in Calvinist culture areas a very strong emphasis on independent

---

[47] Recent ethnographic research in the Netherlands suggests that Dutch social relations may in some respects evince more "interdependence" and "cooperation" than do those of Americans. See, e.g., Peter Stephenson, "Going to McDonald's in Leiden: Reflections on the Conception of Self and Society in the Netherlands," *Ethos*, vol. 17, no. 2, 1989, pp. 226–47.

[48] In fact, Kant's principles of moral autonomy and rationality derive much from Protestant doctrines, particularly Pietistic inner light mysticism. For further discussion of this connection, see the following section of this chapter, on "self-direction."

[49] Nelson, "Self-Images," p. 75.

[50] Max Weber, *The Protestant Ethic and the Spirit of Capitalism* (New York: Charles Scribners' Sons, 1958).

[51] Perry Miller, "The Marrow of Puritan Divinity," *Publications of the Colonial Society of Massachusetts*, vol. 32, 1937, pp. 245–300; Perry, *Puritanism and Democracy*; Lukes, *Individualism*.

achievement in this world. This is because one's worldly activity and success, apparent confidence, and capacity to improve one's life *through one's own initiative* were construed as evidence that one was among the elect, marked for redemption: "God helps those who help themselves." This was perhaps most extremely true of American Puritanism, i.e., the culture of New England where, as Ralph Barton Perry pointed out, Puritanism could develop "unhampered" upon favorable soil.[52]

Perry wrote of the "Puritan temper of personal independence. For though he was willing to admit his dependence on God, he looked to this as a means of emancipation from dependence on man and on nature. Salvation was the only gratuity he was willing to accept."[53] This view of the individual as very much "on his own" became even more marked as Puritanism became divested of its original communitarian and worldly utopian aspirations, which had perhaps mitigated somewhat the "unprecedented inner loneliness," which according to Weber was the lot of the Puritan and "can even today be identified in the national character and institutions of the peoples with a Puritan past."[54]

The contemporary American analyst Robert Holt has suggested that "autonomy is the utopian ideal of ego psychology."[55] Insofar as he asserts that in psychoanalysis there is a "utopian" ideal at all, of course, one might argue that Freud's message has been somewhat misread – "Americanized." But even if we accept Holt's viewpoint (perhaps on the grounds that many Anglo-American psychoanalytic theories are indeed more congenial to utopianism), I would propose that the utopia of ego psychology ("later" ego psychology, at least), self psychology, and object-relations theory is not autonomy alone. Rather, it is the supplementation of autonomy with "intimacy." By this term I mean the capacity for relationship, in which one may experience sustained connection to another person and, within limits, longed-for "regression" and "oneness," while simultaneously retaining one's essential distinctiveness, integrity, and autonomy. Thus, as was discussed above, Anglo-American psychoanalytic theory has become both an explication and rationalization of the ideal of self-reliance, and a subtle critique and tempering of this ideal via acknowledgement of the costs and losses inherent in its promotion.

---

[52] Perry, *Puritanism and Democracy*, pp. 93–4 (following Miller, "Marrow"), also points out that "the form of Calvinism which prevailed in New England was the so-called covenant or federal theology." It is this type of Calvinism which most exemplifies and promotes the notion that one's independent efforts and successes – one's material, moral, intellectual, and spiritual achievements – all give evidence of the salvation of one's soul.

[53] Ibid., p. 301.

[54] Weber, *Protestant Ethic*, p. 105.

[55] Holt, *Freud Reappraised*, p. 229. Actually, Holt here is answering Erikson, who had suggested that "for psycho-analysis [that is, for id-psychology] the utopia is 'genitality.'"

Self-direction

Self-direction encompasses two imperatives: first, that one should know what is in one's heart and mind and second, that one should make choices and (insofar as is possible) live one's life in accord with these inner beliefs and feelings, rather than in compliance with some external standard or with another person's wishes. The opposite of self-direction, compliance, signifies not merely behavioral conformity to some external authority but also (and this is considered more pernicious and psychologically undesirable) a confusion of the other's desires with one's own in a way that distorts, constricts, or suppresses one's true self and its unique personal experience.

In psychoanalytic theories, there are two eras of life in which the theme of self-direction is particularly emphasized. One is the preoedipal era and the other is adolescence. During infancy and early childhood, parental failure to encourage and promote in the child a sense of his true needs, feelings, and preferences is considered to be highly pathogenic. Winnicott[56] asserts that the child who is forced to respond too early in life to his mother's needs does not have sufficient attention paid to his own. Consequently his "true self" – the seat of his own wishes, and of his unique and spontaneous feelings and gestures – becomes submerged and inaccessible, and cannot develop properly. Kohut[57] claims that the narcissistically disturbed self has not received sufficient empathic responsiveness and "mirroring" from his parents, and that this is why such a child cannot develop an adequate self structure. Erikson[58] posits an early developmental tension between autonomy on the one hand, and shame and doubt on the other. He suggests that if the very young child is denied the "gradual and well-guided experience of autonomy and free choice," as embodied in the proper balance between parental limitation and promotion of his free expression, the child will not grow up to know his own mind and feelings.

The particulars of this miscarriage of development thus are conceptualized differently in these various theories. But whether we are looking at Winnicott's overly compliant false self, Kohut's narcissistically disturbed self, Erikson's imbalance of shame and doubt versus autonomy, or still other clinical entities, we find that despite differences in the timing and severity of these pathologies a feature that they share is an inability on

---

[56] D.W. Winnicott, "Ego Distortion in Terms of True and False Self," in *The Maturational Processes and the Facilitating Environment* (New York: International Universities Press, 1960) pp. 140–52.

[57] Kohut, *Analysis* and *Restoration*.

[58] Erik Erikson, *Childhood and Society* (New York: Norton, 1963).

the part of the self to develop or discriminate his true feelings and desires, as well as a stunted capacity for free choice, spontaneity, and creativity.

The other era when the individual is supposed to learn a great deal about what is in his mind and heart is, of course, adolescence, which the analyst Peter Blos has called "the second individuation."[59] Erikson, who devoted so much attention to this stage of life, suggests that the task of the adolescent era is the development of a sense of identity. He defines "the sense of ego identity" as "the accrued confidence that the inner sameness and continuity prepared in the past are matched by the sameness and continuity of one's meaning for others."[60] As I understand him, he asserts that the task of the adolescent and young adult is not only the achievement of a greater separation and individuation from his or her primary object ties, but also the expression and integration of the self within the larger society. One must somehow find a way for the inner sense of self to connect to the world in a meaningful, satisfying, and socially responsible way. Erikson's seeming optimism about the possibility (indeed, the imperative) of connecting the inner self to the outer social world indicates one important difference between the idea of individuality in the United States and that in many other culture areas, including Japanese, Mediterranean, and even English societies.[61]

This general emphasis on the psychological and moral value of being attuned to one's true beliefs, feelings, and preferences appears in large measure to be a secular, modern-day transformation of the "nonconforming" Protestant doctrines which have played such an important role in American cultural life. I have described how certain non-Puritan dissenting Protestant groups which settled in the New World (including the Quakers and the Methodists) emphasized Luther's principles of the priesthood of all believers and respect for individual conscience in a

[59] Peter Blos, "The Second Individuation Process in Adolescence," in *The Psychoanalytic Study of the Child*, vol. XXII (New York: International Universities Press, 1967), pp. 162–86.

[60] Erikson, *Childhood and Society*, p. 263.

[61] Gaines ("Cultural Definitions") has contrasted the Northern European Protestant "referential" self to the Latin "indexical" self of French ethnopsychology. He asserts that for the French, as for other Latin cultures, the inner self is considered to be fixed at birth, immutable, and essentially not in commerce with one's outer self, which changes in relation to the interpersonal and "role" situations in which one finds oneself. Lebra (*Japanese Patterns*, p. 158) suggests that, despite the common description of Japanese culture as characterized by "groupism" and "social orientation," the Japanese "are not indifferent to individuality and autonomy." However, "[i]ndividuality for the Japanese is at the opposite pole of social involvement. Individuality lies not in society but away from it." In English society, in spite of its strong radical Protestant and Romantic traditions, the imperative of self-expression and self-actualization in one's daily life is likewise not as strong as it is in America.

manner which was even more extreme than in Lutheran and Calvinist versions of these principles. These sects' doctrines tended to be more "emotional," compassionate and optimistic than those of the Puritans, and often had strong mystical overtones.[62] For them, intimations of one's salvation arise not (or not only) as a by-product of worldly activity and achievement, but rather in the experience, accessible to all, of contact with God within one's soul. The individual human spirit can be illuminated by the divine spark such that one may apprehend God and one's connection to him, and thereby have an intuition and foretaste of a more definitive salvation to come. This is the doctrine of the inner light,[63] which predated Protestantism by many centuries but also became a centerpiece of these post-Reformation doctrines and thereby took on an increasingly "this-worldly" cast. Eventually, the belief that the individual must look inward to discover God's truth within himself became completely secularized, so that it was not God and an intimation of literal salvation one sought by looking within, but rather one's *self*. In the nineteenth century, American philosopher Ralph Waldo Emerson helped to transform the religion of the inner light into a literal worship of the self, with his exhortation that "a man should learn to detect and watch that gleam of light which flashes across his mind from within ... Nothing is at last sacred but the integrity of your own mind." Correspondingly, he asserted, "Whoso would be a man, must be a nonconformist ... What I must do is all that concerns me, not what the people think."[64] Today, this creed remains one of the foundations of our culture: Robert Bellah describes "finding oneself," and attempting to be faithful to that self in one's "lifestyle," as central aims of contemporary Americans.[65]

---

[62] The powerful influence of worldly mystical Protestant strains on American ethnopsychology and Euro-American high culture has rarely been directly assayed. Benjamin Nelson exhibited characteristic perspicacity when he noted that "Weber was so intent upon the unique predominance in the West of the penetration and remaking of the world to innerworldly asceticism that he failed to give enough weight to another fact ... Weber does not...sufficiently stress the significance of *innerworldly mysticism* ..." Nelson, "Max Weber, Ernst Troeltsch, Georg Jellinek as Comparative Historical Sociologists," *Sociological Analysis*, vol. 36, no. 3, 1975, p. 236.

[63] See Paul Tillich, *A History of Christian Thought From its Judaic and Hellenistic Origins to Existentialism* (New York: Touchstone, 1968); see also Nelson, "Self-Images."

[64] Ralph Waldo Emerson, "Self-Reliance," in *Selected Essays, Lectures and Poems* (New York: Bantam, 1990).

[65] Bellah et al., *Habits*. Of course, in spite of our individualistic ideology, and the use of rationales and judgements (of ourselves and others) which invoke the concepts of "self-direction" and "self-expression," at another level of ethnographic analysis one finds that Americans are no more tolerant of truly deviant behaviors than are members of any other society. What is so interesting (and cultural) is that we think we are, should be, or could be.

In addition to these Protestant sects' direct bequest to American ethnopsychology of the belief that the individual must look inward to discover (God's or his own) truth within himself, there are at least two other secular strains of thought that grew out of Protestant "inner light" mysticism[66] and have also influenced American high and popular culture. One is Enlightenment (including Kantian) political and moral philosophy: the social and political principles of liberty and freedom of conscience upon which this country was founded owe a great deal to Protestant sectarian thought. Kantian philosophy, with its idea of the autonomous "will of every rational being which makes universal law,"[67] owes more to the doctrine of the inner light (mediated via German Pietism) than is often acknowledged.[68] Phrasing the spiritual imperative of self-direction in more explicitly political terms, Thomas Jefferson wrote, "Rebellion to tyrants is obedience to God."

The other secular transformation of this aspect of nonconformism can be found, paradoxically, in a critique of Enlightenment rationalism: high Romantic thought. There is an indigenous Romantic strain in American culture that Robert Bellah calls "expressive individualism" (Emerson and Walt Whitman exemplify this tendency). High-cultural English and German Romantic themes and patterns also are prominent in Anglo-American psychoanalytic theories of development. In part, this is due to the straightforward congruence of some of these European motifs with American Romantic themes (for example, that of self-expression).[69] It is also due to the fact that the high Romantic vision, with its depiction of a quasi-mystical striving towards a "higher" reunion of subject and object in which the subject's individuated distinctiveness also is preserved, provided a dynamic, dialectical (and hence psychoanalytic) "understructure" to the American emphasis on separate-selfhood and independence. For these reasons, English and German high Romantic

---

[66] The influence of nonconforming Protestant ideas on a variety of Northern European and American popular and folk cultural discourses has been noted by Nelson, "Self-Images." On the connection between Protestant sectarian mysticism and rationalism, see Tillich, *History of Christian Thought.* On the transmission of Christian mystical themes to the Romantics via their contact with Protestant sectarian doctrines, see M.H. Abrams, *Natural Supernaturalism* (New York: Norton, 1973). See also Charles Taylor, *Sources of the Self* (Cambridge, MA: Harvard University Press, 1989).

[67] Quoted in Lukes, *Individualism*, p. 45.

[68] Nelson, "Self-Images"; Taylor, *Sources.*

[69] Louis A. Sass has explored how Heinz Kohut's theory embodies Romantic and "expressivist" themes. Perhaps these particular Romantic dimensions were expanded in (and to some extent grafted onto) Kohut's and other, similar, psychoanalytic theories in conjunction with these theories' taking root in American cultural soil. See L.A. Sass, "The Self and its Vicissitudes: An 'Archaeological' Study of the Psychoanalytic Avant-Garde," *Social Research* 55 (Winter 1988), pp. 551–607.

themes (and in particular the narrative pattern which is the central focus of this book) have become elaborated in Anglo-American psychoanalysis to a greater degree than they were in Freud's texts. [70]

The term "nonconforming" originally was applied to these Protestant groups because they dissented and broke away from the Church of England. It is interesting to note that, of the leading British-born object-relations theorists, Winnicott was raised as a Methodist and Guntrip a Congregationalist (both "dissenting" denominations), and Fairbairn's primary religious affiliation was with the Scottish Presbyterian Church. Of course, they also were exposed (particularly Winnicott) to a celebration of the "true" self in English Romantic poetry and literature.

Verbal expression

The importance that Westerners in general attach to verbalization has been noted by many writers.[71] In contemporary American culture, verbalization of one's thoughts, feelings, and opinions is encouraged as a means of serving the values of self-expression and freedom of choice, both of which have been discussed above. The anthropologist Joseph Tobin and his associates have described how, in the contemporary American preschools they studied, the use of language is emphatically encouraged as a means of expressing one's opinions and feelings in a way that it is not in the mainland Chinese or Japanese settings that they also studied. Tobin reports a bit of dialogue from an American school in which the teacher asks, "Do you want juice, Rhonda? Milk? A cracker? What do you want? Don't just keep shaking your head. How am I supposed to know what you want if you don't tell me?"[72] Embedded in this utterance are two assumptions: first, everyone is entitled to freedom of choice and a variety of options; second, you cannot expect another to intuit or anticipate your preferences: you must state them explicitly.

As a substitute for the acting out of impulses, and as an expression of insight, verbalization has always been deemed of central importance in

---

[70] Romantic themes present in German literature and philosophy are by no means absent from Freudian texts: see Thomas Mann, "Freud's Position in the History of Modern Thought," in *Past Masters and Other Papers* (New York: Alfred A. Knopf, 1931) and "Freud and the Future," in *Freud, Goethe, Wagner* (New York: Alfred A. Knopf, 1937); Lionel Trilling, *Freud and the Crisis of our Culture* (Boston: Beacon Press, 1955); Trosman, "Freud's Cultural Background"; Holt, "Ideological and Thematic Conflicts" and "Ego Autonomy"; McGrath, *Freud's Discovery of Psychoanalysis*; and Vermorel and Vermorel, "Was Freud a Romantic?"

[71] See Joseph Tobin, David Y.H. Wu, and Dana Davidson, *Preschool in Three Cultures: Japan, China and the United States* (New Haven: Yale University Press, 1989); Roland, *In Search of Self.*

[72] Tobin et al., *Preschool*, p. 134.

psychoanalysis. But in the context of American culture, where verbal communication has come to connote an acknowledgement of one's radical separateness, and to serve as a vehicle for one's freedom of choice and self-expression, verbalization in psychoanalysis has acquired additional import: the use of language for communication is now highlighted as an expression of one's awareness that one is separate and different from the other. To communicate verbally is a sign of higher development because it is taken to mean that one is aware that preverbal gesturing or empathic communication (associated with lower-level fantasies of symbiosis and merger with the object) cannot be relied upon to communicate needs and wishes to the other. This emphasis is evident in the developmental theories of ego psychologists Rene Spitz and Margaret Mahler. Spitz, in his genetic field theory of ego formation,[73] asserts that semantic communication is the third (relatively advanced) level of ego development:

The use of speech for semantic communication involves awareness that object images are separate from self-images, and includes the intention to communicate across ego boundaries. This will remain the principal mode of communication throughout life, with certain exceptions when there is a temporary and reversible merger for pleasure or for artistic creation.[74]

Verbal communication is emphasized in British culture at least as much as in America, but verbalization of feelings is not: Britons are not known for their emotional expressiveness, verbal or otherwise.[75] As for Americans, it may be that the dissemination of psychological and psychodynamic ideas in the United States over the past several decades has helped to promote the idea that such emotional expressiveness is desirable and "healthy." (This would be another example of the characteristically psychoanalytic endeavor to effect a better balance between manifest and repudiated cultural elements, while still fundamentally upholding the status quo.) Certainly there are older Anglo-American sources of expressiveness too, such as the aforementioned Romanticism and expressive individualism. In any case, the emphasis on the verbal expression of sentiment preserves and reinforces assumptions about our radical separateness, even as it to some extent challenges or modifies views about the appropriateness of expressive and emotional display.

---

[73] Rene Spitz, *A Genetic Field Theory of Ego Formation* (New York: International Universities Press, 1959).
[74] Blanck and Blanck, *Beyond Ego Psychology*, p. 12.
[75] See, e.g., David McGill and John K. Pearce, "British-American Families," in Monica McGoldrick, John K. Pearce and Joseph Giordano, *Ethnicity and Family Therapy* (New York: The Guilford Press, 1982), pp. 457–79.

It is important to acknowledge that these ideals of the self that I have called contemporary derivations or descendants are quite different from their literal theological forebears. The dark night of the soul that preceded the intuition of the inner light is a far cry from the modern identity crisis; and key ideas about self and its relation to community, as these ideas were lived out in the older religious communities, bear little relation to the world view of the contemporary expressive individualist. But what have been retained – at the very least – are certain ways of structuring the idea of the soul (now re-cast as the self) and the possibilities of and routes to its salvation (i.e., its moral goodness and spiritual fulfillment). Also retained is the meaning of these structures as crystallizations of issues of ultimate concern (this is not their only contemporary meaning, but it remains a basic one). Characteristics such as self-reliance and identity, then, have become among the most important means through which those who are seen to possess them may acquire such moral and emotional "salvation" as is still available in this disenchanted world.

If my analysis is correct – that the ascendance of "ego" and "self" theories in North American and British psychoanalysis is a testament to our hyperindividualism, which in turn is traceable to our radical Protestant heritage and its secular offshoots – then we would not expect to find that psychoanalytic theory has developed along the same lines (if indeed it has caught on at all) in a non-Protestant nation. The case of psychoanalysis in France would seem to confirm this hypothesis. Marion Olinor points out that "concepts such as separation-individuation, object constancy, or self-object ... are foreign to ... French" analytic theorists, Lacanian and non-Lacanian alike.[76] This is not a superficial linguistic difference. In general, the Anglo-American preoccupation with strengthening the ego and/or the self is absent from the French analytic attitude. This is of course most radically true in the case of that most notorious and celebrated of French analysts, Jacques Lacan, for whom the self or subject is an illusion to be dissolved, itself the problem (or rather the symptom). Particularly the notion of self-direction I described above – the idea of a "true" or "real" self that is the repository of one's "authentic" feelings and may even be present in nuclear form at birth – is disdained by many French analysts, even those who are not exclusively Lacanian. In commenting on the initial foreignness and distastefulness of the emphasis in recent Anglo-Saxon psychoanalysis on the "self" (for

---

[76] Marion Olinor, *Cultivating Freud's Garden in France* (New York: Jason Aronson, 1988). p. 12; see also Sherry Turkle, *Psychoanalytic Politics: Freud's French Revolution* (Cambridge, MA: Harvard University Press, 1981).

which there is no precisely equivalent word in French), J.-B. Pontalis
wrote: "Thus the French psychoanalyst is, from the start, disconcerted
by the notion of *self* ... One should therefore talk of a return of the
repressing rather than that of the repressed: a return masked by nostalgia, a nostalgia for the good old self which would have been lost through
too much analysis."[77]

Finally, one might wonder how it could be that a group of analysts,
many of whom were neither born nor trained in the United States or
England, and many of whom were not even Christian let alone
Protestant, could have become the bearers of these quintessentially
Anglo-American ideals. In response to this question, I invoke the words
of Margaret Mahler[78] with which I began this chapter. "If I had not come
to America," she wrote, "I would have accomplished very little." In
Vienna, "I reached an impasse, unable to find a voice to express the
developmental and clinical insights toward which I was then groping."
Upon her migration to America, however, she found "vital new sources
of collegial support. It was only in America, and only owing to the
tremendous professional encouragement I received in America," that she
really found her "voice" and became professionally productive and
influential. As I have shown, themes of the self and its individuation, of
oneness and separateness, are highly salient for Anglo-Americans
because of their relation to our ideals of independence and self-direction.
American mental health professionals appear to have discerned in
Mahler's preexisting interests and interpretive tendencies a resonance
with some of their own ingrained ethnopsychological concerns. Thus
provided with the necessary support of all kinds, she was induced to
further pursue these issues and to elaborate upon her original insights to

[77] J.-B. Pontalis, *Entre Le Rêve et La Douleur* (Paris: Gallimard, 1977), p. 127 (emphasis
in the original). While one would hardly want to call Lacanian analysis a French folk
psychology, it *is* true that not only is it extremely un-Protestant (in spite of Sherry
Turkle's characterization of it as "psychoanalytic protestantism") but also it embodies
certain assumptions about the person which are characteristic of the Latin self as
described by Gaines ("Cultural Definitions"). He asserts that "the boundary of the Latin
self is not drawn around a single biological unit, but around the 'foyer.' The self consists in part of significant others, primarily family. Thus, the self is partly composed of
elements over which the individual has no control ... This self stands in stark contrast
with the bounded, autonomous and, therefore, self-regulated and self-reflective protestant individual ... The unchanging and unchangeable self which is in part composed of
seemingly external social and spiritual elements is the self of Lacan's French version of
psychoanalysis." (p. 184).

[78] *Memoirs*, pp. 120–2. Of course, Mahler was not herself referring to the influence of cultural values on the cultivation and reception of her work, which she considered to be
universally important and applicable. Rather, she emphasized that the "psychoanalytic
politics" in Vienna at that time (dominated by Anna Freud and Helene Deutsch) were
antipathetic to her and her ideas.

a far greater extent than she had before. In so doing, she not only absorbed and underscored the fundamental American concern with self-reliance and separateness, but also drew upon her acquaintance with the Romantic literary and philosophical discourses about oneness and separateness which were part of the cultural background of any educated Austro-Hungarian (in fact she had studied philosophy).

A similar dialectic of reception and creation may be found to obtain for other celebrated immigrant analysts such as Erikson, Kohut, and Kernberg (and Horney before them). The paradigm shift embodied in their theories initially was resisted by Anglo-American psychoanalytic orthodoxy. Yet the eventual ascendance of that paradigm, an ascendance that has occured over the past several decades, would appear to have been inexorable. I have argued in this chapter that this is due to the pressure of selection exerted by Anglo-American cultural ideals and ethnopsychological themes.

3

The developmental narrative: The design of psychological history

Chapter 2 was an exploration of the recent psychoanalytic preoccupation with the bounded, independent, and autonomous self. In this chapter, the focus shifts to a second essential dimension of contemporary psychoanalytic theory, one that has been expanded and elaborated in tandem with the first. This is the narrative pattern that traces the development of these desired, culturally valued characteristics and capacities of the self. In virtually all of these theories, the mature ego or self is said to develop out of an original state in which it does not experience differentiation between itself and the other, and in which it experiences a sense of omnipotence that is concomitant to its actual situation of extreme dependence. According to psychoanalytic theory, the desire for, and movement in the direction of, separation and individuation always stands in tension with more "primitive" or "archaic" tendencies and wishes – for fusion, merger, extreme dependence. In these theories, the pinnacle of personality and emotional development is not simply autonomy and independence, but rather a more complex, dynamic state. The truly mature self, then, is seen to be characterized by a relative integration of divergent or opposing needs and tendencies, and by a more or less stable resolution of the ongoing tension between the self's infinity of wishes and the limitations of reality.

Chapter 2 was framed in terms of how psychoanalytic theory has been altered to "fit in" with American or Anglo-American values and assumptions about the self. But as was noted there, one cannot consider how our concerns about autonomy have intensified this emphasis within psychoanalysis without acknowledging that in this commingling the American ideals also have been modified, at least as they are manifest in the psychoanalytic discourse. In addition to "canonizing" the imperative of autonomous behavior and thought, contemporary psychoanalytic thought also insists that a balance – a compromise – must be struck between these sociocultural and developmental demands, and the opposing wishes and desires that forever persist in the human psyche. Thus, the highest, most mature forms of development are seen to be those in which there is an integration of both fusion and separation, of both dependency needs and autonomy. The course of individual development necessitates individuation, but towards the end of that perhaps-limitless trajectory, the individual may attain the capacity to engage in certain types of circumscribed experiences of reunion with his or her objects, reunions in which the sense of bounded individuality nevertheless remains intact. Such reunion-in-separateness may take several different forms of varying intensity. First, there are actual "regressions in the service of the ego" – falling-in-love, artistic creativity, orgasm, some aspects of the mother–infant relationship. Second, there is a more limited and partial type of "reunion with the object" which is part of any intimate relationship. For in any such relationship, although one must keep one's sense of separation and distinctiveness, if one does not possess the capacity to display some dependency, "regression," and permeability of ego boundaries, then one also is not considered fully healthy and mature. Finally, let us not forget that in personality formation itself there occur subtle forms of reunion-with-the-object: personality development is seen by psychoanalytic theorists to entail an internalization of the mothering figure such that one increasingly becomes one's own parent. Kohut called his version of this dynamic "transmuting internalization": the individual comes to depend less intensely and completely on others for the fulfillment of her narcissistic needs; she comes more and more to rely on internalized representations of such self-object relationships, which have become part of her character structure.

The inclusion of this dimension alongside the dominant emphasis on independence and individuation, then, underscores the fact that Anglo-American psychoanalytic developmental psychology remains, in at least a broad and generic sense, a *psychodynamic* theory. As was noted in Chapter 2, psychoanalysis is called a "dynamic" theory of mind[1] because it postulates that the "normal" and the "mature" do not consist of a

---

[1] Otto Fenichel wrote that psychoanalytic psychology "explains mental phenomena as the result of the interaction and counteraction of forces, that is, in a *dynamic* way." (*The Psychoanalytic Theory of Neurosis*. New York: W.W. Norton and Co., 1945) p. 11. Fenichel, of course, notes that Freud took this idea from the natural sciences – physics, biology, psychophysics. But he also states that originally, physics got the idea from ethnopsychology: "the idea of looking at mental phenomena as a result of interacting forces certainly was not derived merely by transferring the concept of energy from the other natural sciences to psychology. Originally it happened the other way around: the

thoroughgoing obliteration of that which is primitive, deviant, or immature. Rather, the ends of development are characterized by intrapsychic states and interpersonal patterns in which opposing tendencies and conflicting trends stand in balance and compromise with one another. Psychoanalytic theory seems at once to have absorbed the Anglo-American preoccupation with and ideology of self-reliance and individuality, and, since it is psychodynamic, to have spelled out a theory of the attainment of these attributes in terms of the persistence of their precursors, their underside, their vicissitudes.

Cultural sources of the psychoanalytic developmental narrative

My argument thus far has been that the increasing emphasis and elaboration of "self," "ego," and "preoedipal" themes has been due at least in part to broad Anglo-American cultural preoccupations with these themes and values. The developmental narrative that likewise has come to prominence is not, however, a popular American or British model.

What sort of model is it? In a general way it is Freud's model: it has a psychoanalytic and psychodynamic structure in the sense that it posits forces in tension with one another, posed in perennial compromise. But although it shares with the central classical Freudian narrative this basic similarity, it is also fundamentally different from it. The Freudian story is framed mainly in terms of psychosexual development, emphasizing the Oedipal era, while the Anglo-American theories deemphasize the instincts and focus more closely on preoedipal development. Of course, Freud himself also dealt with so-called "preoedipal" issues: primary narcissism and object choice, the "undifferentiated" origin of psychic structure (id/ego/superego) and of the sense of self–world relationship, and other "archaic" aspects of human development. And among his first

---

everyday assumption that one understands mental reactions when one understands their motives has been transferred to physics." In fact, physics may have inherited the dynamic model from esoteric religious and philosophical doctrines, rather than from "everyday" assumptions. M.H. Abrams points out that this "esoteric view of the universe as a plenum of opposed yet mutually attractive, quasi-sexual forces – which was discredited and displaced by Cartesian and Newtonian mechanism, but was revived, in a refined form, in the *Naturphilosophie* of Schelling in Germany and of Coleridge in England – proceeded, by peripety of intellectual history, to feed back into scientific thought some of the most productive hypotheses of nineteenth century and modern physics." (*Natural Supernaturalism* [New York: W.W. Norton, 1973]) p. 170. He cites L. Pearce Williams, *Michael Faraday* (New York: Basic Books, 1965), who demonstrated that "Faraday and other pioneers of electromagnetic theory profited from *Naturphilosophie*."

disciples, Ferenczi[2] and Rank[3] can be singled out as two of the earliest explorers of this theoretical terrain. Moreover, Hartmann and Anna Freud initiated their investigations into the psychology of the ego (following Freud's directive) during their final years on the Continent. Thus, it is certainly possible to cite important precursors to the current emphasis on preoedipal developmental trajectories, including some theories which were formulated while the analysts were still living in Europe. Nevertheless, the narrative of the development of the individual's sense of differentiation from objects – less central, less elaborated in Freudian texts and in the classical corpus – has been seized upon and has become increasingly elaborated in the United States during the past several decades, eclipsing the psychosexual trajectory or revising its meaning.

Thus, while the more popularly diffused cultural preoccupations discussed in Chapter 2 may be responsible for the coming-to-prominence of this narrative pattern in psychoanalytic theory, we need to look elsewhere to seek the sources of that narrative pattern. As I demonstrate in the remainder of this book, the pattern is derived from a root metaphor that is at once more cosmopolitan and more esoteric than are the modern American ideals of maturity that it has been harnessed to promote. It is "esoteric" in both senses of the word. In the literal sense, it is descended from mystical doctrines that were considered secret, accessible only to the initiated. And in the figurative sense, these doctrines were, and have remained, the province of more educated, intellectual, or artistic groups rather than part of folk or popular culture.[4] The relatively close ancestor of psychoanalytic developmental theory is a generic narrative pattern that can be found in Romantic and post-Romantic literature and philosophy. Its more distant ancestor is the Christian

---

[2] Sandor Ferenczi, "Stages in the Development of the Sense of Reality," in *Sex in Psychoanalysis* (New York: Basic Books, 1950), pp. 181–203.

[3] Otto Rank originated the terms "birth trauma" and "separation anxiety" in psychoanalysis. On Rank and Ferenczi, see Paul Roazen, *Freud and His Followers* (New York: New American Library, 1976). On Rank, see Esther Menaker, *Otto Rank: A Rediscovered Legacy* (New York: Columbia University Press, 1982) and E. James Lieberman, *Acts of Will: The Life and Work of Otto Rank* (New York: Free Press, 1985).

[4] Just as the culture concept has been called into question by some anthropologists (see Chapter 1, footnotes 39 and 54), the distinction between "high" culture on the one hand, and "folk" or "popular" culture on the other, has been "deconstructed" in recent years by various literary and cultural studies scholars (see, e.g., Chandra Mukerji and Michael Schudson [eds.], *Rethinking Popular Culture: Contemporary Perspectives in Cultural Studies* [Berkeley: University of California Press, 1991]). Although I retain the terms "high," "folk," and "popular" as expository conveniences, my project also participates in the undermining of a rigid separation between these domains. I emphasize the affinities and cultural kinship of American ethnopsychology and high Romanticism, and the role of their mutual interpenetration in the development of psychoanalytic theory.

mystical narrative of the history and destiny of mankind and the individual soul.

Obviously this suggestion that psychoanalysis has sources in Romanticism and, especially, in mystical Christianity, is a radical claim to make about any psychoanalytic theory, even a post-Freudian one.[5] I attempt to buttress this claim in two ways. First, in the chapter that follows this one, I review a growing body of literature in the history of social science and psychology that takes seriously the influence of religious and other culturally constituted narrative patterns on contemporary psychological theory. Second, I trace the cultural genealogy of contemporary psychoanalytic theory by examining earlier (theological and Romantic) versions of the narrative and demonstrating structural and thematic parallels between them and the psychoanalytic version. Thus, I trace the series of transformations by means of which this spiritual narrative pattern has become secularized and "psychologized" and now constitutes the implicit root metaphor in terms of which psychoanalytic developmental theory is structured.

The psychoanalytic developmental narrative

There is a generic narrative pattern the broad outlines of which are present in virtually all Anglo-American psychoanalytic developmental theories. I begin discussion of key structural and thematic features of this

---

[5] In Chapters 1 and 2 I noted various scholars who have explored Freud's contact with and appropriation of Romantic thought. There are also scholars who have noted the "Romanticism" inherent in Freudian psychoanalysis without pinpointing specific or direct transmission: e.g., Thomas Mann ("Freud's Position in the History of Modern Thought," in *Past Masters and Other Papers*, trans. H.T. Lowe-Porter [New York: Alfred A. Knopf, 1933], and "Freud and the Future," in *Freud, Goethe, Wagner* [New York: Alfred A. Knopf 1939]) and Lionel Trilling, *Freud and the Crisis of our Culture* (Boston: Beacon Press, 1955).

I also noted that psychoanalytic theory is "shot through" with myriad cultural discourses; various lines of influence have been explored (some more convincingly and/or controversially than others) by scholars too numerous and diverse to mention here. It is germane for our purposes, however, to note those who have attempted to detect the influence of Freud's (or other analysts') Jewish background on psychoanalytic theory. This is not my project, since my focus is neither on Judaism (or Christianity) per se nor on individual psychoanalysts' backgrounds. For the record, however, those who have attempted to connect Freud's Jewishness to his theories include: Marthe Robert, *From Oedipus to Moses: Freud's Jewish Identity*, trans. Ralph Mannheim(Garden City: Anchor Press, 1976); John Murray Cuddihy, *The Ordeal of Civility: Freud, Marx, Levi-Strauss and the Jewish Struggle with Modernity* (New York: Basic Books, 1974); Dennis Klein, *Jewish Origins of the Psychoanalytic Movement* (New York: Praeger, 1981); William McGrath, *Freud's Discovery of Psychoanalysis: The Politics of Hysteria* (Ithaca: Cornell University Press, 1986); Yosef Hayim Yerushalmi, *Freud's Moses: Judaism Terminable and Interminable* (New Haven: Yale University Press, 1991); and of course, in a different vein, David Bakan, *Sigmund Freud and the Jewish Mystical Tradition* (London: Free Association Books, 1990).

narrative form, by explicating the theory of ego psychologist Margaret S. Mahler. Her "separation-individuation" theory[6] not only exemplifies many of the strongest tendencies in psychoanalytic developmental psychology, but also provides a particularly clear and coherent exposition of them. This is followed by a discussion of the developmental trajectories of the self and relationships offered by two highly influential theorists of different schools, the object-relations theorist D.W. Winnicott (arguably the most noted and influential of the British "middle school" theorists) and the founder of self psychology, Heinz Kohut. It is shown that whatever their differences, they too share certain key features with Mahler's trajectory.

Margaret S. Mahler (1897–1985) was an Austrian-born pediatrician and psychoanalyst who studied philosophy before taking her degree in medicine.[7] She arrived in the United States via England in the early 1940s. It was in the United States that she, along with several collaborators including Anni Bergmann and Fred Pine, conducted most of the research and writing for which she has become famous.

Mahler's theory has been selected for scrutiny because it is a particularly clear and coherent version of the psychoanalytic developmental narrative, and has been popular among professional clinicians and educators. It has had a strong impact on psychoanalytic clinical theory and practice, and a significant influence on early childhood education.[8] Since it shares certain basic assumptions about development with theories that focus on the growth of cognitive functioning rather than affect, it has been used to combine cognitive-developmental and psychoanalytic paradigms into a single unified theory.[9]

Mahler's theory also can be seen as an important bridge between divergent paradigms within psychoanalysis. On one hand, it maintains allegiance to, and utilizes the vocabulary of, orthodox Freudian metapsychology. At the same, it embodies the important and innovative deviations from that metapsychology that characterize a much broader array

---

[6] The term "individuation" was first used by Jung to denote "the process by which individual beings are formed and differentiated; in particular, it is the psychological *individual* as a being distinct from the general, collective psychology."(Jung, *Psychological Types*, in *The Collected Works of C.G. Jung*, vol. vi [London: Routledge and Kegan Paul, 1981], p. 448). In her memoirs, Mahler stated that this phrase was first applied to her own work by Annemarie Weil, who heard Mahler and Gosliner read a paper at the New York Psychoanalytic Society in 1945 (Margaret S. Mahler, *The Memoirs of Margaret S. Mahler*, ed. Paul Stepansky [New York: Free Press, 1988], pp. 138–9).

[7] For biographical information, see ibid.

[8] "Analyst Focuses on Life's Early Years," *New York Times*, 13 March 1984.

[9] See, e.g., Robert Kegan, *The Evolving Self* (Cambridge, MA: Harvard University Press, 1982).

of Anglo-American psychoanalytic models. According to Jay Greenberg and Stephen Mitchell in their 1983 comparative study of recent trends in psychoanalytic thinking, Mahler's system employs what they term a "strategy of accommodation."[10] By this they mean that her focus on the development of identity and object relations "sits" on classical Freudian metapsychological assumptions about drives (libido and aggression) and psychic structure (ego/id/superego). As was noted above, she comes out of the tradition of ego psychology: theorists aligning themselves with this tradition see themselves as elaborating upon certain issues within the broader scope of Freudian theory. They consider themselves to be further detailing the development and functions of the ego, which is that portion of the psychic structure responsible for relating to reality. Indeed, the title of Heinz Hartmann's most famous book is *Ego Psychology and the Problem of Adaptation*. As this title indicates, his concern is with the ego as the mediator between the inner world of drives, wishes, and fantasies, and the demands and constraints imposed on the individual by the environment, or "real world." Mahler, along with the other "later" ego psychologists – Rene Spitz, Edith Jacobson, Otto Kernberg – took as her focus a subset of the "environment": human relationships.

As was noted in Chapter 2, Mahler (like many other post-Freudians including Winnicott, Fairbairn, and Kohut) came to suggest in her later years that not only borderline and psychotic illnesses, but perhaps neurotic conditions also, can be better understood in terms of the vicissitudes of the separation-individuation process:

There is much in the neurotic development we see daily that derives as well from the prephallic, preoedipal periods, during which crucial forms of psychic organization and reorganization are structured.[11]

Mahler's emphasis on the period of life from birth to about age 3 was derived from her interest in the origins of severe psychopathology in young children (autistic and symbiotic psychoses). She felt that by studying both disturbed and "normal" infants and toddlers in interaction with their mothers, she could learn about both normal and deviant patterns of mother–infant interaction, and the relationship of those patterns to the emotional development of the young child. During the 1960s, Mahler and her colleagues conducted several longitudinal, observational studies

[10] *Object Relations in Psychoanalytic Theory* (Cambridge, MA: Harvard University Press, 1983).
[11] Mahler, "On the Current Status of the Infantile Neurosis," in *The Selected Papers of Margaret S. Mahler* (New York: Jason Aronson, 1975), p. 302. Mahler also makes this point in the final chapter of her memoirs ("Epilogue: Thoughts on Separation-Individuation," in *Memoirs*).

of "normal" mother–infant interaction. These studies were designed to test and elaborate upon hypotheses that she had introduced as early as 1955: that of the "universality of the symbiotic origin of the human condition, as well as the hypothesis of an obligatory separation-individuation process in human development."[12]

The purpose of the following recounting of her theory is not to criticize, or even to describe in detail, the research methods or inferential processes employed by Mahler and her associates. Rather, it is to suggest that certain broad, culturally constituted narrative patterns and motifs, manifest in these models of development, appear to have shaped and conditioned the selection and structuring of her research questions, as well as how she and her associates interpreted their observations.

The basic plot of the separation-individuation story traces the evolution of the child's subjective sense of separate-selfhood from an earlier, more primitive sense of *not* being separate from mother (or from anything else). In her most important book, *The Psychological Birth of the Human Infant: Symbiosis and Individuation* (1975), Mahler and her associates draw on their research to describe the separation-individuation process and its antecedents. In this book she illustrates her contention that the sense of being a separate self is attained (normally) by the age of 3:

> we refer to the psychological birth of the individual as the separation-individuation process: the establishment of a sense of separateness from, and relation to, a world of reality, particularly with regard to the experience of one's own body and to the principal representative of the world as the infant experiences it, the primary love object usually the mother ... the principal psychological achievements of this process take place in the period from about the fourth or fifth month to the thirtieth or thirty-sixth month, a period we refer to as the separation-individuation phase.[13]

This subjective ("intrapsychic") sense of separate-selfhood, or identity, gradually emanates out of an earlier phase during which the baby's intrapsychic self-representation is one of omnipotent fusion with the mother.[14] At the age of about 3 or 4 weeks,[15] Mahler asserts, the baby

[12] Margaret S. Mahler, Fred Pine and Anni Bergmann, *The Psychological Birth of the Human Infant: Symbiosis and Individuation* (New York: Basic Books, 1975), p. ix.

[13] Ibid., p. 3.

[14] Or, as Mahler et al. put it, the baby's self-representation is one of "hallucinatory or delusional somatopsychic *omnipotent* fusion with the representation of the mother and, in particular, the delusion of a common boundary between two physically separate individuals" (ibid., p. 45; emphasis in the original).

[15] Mahler also posits an earlier period, the "normal autistic" phase. This lasts from birth to 3–4 weeks. During this period, the infant is considered to be relatively oblivious to external stimulation. Mahler considers the symbiotic phase which follows it to constitute the true origin of human relationship, for it is then that the infant is more aware of the external world and can thus "cathect" onto mother such that baby and mother are intrapsychically imaged as "one."

invests the mother "with a vague dual unity that forms the primal soil from which all subsequent human relationships form."[16] *Symbiosis* thus refers to an "intrapsychic state rather than a behavioral condition; it is thus an inferred state."[17]

The term *symbiosis* in this context is a metaphor. Unlike the biological concept of symbiosis, it does not describe what actually happens between two *separate* individuals of a different species. It describes that state of undifferentiation, of fusion with the mother, in which the "I" is not yet gradually differentiated from the "not-I" and in which inside and outside are only gradually coming to be sensed as different.[18]

Mahler contends that the baby's initial experience of this blissful, euphoric dual-unity instills in him a sense of basic trust and "goodness." This fundamental trust will persist throughout his future development, embodied both in his sense of self, and in his sense of relation to that which is not-self (at this point, self and not-self are not yet cognitively or affectively differentiated).

What, then, gives impetus to the baby's moving out of this subjective state of blissful, omnipotent dual-unity? Mahler suggests that the child's "gradual emergence, or 'hatching,' from the common symbiotic membrane" is motivated by the normal infant's *"drive for and toward individuation."* This maturational thrust, asserts Mahler, *"is an innate,* powerful *given,* which, although it may be muted by protracted interference, does manifest itself all along the separation-individuation process."[19]

Individuation "consists of those achievements marking the child's assumption of his own individual characteristics"[20] – it entails the innately programmed maturation of his autonomous ego (cognition, perception, memory, reality testing) and motor (especially walking) functions. Individuation and separation are "intertwined, but not identical, developmental processes." Unlike individuation, *separation* is not a primary driving force, but rather a necessary consequence of the child's individuating capacities and achievements. It consists of "the *intrapsychic* achievement of a sense of separateness from mother and, through that, from the world at large."[21]

Mahler contends that "normal autism and normal symbiosis are prerequisite to the onset of the normal separation-individuation process." Moreover, the design of development is such that

[16] Mahler et al., *Psychological Birth*, p. 48.
[17] Ibid., p. 8.
[18] Ibid., p. 44.
[19] Ibid., p. 206 (emphasis in the original).
[20] Ibid., p. 4.
[21] Ibid., p. 8.

Neither the normal autistic, the normal symbiotic, nor any subsequent phase of separation-individuation is completely replaced by the subsequent phase ... they overlap considerably. However, from a developmental point of view, we see each phase as a time when a qualitatively different contribution is made to the individual's psychological growth.[22]

The phase of separation-individuation consists of three distinct but overlapping subphases: differentiation (from 4 or 5 months until about 10 months), practicing (from about 10 to between 15 and 18 months), and rapprochement (from about 16 to about 24 months).

The *differentiation* subphase begins while the baby is still enmeshed in "safe anchorage within the symbiotic orbit."[23] As his ego functions begin to develop, he starts to expand his attention and awareness beyond the symbiotic boundary. A phenomenon known as "hatching" takes place, in which the infant appears markedly more alert and attentive; he appears to explore both his mother (thereby beginning to differentiate her body from his own) and people and things outside the symbiotic (mother–baby) common membrane. All the while, he still remains physically close to mother. As he begins to differentiate his body from his mother's, "he [also] starts to discriminate between mother and he or she or it that looks, feels, moves differently from, or similarly to, mother."[24] He compares others to mother via "checking back" to her, and expresses curiosity and, at times, apprehension about these "strangers."

The early *practicing* subphase overlaps the differentiation subphase. During the practicing period, the child begins to walk. His first steps, according to Mahler, are away from mother, and towards a new world of objects that he eagerly begins to explore.

With the spurt of autonomous functions, such as cognition, but especially upright locomotion, the "love affair with the world" begins. The toddler takes the greatest step in human individuation. He walks freely with upright posture ... The central feature of this subphase as we see it, [is] the elated investment in the exercise of the autonomous functions, especially motility, to the near exclusion of apparent interest in the mother at times.[25]

His elation and enjoyment of his new autonomous functioning and mastery is inferred to be all the more pure and grandiose because he does not yet much experience the perils, conflicts, and limits inherent in individuation. He has not yet been decisively confronted with the fact of his, his mother's, or the world's limitations:

22 Ibid., pp. 47–8.
23 Ibid., p. 53.
24 Ibid., p. 56.
25 Ibid., pp. 69–71.

the child concentrates on practicing and mastering his own skills and autonomous (independent of other or mother) capacities. He is exhilarated by his own abilities, continually delighted with the discoveries he makes in his expanding world, and quasi-enamored with his own grandeur and omnipotence.[26]

But this period of exhilarated pleasure in his own expanded powers and in his discovery of the world around him does not last forever. By about the fifteenth or sixteenth month of life, Mahler infers from her observations, the toddler begins to have intimations of a reality which will prove a terrible letdown for him:

Concomitant with the acquisition of primitive skills and perceptual cognitive faculties, there has been an increasingly clear differentiation, a separation between the intrapsychic representation of the object and the self-representation.[27]

This cognitive and perceptual advance leads not only to the recognition of child–mother separateness *per se*, but also to a dawning awareness of some rather distressing consequences of this separateness:

At the very height of mastery, toward the end of the practicing period, it had already begun to dawn on the junior toddler that the world is *not* his oyster, that he must cope with it more or less "on his own," very often as a relatively helpless, small and separate individual, unable to command relief or assistance merely by feeling the need for it, or giving voice to that need.[28]

In other words, the child is faced with his most decisive experience yet of a rupture of this sense of dual-unity with mother. During the practicing subphase, while the child is preoccupied with the exercise of his own emerging skills, his intrapsychic sense of relationship to mother (although not a major focus of his attention at this time), and to the world, still provides him with many of the benefits and reassurances of the earlier period when he was "held" by the symbiotic mother. Indeed, that he "has it both ways" is what makes the practicing subphase so glorious and grand! The ensuing era of crisis – considered to be a real crossroads in terms of future development – is called the *rapprochement* subphase, precisely because the hurdle to be overcome entails a re-connection. The period is characterized by the re-negotiation of the child's sense of self and connectedness-to-mother (and to the rest of the world), once his loss of the original sense of oneness has become irrevocable and undeniable.

At first, the toddler attempts to defend himself against the knowledge that he and mother are separate, i.e., that their interests often differ and

---

[26] Ibid., p. 71.
[27] Ibid., p. 78.
[28] Ibid.

even conflict, and that he is helpless and cannot control mother. The "rapprochement crisis" (usually lasting from about 18 months to 20-to-24 months) is characterized by various behavioral and intrapsychic attempts to deny and "undo" this new subjective sense of separation and limitation. These attempts express not only the wish to restore the lost unity via "magical" means, but also a contradictory desire to resist the reengulfment of the autonomous self that such re-fusion would entail.

On the one hand is the toddler's feeling of helplessness in his real realization of separateness, and on the other hand is his valiant defense of what he cherishes as the emerging autonomy of his body.[29]

The resolution of this struggle to renegotiate closeness and separateness is achieved when the toddler finds an "optimal distance" from the mother. By "optimal distance" Mahler refers to the toddler's capacity to retain a sense of relatedness while preserving the sense of individual integrity and separateness achieved during the separation-individuation phase. The toddler begins to build new "bridges," higher-level forms of connection, to mother and others. These are made possible by the maturation of three new individuation functions. The first of these is *the capacity for verbal communication*. The rapprochement child has been forced to recognize that preverbal gesturing or empathic communication frequently cannot communicate needs and wishes to the other. The use of language integrates awareness of separateness with the attempt at connection. Second, the child develops *the capacity for symbolic play*: Mahler emphasizes that "the ability to express wishes and fantasies through symbolic play, as well as the use of play for mastery,"[30] constitute a developmental achievement. Third, there is the growth of *the capacity for "internalization."* Assuming that the actual mother–child interaction has been adequate, the child now begins to internalize a representation of the "good" mother, an image that "supplies comfort in the mother's absence ... This, to begin with, permits the child to function separately despite moderate degrees of tension (longing) and discomfort."[31] The child begins to be able to better tolerate not only the ongoing sense of separateness, but also actual separations.

With the beginning of the capacity for this kind of internalization, the child enters the fourth subphase of separation-individuation, which is open-ended. Mahler calls this the subphase of *consolidation of individuality and the beginnings of emotional object constancy*. The capacity to

---

[29] Ibid., p. 95.
[30] Ibid., p. 101.
[31] Ibid., p. 109.

internalize "a constant, positively cathected inner image of the mother"[32] is an important first step towards the development of what Mahler calls "libidinal object constancy":

But the constancy of the object implies more than the maintenance of the absent love object ... It also implies the unifying of the "good" [satisfying] and "bad" [frustrating/disappointing] object into one whole representation ... In the state of object constancy, the love object will not be rejected or exchanged for another if it can no longer provide satisfaction; and in that state the object is still longed for, and is not rejected (hated) as unsatisfactory simply because it is absent.[33]

This fourth subphase has no definite termination point. While the sense of individual identity and the capacity for emotional object constancy "should have their inception" at this age, Mahler emphasizes that "both of these structures represent merely the beginning of the ongoing developmental process."[34] In other words, the initial and somewhat fragile reconciliations effected at this stage – of self and other, and of good and bad – are only early precursors to the more stable and enduring emotional and interpersonal capacities of adulthood. Adolescence, in particular, is considered to recapitulate the "separation-individuation" era at a more sophisticated level. It is only as this later developmental period's crises and struggles begin to be resolved that a mature sense of individual identity, and of the constancy necessary for mature intimacy, are attained. And even then, these accomplishments are a matter of degree rather than the enduring attainment of an absolute. For in addition to being gradually rather than abruptly attained, these achievements are approximate.

Mahler does emphasize that there is a qualitative difference between the relative contributions to individuality and object-constancy made during the first three years of life, and the developmental achievements that occur thereafter.

We wish to emphasize our focus on *early* childhood. We do not mean to imply, as is sometimes loosely done, that every new separation or step toward a revised or expanded feeling of self at any age is part of the separation-individuation process. That would seem to us to dilute the concept and erroneously to direct it away from that *early intrapsychic achievement of a sense of separateness that we see as its core.*[35]

This early "core" accomplishment of a sense of separateness, along with more advanced forms of autonomy and identity, are necessary

---

[32] Ibid.
[33] Ibid., p. 110.
[34] Ibid.
[35] Ibid., p. 4 (emphasis in the original).

aspects of the self's maturity. But there is an additional capacity (one for which identity and constancy are essential prerequisites) that is necessary for successful emotional development. This is what Mahler calls the capacity "to make commitments [and] form warm, intimate relationships."[36] Such mature intimacy involves the ability to feel closely connected to another person in what, at times (e.g., during "falling-in-love," and also during the experience of orgasm), may include a feeling of ecstatic fusion, evocative of the symbiotic phase of early infancy. In his Mahler-inspired essay, "Psychoanalytic Observations on the Capacity to Love," Martin Bergmann asserts that

When the symbiotic phase gives way to further development, it leaves as a residue a longing which remains ungratified until love comes ...

Love revives, if not direct memories, then feelings and archaic ego states that were once active in the symbiotic phase ... Therefore it is often feared as endangering the boundary of the self.[37]

It revives these feelings – but with a difference: "the psychopathology of love teaches us that love can take place only if every psychic event does not exceed a certain limit."[38] The longed-for regression to symbiosis does not, in the case of "normal" love, lead to a total or enduring sense of re-fusion with the love object (nor, of course, is the object the original symbiotic partner, i.e., the mother). Rather, the transient or partial subjective sense of "oneness" is incorporated within the larger context of a "relationship." In a healthy relationship, the individual's intrapsychic sense of separateness and individual identity is preserved (simultaneously with the revived "archaic ego states," and/or sequentially preceding and following such states), as are the autonomous ego functions associated with individuation:

feelings belonging to the symbiotic phase of development must be reawakened but without bringing with them a dangerous ego regression. It should be added that certain ego functions must be temporarily suspended, for example, reality testing must be given up if the necessary idealization is to take place, and yet, paradoxically, this very ego function must simultaneously make possible the selection of a good mate.[39]

---

[36] *New York Times*, March 13, 1984.
[37] Martin Bergmann, "Psychoanalytic Observations on the Capacity to Love," in John B. McDevitt and Calvin Settlage (eds.), *Separation-Individuation: Essays in Honor of Margaret S. Mahler* (New York: International Universities Press, 1971), pp. 15–40, pp. 32, 39.
[38] Ibid., p. 38.

The design of psychological history: Basic features of the post-Freudian psychoanalytic developmental narrative

Mahler's separation-individuation theory is characterized by several basic structural and thematic features, five of which are highlighted below:

The developmental spiral

Human psychological birth is a process in which the infant's psychic representation of itself and the world as an undifferentiated unity (symbiosis) undergoes differentiation and individuation (differentiation and practicing subphases). This is followed by a growing "crisis of confidence" – a new, problematic consciousness of the separateness of self and other, which is linked to a disillusionment with both the self's and the other's powers (the rapprochement crisis). This crisis is resolved as the self begins to consolidate its sense of identity, and to re-work its sense of connection to others, in a manner which preserves the intervening differentiations (self and other, good and bad self- and object-representations). This "consolidation of individuality and development of emotional object-constancy" is an open-ended process, however, and much further maturation and development must take place before a truly mature integration of these oppositions (e.g., in intimacy) can become possible.

Emotional development, in this system, involves the forging of new connections to the object world as that world becomes progressively differentiated from the self. More archaic, less differentiated intrapsychic representations of self-object unity are supplanted by modes of connection that are more sophisticated in a cognitive and moral sense. These modes of connection include verbal communication and internalization of the representation of the other, as well as various forms of relatedness. These are "higher level" in the sense that they enable the individual to recognize, both intrapsychically and behaviorally, the distinction between self and object, while simultaneously mitigating the pain and anxiety engendered by the "minimal threats of object loss – which probably each new step of progressive development entails."[40]

[40]Mahler et al., *Psychological Birth*, p. 71.

The self's development out of the baby's sense of undifferentiated unity

Mahler asserts that

separation and individuation derive from and are dependent upon the symbiotic origin of the human condition, upon that very symbiosis with another human being, the mother. This creates an everlasting longing for the actual or coanesthetically fantasized, wish-fulfilled and absolutely protected state of primal identification...for which deep down in the original primary repressed realm, every human being strives.[41]

This "symbiotic origin of the human condition" refers to that immediate and necessary precursor to separation-individuation, "the normal symbiotic phase," during which the infant must "invest the mother within a vague dual-unity that forms the primal soil from which all subsequent human relationships form."[42]

A period of rupture and disillusionment, hinging upon the self's recognition of separateness and limitation

In Mahler's scheme, this is a distinct episode of crisis, which she calls the rapprochement crisis and subphase. It follows a period of elation and relative confidence in one's own powers and invulnerability. For a brief time the toddler both "walks alone" and is intrapsychically connected to mother and the world in a reassuring way. But with the dawning of the rapprochement era, this confident trust in one's own powers and in the world's relative benevolence is severely undermined. The child perceives for the first time how decisive and limiting his separateness is, and how vulnerable and alone this makes him. He begins to experience conflicts related to this newly highlighted separation between self and other. At the same time, opposing (good and bad) images of other and of self also begin to be a problem for him (such "splitting" of the object-world persists past the rapprochement period).

The constructive role of individuation, separation, and conflict in the developmental movement towards maturity

In Mahler's developmental psychology, development proceeds as a function of two types of interrelated imperatives. These are the innate thrust towards individuation, and the individuating toddler's inevitable

[41] Ibid., p. 227.
[42] Ibid., p. 40.

recognition that his objects are limited and often disappoint and frustrate him (this recognition culminates in the rapprochement crisis). The child is on the road to maturity (identity and object-constancy) when he begins to tolerate the imperfections of his existence and relationships and, at an intrapsychic level, to integrate the oppositions and splits that such disappointments and imperfections imply. In other words, maturity is seen by Mahler and her colleagues to entail an integration of the necessary contraries that comprise the human condition. The existence of both self and object, of both good and bad aspects of self and others, and of one's capacity for both aggression and love, must be faced, and these polarities ultimately must be integrated in a manner that preserves their differentiated distinctiveness. Both the rich intrapsychic life characteristic of maturity, and the capacity to have stable and intimate relationships, are seen to be contingent upon the acknowledgement of such opposing elements and upon their reconciliation at a higher, more complex level.

The ends of development: autonomy, constancy and intimacy, creativity

As I have emphasized, autonomy – independence, self-reliance, self-direction – is a necessary but not sufficient goal of the developmental process. Two other such goals highlighted by Mahler are "constancy" and "intimacy." As the rapprochement struggle is resolved, the toddler begins to develop a form of integration called "constancy." "Libidinal object constancy," in Mahler's usage, can be understood, on the one hand, as evidence of increased *independence* from the environment (a salient American ethnopsychological goal), since it involves the internalization of certain mothering functions. But on the other hand, it can be viewed as a *reunion* of self and other on a more subtle and sophisticated level: the child becomes able to tolerate actual separateness from the other, precisely because he has "taken in" a representation of the other, and made it a part of his self. Constancy also entails another kind of synthesis – of contrasting, "good" and "bad" images of the other and the self. Finally, constancy helps the individual to cope with other forms of loss, disappointment, and frustration encountered throughout life. The dynamic underlying all these aspects of constancy thus involves the ability to reconcile and transcend split and estranged elements whose divisions and differentiations are associated with loss and limitation.

In addition to constancy, there exists in ego-psychological theory a further goal of emotional development: intimacy, or what Mahler calls "the ability to make commitments [and] form warm, intimate relation-ships."[43] As was described earlier, mature intimate love (considered to be at best an approximate rather than absolute state) is seen to involve an integration of self and other, and of oneness and separateness, such that the "symbiotic longing" is somewhat mitigated, and the painfulness of individual existence somewhat assuaged. Yet simultaneously, the ego functions and sense of individuality must be, for the most part, retained.

Finally, the creative process – for some individuals, at least – is also seen to entail a kind of experience of reunion of the individual self with the object world, a reunion in which the self's awareness of its true boundaries is simultaneously (paradoxically) preserved. This is empha-sized more by various other theorists than by Mahler, and is discussed later in this chapter and in Chapter 8.

Different theorists offer differing versions of the developmental pattern explicated above. My aim in the present chapter, as in the previous one, is to highlight their theories' fundamental similarities. However, it also must be noted that the developmentalist visions of Anglo-American psy-choanalytic theorists (even theorists considered to be of the same school, e.g., Winnicott and Fairbairn) diverge from one another in significant ways. One source of variation derives from the fact that some theorists have devised their own terminology to denote what is at stake in the developmental process. Moreover, even theorists who make use of the same word may diverge in the precise meaning they give to it and the way they envision its role in the dynamics of psychic maturation. For exam-ple, Winnicott (most of the time) uses the concept of "aggression" to denote the baby's self-assertive and individuating energies, while Klein and Kernberg give the term a more sadistic and potentially pathogenic cast. Theorists differ, too, in the relative weight they give to environ-mental factors (i.e., the quality of mothering or parenting) versus "con-stitutional" ones (e.g., the strength of the aggressive drive), as well as in the way they envision the etiology and dynamics of various clinical enti-tites (e.g., Kernberg and Kohut have a well-known disagreement about narcissistic pathology[44]).

Moreover, the features of Mahler's narrative that I have delineated are in a sense ideal-typical; certainly not all of the theories fit the template equally well, though few contain elements that sharply contradict it. One feature of Mahler's narrative that is not shared by the other

---

[43] *New York Times*, March 13, 1984.

[44] See Gerald Adler, "Psychotherapy of the Narcissistic Personality Disorder Patient: Two Contrary Approaches," *American Journal of Psychiatry*, vol. 143, no. 4, April 1986, pp. 430–6.

theories is her delineation of a sharp period of crisis hinging upon the child's recognition of its separateness. However, the issues at stake during her rapprochement subphase, and their "fraught" quality, are also present in other theorists' depictions of development, as is shown later in this chapter.

Kohut's theory might be seen to deviate significantly from the Mahler-derived template insofar as he tends to underplay the tragic dimension of the healthy developmental process.[45] Above all else, he emphasizes that if the parents are sufficiently empathic and responsive, the child's self will develop in a felicitous manner. This theme eclipses the idea that conflicting and contrary forces (both within the psyche and between the self and others), and experiences of loss and limitation, play a necessary and constructive role in development. Kohutian analyst Marian Tolpin expresses this optimistic vision when she writes:

> When reasonably attuned selfobject responses meet the baby's active initiative and his normal expectations part way, his inherent vitality is simply preserved; and when this is the case, he automatically continues to exercise to the hilt all of his progressively growing and unfolding capacities and all of the expanding signals and signs at his disposal in order to continue to assert himself and to announce his legitimate developmental needs.[46]

Such statements seem to imply that healthy development (undistorted by inadequate parenting) is preprogrammed to lead to a natural unfolding of a "cohesive" self and to a harmonious fit between self and others (and between self and society). Such a self is constructively assertive and is characterized by a relative absence of inner conflict.[47]

Yet, at other points in self psychologists' writings, the template I have described is indeed present. For example, Kohut does allude to the role of frustration and disillusionment in the developmental process. He writes of the "optimum (nontraumatic, phase-appropriate) failures of the self-object [that] lead, under normal circumstances, to [psychic] structure

---

[45] Fairbairn's writings contain some similarly "utopian" ideas; see Morris Eagle, *Recent Developments in Psychoanalysis* (New York: McGraw Hill, 1984), p. 85; Greenberg and Mitchell, *Object Relations,* pp. 180–1.

[46] Marian Tolpin, "Discussion of '*Psychoanalytic Developmental Theories of the Self: An Integration'* by Morton Shane and Estelle Shane" in Arnold Goldberg (ed.), *Advances in Self Psychology* (New York: International Universities Press, 1980), pp. 47–68, p. 55.

[47] Louis Sass, in "The Self and Its Vicissitudes: An 'Archaeological' Study of the Psychoanalytic Avant-Garde," *Social Research* 55 (4) (1988), pp. 551–607, links Kohut's lack of a tragic sense to the latter's (unacknowledged) championing of Romantic cultural themes and values. It is also important to note (following Abrams, *Natural Supernaturalism*) that many of the greatest and most influential Romantics did incorporate a tragic sense into their work. (See Chapter 7 of this book.)

building via transmuting internalization."[48] At such moments of "optimal frustration," the self's healthy assertiveness – what Kohut terms "nondestructive aggressiveness" – comes into play in a manner that ultimately strengthens the "cohesiveness" of the self.[49] Thus even Kohutians include some mention of the role of disappointment, limitation, and conflict in promoting necessary and constructive growth. It is surely of note that Kohut gives relatively short shrift to these dimensions of the developmental narrative, but clearly they do form part of his background understanding of the nature of self, relationship, and reality.

The two theories I discuss below are those of the British object-relations theorist D.W. (Donald Woods) Winnicott (1896–1971) and the self psychologist Heinz Kohut (1913–1981). Winnicott, an English pediatrician and psychoanalyst, is arguably the most well known and influential of the British object-relations theorists. His approach is classified by Greenberg and Mitchell as an "alternative" to classical drive theory – it departs from Freudian psychoanalysis more fully and innovatively than do the approaches of Mahler and the other ego psychologists. Like Mahler, however, Winnicott never explicitly broke from orthodox psychoanalysis, continuing to claim his continuity with and allegiance to both Freudian and (more ambivalently) Kleinian approaches (Melanie Klein, a dominant figure in British psychoanalysis during Winnicott's lifetime, was one of his supervisors). Heinz Kohut was a Czech-born psychiatrist who emigrated to America via England in 1940,[50] and whose "self psychology" has been extremely influential in American psychoanalysis since the 1970s. He posited a discrete "narcissistic" line of development through which he traced the development of the self. As was noted in Chapter 2, Kohut first conceived his theory as a supplement to classical psychoanalytic theory, but in later work he moved towards making this narcissistic line preeminent.

I do not presume here to do full justice to the distinctive voice of each theorist (this is particularly challenging in the case of Winnicott, who wrote about development and the self from several different angles, often in an epigrammatic and even cryptic style). Nor do I aim to fully describe the intricacies of the trajectory each theorist traces, his unique

---

[48] Heinz Kohut, *The Restoration of the Self* (New York: International Universities Press, 1977), p. 87.

[49] See Ernest Wolf, "On the Developmental Line of Selfobject Relations," in A. Goldberg, *Advances in Self Psychology* (New York: International Universities Press, 1980), pp. 117–30, p. 126.

[50] Biographical information on Kohut can be found in Geoffrey Cocks (ed.), *The Curve of Life: Correspondence of Heinz Kohut, 1923–1981* (Chicago and London: University of Chicago Press, 1994). See especially the Introduction, pp. 1–32.

theoretical preoccupations, or the particularities of his vision of the healthy self (though I hope to convey some sense of all of these). Rather, my goal is to show the common thread of developmental history that runs through both of their theories as it does through Mahler's. For in spite of all the variations, the features I have distilled from Mahler's narrative do form an underlying frame of assumptions upon which the more varied assortment of theoretical forms have been draped. I explore these fundamental structural and thematic affinities in terms of the features already discussed: the developmental spiral, the self's origin in undifferentiated unity, the constructive role of rupture and individuation, and the goal of development as both autonomy and re-connection at a higher level.

The developmental spiral

Winnicott refers to development as a three-moment progression, in which the individual moves from the stage of *absolute* dependence, through *relative* dependence, and finally into a way of being he calls *towards* independence.[51] As is described below, this trajectory also entails a movement from a sense of omnipotent merger with the object world towards gradual disillusionment and awareness of separate-selfhood and limitation. And as in the case of Mahler's separation-individuation theory, the apparent linearity of this trajectory is seen to be mitigated when one takes a closer look at the dynamics and ends of the developmental process. Winnicott's narrative, like Mahler's, merits the label "spiral" in that development and maturity are seen to include the capacity (and the opportunity) both for benign regression and for higher forms of re-connection (these higher reunions are discussed below).

Kohut, too, posits a developmental trajectory in which the individual moves from a state of dependence upon what he calls one's "self-objects" (one's caretakers who are not yet experienced as differentiated from the self) to a condition of relatively greater independence. For Kohut, development entails a movement from an original sense of grandiosity and lack of self-object differentiation, through a series of increasingly differentiated (but still immature) self-object configurations, and (under optimal conditions) towards a more mature and "cohesive" self. This mature self has internalized the caretaker's psychological sustenance to the extent that it is not as dependent upon support from others to main-

---

[51] "From Dependence Towards Independence in the Development of the Individual," in *The Maturational Processes and the Facilitating Environment* (New York: International Universities Press, 1965), pp. 83–92.

tain its equilibrium or self-esteem in the face of frustration or disappointment. Thus Kohut too writes of a process of separation and individuation, of the "independent self ... [rising] out of the matrix of mirroring and idealized self-objects."[52]

In later writings Kohut attempted to distance himself from a developmentalist orientation, suggesting that the continuing need of all adults for "a milieu of responsive selfobjects"[53] seems to offer evidence against the idea of development altogether. However, as Greenberg and Mitchell have pointed out, this is a somewhat ingenuous characterization of the self-psychological perspective, one that contradicts some of its own basic premises:

To say that there is a continuous need for selfobject relations throughout life says nothing about change *within* those relations, and all of Kohut's formulations concerning development suggest a progression in health from "archaic," "infantile" forms of selfobject relations to more mature, differentiated resilient forms ... Kohut has portrayed development as a move from addictive dependence to greater resilience and independence ... Thus, while the need for others remains throughout, the quality of the need changes.[54]

They cite Kohut's close collaborator, Ernest Wolf who, in the same volume in which Kohut disassociates himself from developmentalism, chronicles the "developmental line" of self-object relations into maturity. Wolf writes that such development, characterized by "substitution of persons, depersonal diffusion, and symbolization[,] create[s] for the adult a whole matrix of selfobject relations that take over much of the function of the originally highly personal, concrete, and focused relation to the archaic selfobjects of childhood."[55] Although it still needs and makes use of self-objects, the mature cohesive self is depicted by Kohutians as being characterized by greater resiliency, more mature forms of perception and relatedness, and more sophisticated and prosocial transformations of narcissism. Thus Kohut's trajectory too is essentially spiral.

The self's origination out of a sense of undifferentiated unity

A famous line of Winnicott's is that "there is no such thing as a baby." He later explained:

---

[52] Kohut, *Restoration*, p. 171.
[53] Heinz Kohut, "Summarizing Reflections," in A. Goldberg (ed.), *Advances in Self Psychology* (New York: International Universities Press, 1980), p. 481.
[54] Greenberg and Mitchell, *Object Relations*, p. 369.
[55] Wolf, "Developmental Line," p. 130.

I once risked the remark, "There is no such thing as a baby" – meaning that if you set out to describe a baby, you will find you are describing *a baby and someone*. A baby cannot exist alone, but is essentially part of a relationship.[56]

Here Winnicott highlights the baby's absolute dependence upon the mother, hence its enmeshment in a dual-unity in the biological sense. If the mother is a "good enough mother," then at this earliest stage she is experiencing "primary maternal preoccupation,"[57] that is, a complete immersion in and devotion to her baby. Not only physically, but intrapsychically too, baby and mother are entwined: Winnicott depicts the infant as beginning its psychic commerce with the world with the aid of the mother; the latter provides a "holding environment" so that the baby does not become overwhelmed by its own as-yet-unintegrated excitations and experiences. By her attunement to and satisfaction of the baby's needs, the mother also ensures that the infant can experience states of fantasied omnipotence:

at the start a simple *contact* with external or shared reality has to be made by the infant's hallucinating and the world's presenting, with moments of illusion for the infant in which the two are taken by him to be identical ...[58]

During such essential "moments of illusion," such experiences of "primary creativity," the infant must feel that she has created the breast which she hungers after, and which responsively appears. The mother must be responsive enough to the baby's needs to sustain such moments. She also must not be too impinging (that is, she must not force the baby into premature responsiveness to and compliance with her needs). Only if the mother is neither unresponsive nor overly intrusive can the baby begin to develop a "true self" (capable of spontaneous gestures and authentic feelings) rather than having that true self remain undeveloped or submerged under a compliant "false self."

In the face of inevitable failures of attunement on the part of the mother (particularly as her primary preoccupation with her infant begins to subside, which is also a part of good-enough mothering), the infant gradually grows to tolerate frustration and disillusionment. "The mother's eventual task is gradually to disillusion the infant," Winnicott wrote,

---

[56] "Further Thoughts on Babies as Persons," in *The Child, the Family and the Outside World* (Harmondsworth: Penguin Books, 1964), pp. 85–92, p. 88; emphasis in the original.

[57] "Primary Maternal Preoccupation," in *Collected Papers: Through Paediatrics to Psychoanalysis* (London: Tavistock, 1958), pp. 300–5.

[58] "Primitive Emotional Development," in *Collected Papers*, pp. 145–56; emphasis in the original.

"but she has no hope of success unless at first she has been able to give sufficient opportunity for illusion."[59]

Similarly to Mahler's and Winnicott's babies, Kohut's infant does not have a differentiated sense of self versus object. Initially it relates to its caretaker(s) as "self-objects," i.e., persons who are not perceived as separate and who perform functions that the self will later gradually internalize and perform for itself. Kohut calls "empathy" the caretaker's necessary attunement and responsiveness to the infant's needs:

The child that is to survive psychologically is born into an empathic-responsive human milieu (of self-objects) just as he is born into an atmosphere that contains an optimal amount of oxygen if he is to survive physically. And his nascent self "expects"...an empathic environment to be in tune with his psychological need-wishes.[60]

The empathic connection works both ways: not only is the caretaker responsive to the infant, but the infant, too, is highly attuned to its caretaker's feeling states.

The functions performed by the caretaker-as-self-object include providing the infant with two forms of archaic relationship that facilitate the development of the self. The earlier and more primitive of these is a "mirroring" of the baby in order to encourage in it a sense of grandiosity and exhibitionism (later transmuted into healthy ambition and assertiveness). Later on the caretaker(s) must provide a focus of idealization, so that the young child may feel itself merged with its idealized self-object, develop the capacity for admiration, and come to possess ideals and values. Only if the child has the opportunity to experience these more primitive and undifferentiated forms of relatedness to the object can a more developed and "cohesive" "nuclear self" emerge.

> *The necessity and inevitability of a painful rupture involving awareness of separateness and limitation; and the constructive role played by individuation in the self's movement towards maturity*

For Winnicott, there is a pivotal era during which the infant begins to negotiate the shift from a sense of omnipotent merger to that of differentiated and limited reality, from subjective illusion to more objective perception. It takes place during the first year of life, although the child

---

[59] "Transitional Objects and Transitional Phenomena," in *Playing and Reality* (New York: Routledge, 1989), p. 11.
[60] Kohut, *Restoration*, p. 85.

participates in more sophisticated forms of it in the years that follow and, indeed, throughout life. It is characterized by "transitional phenomena," i.e., those activities that involve an "intermediate state between a baby's inability and his growing ability to recognize and accept reality."[61] Such phenomena usually involve "transitional objects," e.g., a favorite doll or piece of cloth. The essence of transitional phenomena and objects is their paradoxical nature: they occupy a liminal imaginative space at the intersection of subjective and objective, illusion and reality, omnipotence and limitation. They help enable negotiation of, and help to soften, the experience of disillusionment that comes with a growing acknowledgement of the nature of reality. In adult life, transitional phenomena continue to play a central role: they are the "necessary" illusions of play, art, religion, and symbolism.

Winnicott also employs another set of concepts to discuss the self's coming to terms with the existence of the subject–object split and with external reality: he discusses the shift from "object-relating" to "object-usage." This is a transition that he characterizes as being potentially fraught with peril and distress but which, in healthy development, results in triumph. The self that can "use" objects has triumphed in that it has attained both a sense of separateness and a capacity to relate to the object (and thus to re-connect to it) at a higher level. An examination of Winnicott's depiction of the shift from object-relating to object-usage indicates that for him, as for Mahler, separation and individuation bring with them danger and pain yet ultimately are necessary and constructive:

In the sequence one can say that first there is object-relating, then in the end there is object-use; in between, however, is the most difficult thing, perhaps, in human development; or the most irksome of all the early failures that come for mending. This thing that there is in between relating and use is the subject's placing of the object outside the area of the subject's omnipotent control; that is, the subject's perception of the object as an external phenomenon, not as a projective entity, in fact recognition of it as an entity in its own right.[62]

What drives the self to place the object outside the area of its omnipotent control, and why is the process so prone to vicissitudes? It has to do with the fact that individuation, for Winnicott, springs out of aggressive energies. "The self is constituted in aggressive assertion," he wrote (in his understanding, these energies are assertive in nature rather than sadistic as in Melanie Klein's sense); "[w]hen the Me and the Not-Me are being established, it is the aggressive component that more

---

[61] Winnicott, "Transitional Objects," in *Playing and Reality*, p. 3.
[62] Winnicott, "The Use of An Object," in *Playing and Reality*, p. 89.

surely drives the individual to a need for a Not-Me or an object that is felt to be external."[63]

Initially this placing the object outside of the subject's omnipotent control – this aggression-driven externalizing of the object – is experienced as a "destruction" of the object ("destructiveness is aggression unmodified by relationship,"[64] explains Winnicott-interpreter Adam Phillips), and thus is potentially isolating for the subject. Thus the peril here (as experienced by the infant) is that the very individuating energies expressed in the need to posit and recognize "others" will destroy those others and leave the self isolated, alone:

> This change (from relating to usage) means that the subject destroys the object. From here it could be argued by an armchair philosopher that there is therefore no such thing in practice as the use of an object: if the object is external, then the object is destroyed by the subject. Should the philosopher come out of his chair and sit on the floor with his patient, however, he will find that there is an intermediate position. In other words, he will find that after "subject relates to object" comes "*object survives* destruction by the subject." But there may or may not be survival.[65]

If in externalizing the object, in placing the object outside of its omnipotent control, the self can appreciate that the object has indeed survived this "destruction," then the self can begin to engage in relationship with the object (e.g., the mother). This survival of the object, and the self's emerging capacity for concern and guilt, also form the foundation of a moral sense. Thus, with the sucessful emergence of the capacity for object use, a more veridical perception of reality, and true relatedness to others, can begin:

> The subject says to the object: "I destroyed you," and the object is there to receive the communication. From now on the subject says: "Hullo object!" "I destroyed you." "I love you." "You have value for me because of your survival of my destruction of you." ... The subject can now *use* the object that has survived. It is important to note that it is not only that the subject destroys the object because the object is placed outside the area of omnipotent control. It is equally significant to state this the other way round and to say that it is the destruction of the object that places the object outside the area of the subject's omnipotent control. In these ways the object develops its own autonomy and life, and (if it survives) contributes-in to the subject, according to its own properties.
>
> In other words, because of the survival of the object, the subject may now have started to live a life in the world of objects, and so the subject stands to gain immeasurably.[66]

[63] "Aggression in Relation to Emotional Development," in *Collected Papers*, p. 215.
[64] Adam Phillips (Cambridge, MA: Harvard University Press, 1988), *Winnicott*, p. 105.
[65] Winnicott, "The Use of an Object," in *Playing and Reality*, p. 90.
[66] Ibid.

Thus, for Winnicott, aggressive energies drive the development (via opposition) of the self and its sense of objects. This necessary emergence of the subject–object opposition, in turn, initiates the possibility of a transcendance or at least mitigation of that opposition (and of the self's individuating aggressiveness) at a more developed, i.e., differentiated, level. Such overcoming of the opposition now begins to be possible via reconnection of self to object through concern, relationship, and love – all of these being higher-level bridges between subject and object.

There is no clear-cut moment or phase of individuation-crisis for Kohut, and in general he plays down the role of contraries and oppositions as being the key to development. What is most crucial, in his view, is that the caretaker be as perfectly empathic, responsive, and admiring as possible. He asserts that such empathic relating should be the rule not only during the earliest symbiosis-like stages (Kohut envisions the infant's earliest experience as being one of "absolute perfection," with its connotations of grandiosity and omnipotence), but also later on during the two aforementioned developmental opportunities for coalescence of the nuclear self (i.e., the mirroring and idealizing forms of self-object relationships). But even Kohut writes of "optimum (nontraumatic, phase-appropriate) failures of the self-object":[67]

a modicum of frustration of the child's trust in the self-object's empathic perfection is necessary, not only in order to usher in transmuting internalizations which build up the structures necessary for the tolerance of delays, but also in order to stimulate the acquisition of responses that are in harmony with the fact that the world contains real enemies, i.e., other selves whose narcissistic requirements run counter to the survival of one's own self.[68]

And the entire developmental movement towards greater self-reliance, towards "transmuting internalization" of the functions of self-objects (i.e., assuming these functions for oneself), bespeaks a greater capacity to tolerate the limitations of other persons and of reality in general.

Kohut is emphatic in his assertion that humans do not have an inborn destructive drive. However, he does write of a "nondestructive aggressiveness" that is characterized by healthy individuation and self-asssertion:

Nondestructive aggressiveness is, in other words, a part of the assertiveness of the demands of the rudimentary self, and it becomes mobilized (delimiting the self from the environment) whenever optimal frustrations (nontraumatic delays of the empathic responses of the self-object) are experienced.[69]

[67] Kohut, *Restoration*, p. 87.
[68] Ibid., p. 123.
[69] Ibid., p. 121.

Thus for Winnicott and Kohut, as for Mahler, disillusionment and individuating energies drive the self towards a recognition of the splits and oppositions inherent in reality and relationships. The capacity to tolerate such oppositions, limitations, and conflicts ultimately enables the healthy self not only to adapt to the boundaries and frustrations that characterize external reality, but also to attain integrations and re-connections at a higher level.

The ends of development: independence, constancy, authenticity, re-connections at a higher level

Independence and constancy

Like Mahler, both Winnicott and Kohut emphasize that the person must develop the capacity to take over the functions of her caretakers and to attain a more veridical appreciation and tolerance of their and her own limitations and imperfections. Thus Winnicott writes of the movement of the developing self "towards independence"; Winnicott-interpreter Simon Grolnick explicates this in terms of a "relative balance of dependence and independence on the side of the latter."[70] Winnicott also stresses "the capacity to be alone" as a crucial index of psychological health. This capacity has two aspects. First, it is similar to Mahler's constancy in that it requires the internalization of intrapsychic functions once performed for the self by the caretaker, so that the individual can now work and play on her own. Second, it entails the ability to be "alone in the presence of another": what is stressed here is that the healthy self has the capacity to exist in relationship, including intimate relationship,[71] while still retaining an unimpinged-upon inner core that remains "unfound" and "incommunicado." (This is further explained below, in the discussions of Winnicott's concept of the "true self" and higher level forms of re-connection.)

Kohut, too (in spite of his sometime-protestations), envisions a movement on the part of the self towards greater independence. He posits "transmuting internalization" as the mechanism by which functions such as self-soothing and self-esteem maintenance, initially performed by the selfobject, are taken inside to form a part of the coalescing nuclear self. A person with a mature, "cohesive" self is assertive and ambitious, has

---

[70] Simon Grolnick, *The Work and Play of Winnicott* (Northvale, NJ: Jason Aronson, 1990), p. 62.

[71] "It is perhaps fair to say," wrote Winnicott, "that after satisfactory intercourse each partner is alone and is contented to be alone. Being able to enjoy being alone along with another person who is also alone is in itself an experience of health." ("The Capacity to be Alone" in *The Maturational Processes*, pp. 29–36, p. 31.

strong ideals and values, and is not compulsively or intensely dependent upon others to bolster self-esteem, contain anxiety, and mitigate frustrations and disappointments. Self psychologists do emphasize the continuing need, throughout life, for self-objects; however, the pressures of such narcissistic needs, and the means through which the self seeks to meet them, are seen to become progressively "more diffuse and less intense."[72] The range of usable self-objects broadens as well; for example, says Wolf, "[i]t is characteristic of the progressive changes in the developmental line of selfobjects that symbols as well are increasingly substituted for persons as selfobjects."

Authenticity

For Winnicott, the essence of being alive is the capacity for spontaneity and "creative originality"; the healthy self also possesses a sense of being embodied and "real." These attributes and experiences are subsumed under the notion of the "true self."[73] Winnicott sees the root of the true self as being present at the very beginning of life; but in order for it to develop and not be crushed under the "false self" (a social self built of compliance to the needs of others), certain environmental conditions must be present. Most importantly, the mother must mirror and validate the baby's emerging self, responding to its requirements rather than allowing her own needs to impinge unduly on her child. She also must "hold" the infant, containing the excitations that threaten to overwhelm him.

As was noted in Chapter 2, Winnicottian authenticity can only be lived out in society to a degree. Living successfully entails a balancing of the true and false selves, the latter embodying what Adam Phillips calls "the healthy compromise of socialized politeness."[74] When this balance leans too far in the direction of the false self – when the development of the true self has not been facilitated – then a personality that is too compliant or "inauthentic" can result.

Thus for Winnicott there exists, inside all healthy persons, an inner core that is not in commerce with other persons and their demands: "Although healthy persons communicate and enjoy communicating, the other fact is equally true, that *each individual is an isolate, permanently non-communicating, permanently unknown, in fact unfound.*"[75] The true

---

[72] Wolf, "Developmental Line," p. 128.
[73] Winnicott, "Ego Distortion in Terms of True and False Self," in *Maturational Processes*, pp. 140–52.
[74] Phillips, *Winnicott*, p. 135.
[75] Winnicott, "Communicating and not Communicating Leading to a Study of Certain Opposites," in *Maturational Processes*, pp. 179–92, p. 187; emphasis in the original.

self, then, has a strong "incommunicado" element – a part of the self that does not want to be found and must be allowed not to be found, a part that does not have to be attuned, or to bend, to the needs or demands of others. In one sense the true self–false self dialectic is similar to Mahler's rapprochement dilemma – i.e., the dilemma of how to be separate while still being connected to others, and how to be connected without being engulfed. But as was noted in Chapter 2, there also seems to be a distinctively British ("indexical") element in Winnicott's notion of the true self.

Similarly to Winnicott, Kohut emphasizes the satisfying and joyous character of creative self-expression as an essential goal of development. Mental health is seen by him to be, in large measure, "the capacity of a firm self to avail itself of the talents and skills at an individual's disposal, enabling him to love and work successfully."[76] Empathic validation – by the caretaker, later self-objects, or the analyst – is seen by Kohut to foster the unfolding of such an authentic self.

Self psychologists also valorize constructive, higher-level transformations of narcissism – the creative self-expression of the artist, and a more general capacity to be self-assertive and ambitious, and to generate and live by one's own values and ideals.[77]

Higher-level re-connections

Winnicott stresses three aspects of separation and individuation: the movement towards independence; the move towards appreciation of the boundaries between self and object and the limits of the self's (and the object's) powers; and the need to preserve the "true self" – the sense of "realness," the inborn "incommunicado" element – from any premature impingement that would suppress or submerge it beneath the compliant facade of the false self. In order for the self to be fully healthy, however, it must integrate these forms of separateness with forms of connectedness to others. As Greenberg and Mitchell have noted, the dilemma of how to sustain contact if one is differentiated (or, conversely, of how to retain the integrity of separate-selfhood in the face of the necessity of relationship with others) is perhaps *the* central theme that runs through Winnicott's work.[78] Thus Winnicott, like Mahler, emphasizes not only independence and authenticity as developmental goals, but also various forms of connection-in-separateness – including the capacities to be

[76] Kohut, *Restoration,* p. 284.
[77] See, e.g., *Restoration,* pp. 17–18.
[78] Greenberg and Mitchell, *Object Relations,* pp. 189–90.

alone, to sustain a balance between the true and false selves, to "use" objects, and to engage in benign regressions (in adulthood) such as transitional phenomena. The self that can be alone in the presence of another, particularly another with whom it has intimate relations, can re-connect without becoming overwhelmed by its own responsiveness to the other's qualities or needs. Similarly, the "true self" portion of a person can just "go on being" without relating to others precisely because that person is secure in her sense that she is not only separate from, but also connected to, other persons. The self that can "use" objects has triumphed in that it has attained both a sense of separateness and a capacity to relate to the object (and thus to re-connect to it) at a higher (more individuated and realistic) level. Finally, the relatively independent and reality-attuned individual can engage in benign regressions – in the form of transitional phenomena (symbols, religion, art), play, all forms of creativity, primary maternal preoccupation, even aspects of intimate relationship – that entail a balancing of oneness and separateness, illusion and reality, boundlessness and limitation. The healthy self, according to Winnicott, can tolerate and be enriched by the paradoxes and suspensions of ordinary logic that characterize transitional and other "regressive" experiences, without having its sanity endangered by them.

The "firm, cohesive" self that is the hallmark of maturity for Kohut likewise is depicted in terms of its capacity for "higher" forms of reunion with its objects. As is the case with Mahler's constancy, transmuting internalization entails a kind of reunion with the object at a more sophisticated level, in the sense that the developed self has "taken in" its care-takers, making them (or some of their functions) a part of its own psychic structure. Kohut also insists that the use of self-objects continues throughout life; but as has been noted, for the developed self, that use is more flexible and less compulsive than is the case with the immature or fragile self. Thus, for the strong, mature self, the reunion inherent in self-object relating is rendered healthy and constructive by virtue of the self having already developed along the lines of resilience and attunement to reality. The healthy self's modes of relating are characterized by a relatively greater degree of "mature tolerance" of the shortcomings of others,[79] by the capacity to tolerate disillusionment and disappointment without "fragmenting." Such healthy self-object relating also character-izes "mature love." Kohut writes:

The psychologically healthy adult continues to need the mirroring of the self by self-objects (to be exact: by the self-object aspects of his love objects), and he

---

[79] Kohut, *Restoration*, p. 125.

continues to need targets for his idealization. No implication of immaturity or psychopathology must, therefore, be derived from the fact that another person is used as a self-object – self-object relations occur on all developmental levels and in psychological health as well as in psychological illness.[80]

As has been noted, there is an ambiguity in self-psychological theorizing concerning the nature and even the existence of "development." But as has also been noted (and as would seem to be indicated in the passage cited above), Kohut does discriminate between self-object relating on the part of a mature and healthy self and such relating on the part of an underdeveloped or "ill" self, even as he considers the difference between health and pathology to be a relative one.[81]

Thus the psychoanalytic developmental narrative, here exemplified by Mahler's trajectory but also evident in the writings of other analysts, highlights the tension between fusion and separation – a tension that heralds the birth of the self and continues to affect its development thereafter. It is the story of a progression from an originally undifferentiated unity, through a painful-but-necessary chain of ruptures, losses, and differentiations, towards a culmination (or several types of culminations) in which the severed elements are reunited, by means of an integration that preserves their differentiated distinctiveness. Since it entails movement from "lower" to "higher" forms of unity, it is considered to be an inherently good and valuable developmental process. This narrative pattern was not conceived first by psychoanalysts, although they acknowledge no earlier ancestry. It is derived from a root narrative that has existed for many centuries, changing over time to increasingly resemble the psychoanalytic version. In Chapters 5, 6, and 7 I trace the genealogy of this narrative form, emphasizing both its continuities and its transformations. First, however, I place this genealogical approach to developmental psychology in an existing context of scholarship: in Chapter 4, I review existing literature which treats "development" as a theologically derived concept, and situate this project in terms of that research.

[80] Kohut, *Restoration,* p. 188 fn 8. See also p. 122 fn 12.
[81] Ibid., p. 188 fn 8.

4

Theological sources of the idea of development

> The process – outside the exact sciences at any rate – has not been the deletion and replacement of religious ideas, but rather the assimilation and reinterpretation of religious ideas, as constitutive elements in a world view founded on secular premises.
>
> M.H. Abrams, *Natural Supernaturalism*, 1973, p. 13

In recent years there has been an upsurge of interest among social science scholars in the cultural and historical sources of their own disciplines. In their quest to elucidate the sociohistorical origins and guiding cultural assumptions of social and psychological models, a number of these scholars – including sociologists Arthur Vidich and Stanford Lyman, political scientist Mona Harrington, and psychologists William Kessen, Bernard Kaplan, and Sheldon White – have drawn inspiration and insight from older, well-known studies in the humanities. Such classic works include Karl Löwith's *Meaning in History* (1949), M.H. Abrams' *Natural Supernaturalism* (1973), Maurice Mandelbaum's *History, Man and Reason* (1973), Norman Cohn's *The Pursuit of the Millennium* (1970), and Michael Walzer's *The Revolution of the Saints* (1965).

In spite of the different theories and disciplines they examine, these classic and contemporary studies underscore a common theme: the vocabulary, guiding questions, and basic concepts and assumptions that characterize a wide variety of post-Renaissance theories about man and society evince a theological ancestry. In other words, these works highlight the extent to which many of our most popular and influential contemporary *secular* models and metaphors of self-understanding are drawn, in large measure, from *religious* sources. In the words of M.H. Abrams:

It is an historical commonplace that the course of Western thought since the Renaissance has been one of progressive secularization, but it is easy to mistake the way in which that process took place. Secular thinkers have no more been able to work free of the centuries-old Judaeo-Christian culture than Christian theologians were able to work free of their inheritance of classical and pagan thought. The process – outside the exact sciences at any rate – has not been the deletion and replacement of religious ideas, but rather the assimilation and reinterpretation of religious ideas, as constitutive elements in a world view founded on secular premises.[1]

Abrams, along with various other scholars who have attempted to trace their disciplines' assumptions and values to their theological roots, argues that many post-Renaissance, post-Enlightenment secular belief systems are still shaped and structured by religious themes, patterns, and metaphors drawn from a much older cultural reservoir. Precisely because patterns and images drawn from this reservoir can be detected in a range of different theoretical systems in several different disciplines (including philosophy, literature, and the social sciences), we are all the more likely to overlook the fact that they are specific to cultures within the Judaeo-Christian orbit.

The Biblical historical narrative: its shape and features

What are the specific features of this "Biblical culture," of our "centuries-old Judaeo-Christian inheritance," which is so widespread as to be unnoticed yet also possesses culture-specific contours? As evidence that theological motifs have been retained in various secular systems of thought, scholars such as Abrams, Löwith, and Kessen highlight a particular view of the nature and structure of history – be it the history of mankind (or a particular people or group), or the history of the individual soul, spirit, or self. Each suggests that a distinctive historical narrative design, patterned after the Biblical saga of creation, fall, and redemption, is detectable in many of our most taken-for-granted ideas about history, society, and psychology.

The Bible contains the definitive Judaeo-Christian story of mankind's history and destiny. Its basic plot is rather simple: God creates the heavens and the earth, culminating in the creation of Adam and Eve (i.e., mankind). Adam and Eve live in paradise – the Garden of Eden – until their fall from God's grace, at which point they are cast out of Eden and into the mortal world of sin, evil, and suffering. Christ's birth is a sign that God has promised redemption. The actual time of that redemption, however, has not yet come.

[1] M.H. Abrams, *Natural Supernaturalism*, (New York: W. W. Norton, 1973), p. 13.

This narrative[2] possesses certain distinctive structural and thematic features. These have been explored in Karl Lowith's *Meaning in History* and, in still greater detail, by Abrams in *Natural Supernaturalism*. In the following discussion of several basic features of Biblical history, I draw upon both of these works, but especially upon the latter.[3]

First, *the Biblical narrative has a distinctive shape*: It is *linear* and *finite*, i.e., "it represents events occurring once and for all in a single, closed temporal span."[4] Moreover, "[i]t has a sharply defined plot with a beginning, a middle and an end, and a strongly accented sequence of critical events."[5] The beginning is the creation of the heavens and the earth by God, climaxing in the creation of man (Adam and Eve). The middle is initiated by the fall, which signifies a precipitous loss of God's grace and of mankind's original innocence, and man's initiation into mortal life. The promise of salvation is signified by the birth of Christ (Abrams calls this event "the crisis, the absolute turning point in the plot which divides the reign of law and promise from the reign of grace and fulfillment and assures the happy outcome."[6]), although the actual climax and end of history – the millennium, heralded by the apocalypse – is yet to come.

The Biblical narrative in its original form is *right-angled*: Rather than "the main line of change" being continuous and gradual, "its key events are abrupt, cataclysmic, and make a drastic, even an absolute difference."[7]

A second distinctive feature of Biblical history is that it is *"prospectivist"* in at least two related senses: First, the present is considered to be the imperfect, "fallen" time, and the future is anticipated with hope and

---

[2] The editors of the *Journal of Narrative and Life History* define "narrative" as "a specific set of discourse sharing the property of temporally sequenced clauses." It is not clear from this definition whether the clauses are meant to represent action occurring temporally, since such a definition would seem to exclude, e.g., the Neoplatonic and Behmenist narratives in which everything is supposed to be happening at once in spite of the fact that it is represented sequentially (see Chapters 5 and 6).

[3] Abrams, *Natural Supernaturalism*, pp. 35–7 ("The Design of Biblical History"), pp. 45–6 ("Christian History and Psycho-Biography"), and pp. 56–65 ("Alternative Ways to the Millennium").

[4] Ibid., p. 35.

[5] Ibid.

[6] Ibid., p. 36.

[7] Ibid., p. 36. Abrams (see especially pp. 56–65: "Alternative Ways to the Millennium") notes that over the course of centuries in which the prophesied apocalypse did not materialize, there was a shift away from the idea that it would be an abrupt, right-angled change, and towards a conception (even within theology) of a more gradual and progressive amelioration of mankind's lot. When the Biblical narrative became secularized, there were translations of both versions of the narrative: a right-angled change can be found in Marx's idea of revolution as the redemptive culmination of history; a more gradual amelioration of the human condition is present in the idea of gradual scientific progress (the incremental progress of knowledge, technology, and human comfort).

optimism. We are always expecting and looking forward to the end of history, which will bring a restoration of pre-lapsarian happiness and well-being to mankind. Abrams writes:

Although its start and finish are symmetrical to the extent that it begins with the creation of the earth and ends with the creation of "a new heaven and a new earth," in this pattern it is the terminal and not the initial felicity that really matters ... Despite the emphasis on a lost paradise in the distant past ... the persistent pressure of the Christian view is not retrospective but strongly prospective; for always, the best is yet to be.[8]

Consequently, Abrams asserts, ours is a culture "long predisposed to expect an inevitable future of moral and material well-being."[9] In the Bible, this renovated end of history is described in terms of the apocalypse ("a vision in which the old world is replaced by a new and better world") and the millennium (the coming of God's kingdom on earth). Over the past two thousand years, there have evolved two alternative interpretations of how the millennium shall be reached: (1) via a sudden, violent revolution which will effect an immediate drastic change in the condition of mankind; and (2) as a result of a less cataclysmic, more gradual progression towards the same redemptive amelioration of the race.[10]

An additional prospectivist feature of Biblical history is that *it evinces an eschatological orientation*: history is a movement towards the last and best things. Karl Löwith wrote that "to the Jews and Christians...history was primarily a history of salvation."[11] He highlights the "eschatological orientation" of the Judaeo-Christian historical design (that is, the orientation of history towards the "last things, the vision of the 'ultimate end' of history as 'both *finis* and *telos*'"):

Not only does the *eschaton* delimit the process of history by an end, it also articulates and fulfills it by a definite goal. The bearing of eschatological thought on the historical consciousness of the Occident is that it conquers the flux of historical time, which wastes away and devours its own creations unless it is defined by an ultimate goal.[12]

Of course, as Abrams points out, God – a personal and anthropomorphic entity – is the "hidden author" of the "plot of history...its director and guarantor of things to come," its "first cause" and its "*telos*."[13]

---

[8] Ibid., p. 37.
[9] Ibid., p. 59.
[10] Ibid., pp. 56–65.
[11] Karl Löwith, *Meaning in History: The Theological Implications of the Philosophy of History* (Chicago: University of Chicago Press, 1949), p. 5.
[12] Ibid., p. 18.
[13] Abrams, *Natural Supernaturalism*, p. 36.

Third, *the Biblical narrative is a theodicy*:[14] Biblical history can be understood in terms of the "problem" that it at once constructs and attempts to resolve. This is the problem of evil and suffering: if God is good (as well as the first cause and *telos* of all things), then why is the human condition one of sin and pain? The answer is that man, through his own sinfulness, has fallen from grace, thereby setting in motion all the vicissitudes of mortal life. Yet at the same time the Biblical theodicy (which means, a justification of "the ways of God" – i.e., evil and misfortune) also holds out the hope for *redemption* of this fallen condition, for salvation. There is a guarantee of future restoration of God's grace and of the ameliorated moral and material conditions that will accompany it.

The fourth and final feature of Biblical history to be noted here is that *the "characters" in the narrative are God, mankind, and the individual soul.* God is conceived as a personal, anthropomorphic entity. As was noted above, he is the "hidden author of history who is also the director and guarantor of things to come." [15]

The primary meaning of the Biblical story is the literal one: it is the story of the actual history of mankind in the world. In the literal Biblical narrative, mankind – a collective subject – has fallen into mortal life and sin, and wishes to regain God's grace and the (material and moral) well-being that will simultaneously be restored. Thus, it is an external history of that collectivity known as mankind. But, as Abrams points out, there is also a long-standing tradition of interpreting the Bible in terms of *psychohistorical parallelism*: By this he means a system of interpretation in which the same text is read to signify not only the "outer events of sacred history ... but also ... the history of the individual spirit."[16]

This, then, is the Biblical historical narrative, which has passed into secular philosophies of history within Judaeo-Christian culture areas. It is by no means universal. In the ancient Greco-Roman world, there were two prevailing views of the course of human history, a "primitivist" or

---

[14] Max Weber wrote of all "rationalized" religions as embodying a "theodicy of suffering," i.e. as positing "rationally satisfactory answers to the questioning for the basis of the incongruity between destiny and merit." Weber suggested that there are three "ideal types" of such "rationally satisfactory" answers: "the Indian doctrine of Karma, Zoroastrian dualism, and the predestination decree of the *deus absconditus* [i.e., the most extreme development of Judaeo-Christianity, found in Calvinism]." ("The Social Psychology of the World Religions," in Hans Gerth and C. Wright Mills (eds.), *From Max Weber: Essays in Sociology* [New York: Oxford University Press, 1958], p. 275).

[15] Abrams, *Natural Supernaturalism,* p. 36.

[16] Ibid., pp. 49 and 83; see also Beryl Smalley, *The Study of the Bible in the Middle Ages* (Oxford: Clarendon Press, 1941) and H. Flanders Dunbar, *Symbolism in Medieval Thought* (New Haven: Yale University Press, 1929).

"degenerationist" view (i.e., the view that the earliest period of history was the best time and things have been getting worse since then) and a cyclical one, which held that things went "from bad to better to best to worse to worst to better, and so on, time without end."[17]

The Biblical narrative of history also differs from the vision of human destiny that is found in non-Western religious traditions. For example, Gardner and Lois Murphy point out that, in contrast to the prospectivist eschatology of Judaeo-Christianity, Buddhist and Hindu conceptions of the history of the universe are neither linear nor finite:

> In most departments of Indian thought...the conception of telos, or purpose, is absent ... For Hindus the world is endless repetition, not a progress toward an end. Creation has rarely the sense which it bears for Europeans. An infinite number of times the universe has collapsed in flaming or watery ruin, eons of quiescence follow the collapse, and then the Deity (he has done it an infinite number of times) emits again from himself worlds and souls of the same old kind.[18]

As we shall see in Chapter 5, Neoplatonism – which interpenetrated with Biblical history to form Christian mysticism – has much in common with these Eastern traditions. Even infused with mysticism, however, Judaeo-Christian philosophies of history, and their secularized and psychologized descendants, retain the linear, episodic, and teleological character which makes them culturally distinctive and in some respects unique.

The persistence of the Biblical narrative in social and psychological theory

At the beginning of this chapter I noted that a number of prominent scholars have explored the connection between the Biblical historical design, and key concepts and themes that lie at the center of their own modern disciplines. In this section I review several of these scholars' analyses; I summarize their claims that some or all of the distinctive features described in the previous section are present in various secular philosophical and social-scientific systems which endeavor to explain the nature of man and his relationship to nature, to other men, and to himself.

---

[17] Abrams, *Natural Supernaturalism*, pp. 34–5. See also A.O. Lovejoy and George Boas, *Primitivism and Related Ideas in Antiquity* (New York: Octagon Books, 1965); E.R. Dodds, *The Ancient Concept of Progress and Other Essays on Greek Literature and Belief* (New York: Oxford University Press, 1973); W.K.C. Guthrie, *In the Beginning: Some Greek Views on the Origins of Life and the Early State of Man* (Ithaca: Cornell University Press, 1957), ch. 4.

[18] Gardner and Lois B. Murphy, *Asian Psychology* (New York: Basic Books, 1968), p. 33. See also A.L. Basham, "Hinduism," and E. Conze, "Buddhism: The Mahāyāna," in R.C. Zaehner (ed.), *The Concise Encyclopedia of Living Faiths* (Boston: Beacon Press, 1967), pp. 225–60 and pp. 296–320.

As a preface to this summary, however, it should be noted that challenges have been raised to the idea that Western secular visions of history and progress, and related concepts, are shaped by earlier theological doctrines. One of the most serious challenges is found in the work of the German philosopher Hans Blumenberg, who offers a lengthy and detailed critique of Karl Löwith's assertion that the idea of historical progress is derived from the design of Biblical history.[19] In *The Legitimacy of the Modern Age,*[20] Blumenberg argues that Löwith's thesis, as well as other secularization theories, rests on a misconception about the genesis of the modern idea of progress. According to Blumenberg's alternative genealogy, the true and "legitimate" notion of progress arose as a function of two developments during the early modern period. The first of these was the rise of modern science, in particular the advances made in astronomy, and consequent attempts to emulate its highly successful scientific method. The second was the "quarrel of the ancients and the moderns" that went on during the late 1600s; this debate within aesthetics gave rise to a more human-centered and progressive image of creativity and of the function and potentials of art. Both of these developments are seen by Blumenberg to have emerged in tandem with the definitive (and "legitimate") feature of the modern era, its celebration of "human self-assertion" – i.e., "an existential program, according to which man posits his existence in a historical situation and indicates to himself how he is going to deal with the reality surrounding him and what use he will make of the possibilities that are open to him."[21] This modernist elaboration and valorization of "self-assertion," he contends, is not a transmutation of religious doctrines, but rather was born as a radical reaction against the extreme turn taken by such doctrines. According to Blumenberg, by the end of the Middle Ages, Christian theology had developed along the lines of an extreme "theological absolutism" (i.e., "the dependence of the individual's salvation on a faith that he can no longer choose to have"[22]). It was this absolutism, he contends – this image of blind submission to the ways of God – that engendered a sharp response in opposition to such a vision of human impotence. In the words of Blumenberg's translator, Robert Wallace, "human self-assertion, as an alternative to this desperate way of being in the world, *had* to interest itself not in fulfillment but in power, and in a world not

---

[19] In *Meaning in History*, Löwith argues that Western renderings of the philosophy of history – from Orosius and Augustine through Marx and Hegel, but also continuing up to the present day – bear the eschatological imprint of the Biblical historical design.

[20] Trans. Robert M. Wallace (Cambridge, MA: The MIT Press, 1991).

[21] Ibid., p. 138.

[22] Ibid., p. 137.

of order but of pure causal contingency – because these were all that were left to man at this point."[23]

Blumenberg argues that these "legitimate," more "partial" notions of progress, and of rational autonomy and self-assertion, were extended, "illegitimately," to attempt to answer sweeping, "premodern" questions about the meaning of history, questions that they were not intended to address. Thus, Blumenberg contends, Löwith is wrong in asserting that philosophies of history are secularized eschatology; rather, they are attempts to stretch or contort the more modest, "legitimate" concepts of progress into forms that they should not be forced to take.

One of the curious features of Blumenberg's argument is that he (implicitly) presents the question of the source of ideas of progress as an either/or proposition: either they are derived from the Biblical model of history, or they embody a wholly modern rupture with the theological past. It is not at all clear why this sort of strict binarism has to obtain for the history of ideas and other cultural forms. Indeed, it is precisely with the aim of highlighting the interplay between rupture and continuity that I delineate in detail the homologies that exist between the Christian mystical, Romantic, and psychoanalytic narratives, and trace the clear directional movement of the template's successive transmutations. The detail with which the features and transformations of this trope can be traced (as is shown in Chapters 5 through 8) serves to weaken any argument that religious themes and patterns are not carried over into at least some secular philosophical and cultural systems that allege the progressive amelioration of the human lot.

Of course, it could be the case that Romanticism and psychoanalytic developmental psychology are, at least in great measure, transmuted versions of the Christian mystical theodicy but that theological themes are not a significant source of the other (non-Romantic) philosophies of history that Löwith highlights, or of the more "modest" notions of progress, rationality, and self-assertion that Blumenberg holds up as the true and radically innovative essence of modernity. But if, as I have suggested, the latter philosopher's "either/or" logic seems overdrawn – if, as Charles Taylor has put it, "the stimulus existed within Christian culture itself to generate these views that stand on the threshold [of secularization and Enlightenment]"[24] – then it seems advisable to retain an openness to exploring the ways in which non-Romantic philosophies of history, non-psychoanalytic developmentalist tropes, and even Blumenberg's more

---

[23] Robert M. Wallace, "Progress, Secularization and Modernity: The Löwith–Blumenberg Debate," *New German Critique*, no. 22, Winter 1981, pp. 63–79, p. 76.
[24] Taylor, *Sources of the Self*, p. 315.

"authentic" rationalist and scientistic systems, embody neither pure reaction and innovation in relation to Judaeo-Christian doctrines, nor simple continuity with them.

Among those scholars who, like Löwith, have highlighted modern social theories' continuity with aspects of Judaeo-Christian doctrine have been the political scientist Mona Harrington and the sociologists Arthur Vidich and Stanford Lyman. Harrington writes of "the dream of deliverance" (from evil) as a pervasive American political "myth." She asserts that a set of assumptions, traceable to the design of Biblical history, informs our political thought up to the present time; these assumptions act as a "screen, allowing some problems through to receive political attention and excluding others."[25] She suggests that this spiritual template was brought to America by the Puritans, "who sought a literal deliverance from the social corruptions of the Old World by leaving it for a new promised land, a new Jerusalem ... following God's law." Harrington further argues that a still more fully secularized version of this Christian prospectivist doctrine was adopted by early American political leaders in the form of eighteenth-century Enlightenment doctrines, as "laws inherent in human nature and the nature of human relations ... embodied in the nature of things on earth ... discernible to those with the capacity to reason."[26] Thus, one of these visions remains explicitly religious (the Puritan worldly utopian aspiration to found a "city on a hill" for the purposes of glorifying God) while the other is secularized (the Enlightenment belief in reason, progress, and natural laws). According to Harrington, these two different worldly prospectivist belief systems complement each other, both of them embodying some taken-for-granted ideas about human nature and destiny that inform much thinking about politics to this day.

Arthur Vidich and Stanford Lyman, investigating the origins and early development of American sociology, make an argument similar to Harrington's. They cite our dual heritage of Protestant worldly "salvationism" (the Protestant sectarians' "hope and expectation" that social problems "could be solved by secular means," perpetuating the "promise of a heavenly kingdom on earth") and nineteenth-century positivistic theories of societal evolution (e.g., Comtean sociology) imported from Europe. Both of these worldly legatees of Biblical history, they suggest, influenced the founders of American sociology, promoting in them a tendency to substitute "'sociodicy' – a vindication of the ways of society

---

[25] Mona Harrington, *The Dream of Deliverance in American Politics* (New York: Alfred A. Knopf, 1986), p. 15.

[26] Ibid., p. 18.

to man – for the theodicy that originally had inspired them ... They substituted a language of science for the rhetoric of religion."[27]

Finally, several scholars have explored how the design of Biblical history also has been imposed on the interpretation of the meaning of *individual* human lives – i.e., how it underlies theories of psychological growth and change over the life course.[28] William Kessen,[29] Sheldon White,[30] Bernard Kaplan,[31] and their associates have made us aware of some broad, theologically derived assumptions and values that inform the idea of "development" as it forms the understructure of our most influential paradigms of child development: cognitive-developmental, organismic, psychoanalytic, and even behaviorist.[32] Kessen argues that Darwin's evolutionary theory was taken up by early child psychologists in an environment already prepared to be receptive to it for "non-scientific" reasons. Early "developmentalists" – Hall, Baldwin, et al. – adopted a nineteenth-century positivistic (Spencerian) reading of Darwin, borrowing the idea of an "end" (eschatology) from moral sciences which, ultimately, were derived from Biblical history.

Of course, after Darwin[33] there was an increasing tendency on the part

[27] Arthur Vidich and Stanford Lyman, *American Sociology: Worldly Rejections of Religion and Their Directions* (New Haven: Yale University Press, 1985), p. 1.

[28] Psychological theories originally traced the development of infants and children (and in some cases adolescents); more recently, they have been reconceptualized to include various phases of adult development: see, e.g., Erik Erikson, *Childhood and Society* (New York: W.W. Norton, 1963); Daniel Levinson, *Seasons of a Man's Life* (New York: Ballantine, 1979).

[29] "The American Child and Other Cultural Inventions," *American Psychologist*, vol. 34, no. 10, Oct. 1979, pp. 815–20; "The Child and Other Cultural Inventions," in Frank Kessel and Alexander W. Siegel (eds.), *The Child and Other Cultural Inventions* (New York: Praeger, 1983), pp. 26–39; Lecture on "The Idea of Development" before the Wellesley Colloquium on the History of Psychology, Wesleyan University, May 1985; Lecture on "The Idea of Development" at Harvard University, March 1986; *The Rise and Fall of Development* (Worcester, MA: Clark University Press, 1990).

[30] Sheldon White, "The Idea of Development in Developmental Psychology," in Richard M. Lerner (ed.), *Developmental Psychology: Historical and Philosophical Perspectives* (Hillsdale, NJ: Lawrence Erlbaum Associates, 1983).

[31] "A Trio of Trials," in Richard M. Lerner (ed.), *Developmental Psychology: Historical and Philosophical Perspectives* (Hillsdale, NJ: Lawrence Erlbaum Associates, 1983), pp. 185–228; "Value Presuppositions in Theories of Human Development," in Leonard Cirillo and Seymour Wapner (eds.), *Value Presuppositions in Theories of Human Development* (Hillsdale, NJ: Lawrence Erlbaum Associates, 1986), pp. 89–103.

[32] Kessen ("Idea of Development," 1985, 1986) argues that B.F. Skinner's "Walden Two" ideal evinces a prospectivist and utopian orientation ultimately derived from the Biblical pattern, even if not perhaps following it as closely as do the other, more strictly "developmentalist" paradigms such as cognitive-developmental, organismic, and – according to Kessen – psychoanalytic psychology.

[33] Perhaps before Darwin too: ever since the scientific revolution and the Enlightenment, "science" has been valued and emulated as opposed to "superstition" and "religion" and other "non-rational" systems of thought and practice. See White, "Idea of Development"; see also Wolf Lepenies' book on the sources of sociology in Europe, *Between Literature and Science: The Rise of Sociology*, trans. R.J. Hollingdale (New York: Cambridge University Press, 1988).

of social theorists to look to scientific models in general, and the theory of evolution in particular, for metaphors to help explain and construct guidelines for many aspects of social life.[34] However, Kessen points out that in the case of child psychology, the welding of Darwin's non-teleological evolutionary theory to the teleological idea of development and "progress" borrowed from the moral sciences harkens back to a much older concept, that of salvationist history. This narrative design, after all, assumes the inevitable progress of mankind towards a stable end point of well-being and moral perfection. Such a framework, Kessen argues, is an artifact of our Biblical heritage.

Similarly, Sheldon White argues that stage theories of cognitive development (beginning with the nineteenth-century writings of Romanes, Sechnov, and Baldwin, and continuing to this day with Piaget's and Kohlberg's work) can be viewed as attempts to reconstitute a basis for ethical values and "the idea of the Good" once Darwin's theory of evolution had struck perhaps the most serious of a series of blows to the traditional theologically derived basis for morality. He contends that during the 1860s and 1870s, many social and psychological theorists looked to the developmentalist model to help them devise theories of individual and collective development that could lead to the discovery of both a means of human betterment[35] and a "source of values" which, because it is based on science, is "stronger than faith,"[36] yet ironically retains some of the central values and assumptions inherent in the Judaeo-Christian historical design.

Thus, in fields of inquiry as disparate as politics, sociology, and developmental psychology, at least some (if not most) theoretical frameworks are seen to be, in various ways and to varying degrees, bearers of the Biblical narrative. They partake of such features as its basic linear design, its prospectivism and future-orientation, and its function as a means of explaining, and offering the hope of amelioration of, the imperfections of the human condition. It is interesting to note that all of these scholars cite two broad types of "worldly revision" that Biblical history underwent before it was incorporated into the social sciences. First, they

---

[34] See Richard Hofstader, *Social Darwinism in American Thought* (Boston: Beacon Press, 1955) and Bernard Wishy, *The Child and the Republic* (Philadelphia: University of Pennsylvania Press, 1968) for discussions of issues surrounding the use of Darwinian theory and evolutionary metaphors to explain social and psychological phenomena.

[35] The promotion of individual development is seen to better the race in two ways: first, simply by raising individuals to a higher level (thereby creating a more civilized and rational group of human beings); second, by making such persons capable of bettering society still further, since they will put their higher intellectual and moral sensibilities to socially constructive use.

[36] White, "The Idea of Development," p. 73.

mention eighteenth- and nineteenth-century philosophical attempts to understand and "perfect" human nature and social life: Harrington and Löwith cite Enlightenment rationalism and views about progress, and Vidich and Lyman, Kessen, and White point to nineteenth-century positivist and social evolutionist schemes such as those of Comte and Spencer. Second, these commentators (largely independently of one another) identify certain tendencies in Protestant (especially the Puritans' "worldly ascetic") thought and culture which apparently helped to promote or facilitate the translation of Biblical history into explicitly secular discourses on the amelioration of "ordinary" life in *this* world.[37]

Does psychoanalytic developmental psychology partake of the Biblical historical narrative?

As was noted above, Kessen, White, and Kaplan have highlighted the fact that Biblical history was translated into secular form in Enlightenment beliefs about reason and progress, and in subsequent nineteenth-century philosophies of history and social evolutionist schemes (which wedded the emergent scientific authority of biological evolution to the neo-eschatology of teleology). They have argued that it was via translation into these secular theories that Biblical prospectivism and eschatology came to influence the child-study and proto-developmentalist movements which emerged in the final decades of the nineteenth century.

---

[37] Scholars tend to agree that Protestantism – painted, admittedly, in very broad and sweeping brush strokes – has been characterized by two orientations or values that have influenced post-Reformation culture in Northern European culture areas (i.e., Western European nations north of the Alps, as well as Switzerland, Great Britain, North America, and Australia): (1) "individualism" – an intensified emphasis (for these tendencies existed in Western culture prior to the Reformation) on the individual's sense of personal responsibility, autonomy, and self-sufficiency, as well as on the personal conscience and inner life (see Chapter 2 of this book); and (2) "worldliness" – a secular thrust, including an emphasis on everyday life in this world (both work and personal [marital and familial] relationships), and a belief that the "Kingdom of God" can be achieved on earth, whether externally, in terms of a genuine betterment of mankind and society, or internally, in the form of certain types of spiritual experiences that the individual can attain even while living a secular, worldly life. See Charles H. and Katherine George, *The Protestant Mind of the English Reformation* (Princeton: Princeton University Press, 1961); Lawrence Stone, *The Family, Sex and Marriage in England: 1500–1800* (New York: Harper, 1979); Ernst Troeltsch, *The Social Teaching of the Christian Churches* (New York: Macmillan, 1931) and *Protestantism and Progress: A Historical Study of the Relation of Protestantism to the Modern World* (Boston: Beacon Press, 1958); Max Weber, *The Protestant Ethic and the Spirit of Capitalism* (New York: Scribners, 1958); Paul Tillich, *A History of Christian Thought from its Judaic and Hellenistic Origins to Existentialism*, ed. Carl E. Braten (New York: Touchstone, 1968).

Kessen and Bernard Kaplan include psychoanalytic theory in the same category as other developmental psychologies: they view it as an heir to Biblical eschatology and prospectivism. Bernard Kaplan argues:

Thus, Freud and Jung both assumed an immanent telos of development – a movement toward genitality or toward individuation – and both worked or claimed to work to remove certain factors inhibiting the relative attainment of such relatively more advanced modes of being-in-the-world. Unfortunately, these two great minds were inclined to take their teloi as immanent in the biographical-historical process: ineluctable, if only the inhibiting forces could be overcome. Freud was, of course, far more pessimistic than Jung concerning the possibility of eliminating the inhibiting forces, and thus his teleological assumption is less obvious.[38]

It is true that psychoanalytic theories partake of the basic developmentalist assumption that the psychological maturity normally characteristic of adulthood is a higher, more advanced, more developed state than childish immaturity, which is more or less equated with primitivity. We also can ascertain a teleological element in psychoanalytic theory, both in the psychosexual movement towards genitality and (most notable in post-Freudian theories) in the movement towards individuation. Phylogenesis as well as ontogenesis move in this direction towards greater rationality and civilization.[39] This assumption is present in Freudian metapsychology, as well as in those ego-psychological, object-relational, and self-psychological theories which I call Anglo-American psychoanalytic developmental psychology. In this sense, then, psychoanalysis is "prospectivist" in the tradition of Biblical history and its Enlightenment and evolutionist descendants.

Yet, although the developmental trajectory in psychoanalytic theory (whether psychosexual or ego-developmental) certainly evinces this inbuilt teleology, and hence can be read as Kaplan reads it, there is nevertheless a significant difference between psychoanalytic developmental psychology and other developmentalisms. In order to highlight this discrepancy, we must look more closely at their respective depictions of the ends of the developmental process.

Kaplan defines developmental psychology as

... a practico-theoretical discipline ... concerned with the perfection (including the liberation or freedom) of the individual. Its aim is to facilitate development

[38] Kaplan, "Trio of Trials," p. 189.
[39] For a detailed examination of Freud's philosophy of history, see Bruce Mazlish, *Psychoanalysis and History* (Englewood Cliffs, NJ: Prentice-Hall, 1963), and Mazlish, *The Riddle of History: Great Speculators from Vico to Freud* (New York: Harper and Row, 1966), ch. IX.

... as an ideal movement toward freedom, autonomy, individuation, liberation from the various forms of bondage, external and internal.[40]

In this definition, I read the assertion that "perfection" in this developmental sense is strongly linked to the attainment of autonomy, as that word has been used in several different senses: a movement towards greater rationality (i.e., the perfecting of one's capacity to apprehend ontological and moral truth), a movement towards greater individuation and independence, and – perhaps as a consequence of these two – a movement towards freedom from external constraint and internal conflict. Additionally, the end-state of development (for example, the perfected capacity to reason) seems to be conceptualized as unitary, untroubled by conflict or qualification (at least in principle).

Do contemporary psychoanalytic theories of development conform to this vision? Post-Freudian psychoanalytic theories which trace the development of the ego and/or the self and its modes of relating to objects also tell a story of psychological development. Yet in these theories we find descriptions of the highest developmental achievements which are framed in terms quite different from those described above. It is true that these psychoanalytic theories do not deny that autonomy – that is, individuation *and* rationality – is a necessary and central aspect of development. Yet their descriptions of the course and ends of development offer a rather more tempered vision, one in which there is an appreciation of the fact that autonomy and rationality always stand in tension with opposing tendencies and longings. Correspondingly, the most developed forms of maturity are seen to entail an integration of both "progressive" and "regressive" tendencies: of individuation *and* fusion, rationality *and* impulse. In the most abstract sense, the highest development is considered, in these theories, to evince a reintegration of severed elements – most notably of self and object – at a higher level than that of the original undifferentiated unity. Most often, this occurs in a "relationship" which preserves the self's individuation and ego functions but also expresses and partially gratifies the psyche's opposing tendencies and longings.

Let us take by way of example Mahler's "separation-individuation" theory. What are the ends of development in her narrative? At first glance, they seem to be similar to those voiced by Kaplan. Certainly one

---

[40] "Value Presuppositions," p. 96. It is true that not all developmentalist theories are self-consciously intended to promote the perfection of the human being or of some particular aspect of him or her: some are merely intended as descriptions of how development does take place. Even such allegedly non-normative theories, however, tend to be more normative, value-laden, and prescriptive than they allege.

crucial end is indicated by the name of Mahler's theory: *separation and individuation*. As was noted in Chapters 2 and 3, psychoanalytic developmental psychologists assert that the development of an enduring sense of separate-selfhood – of independence and self-direction – is an absolutely essential aspect of maturity. *Rationality* also is valued as an end of development: all of these psychoanalytic theories partake of the Freudian tenet that the improved rationality and enhanced insight of the strengthened ego endow the individual with a bit more control and freedom, and hence the capacity for greater satisfaction of his needs, if not his fantasies. There is a teleological aspect to these theories as well: for example, in Mahler's notion that strivings towards individuation are innately programmed into the individual. So far, then, the "ends" of development in these psychoanalytic theories seem similar or analogous to the ends of development as I described them for the non-psychoanalytic theories.

Yet the maturity that they conceptualize is actually more complex than this. This is a vision of human development in which the self – even if manifestly at a pinnacle of autonomy, self-reliance, and rationality – is always beset by opposing tendencies and inclinations, tendencies which are not eradicated but rather stand perennially in tension with these manifestly "desirable" ends.

According to psychoanalytic metapsychology (beginning with Freud), the human condition is essentially a tragic one. This is so for several reasons: first, because by nature the human being has within him conflicting tendencies, wishes, and needs; second, because the longings and fantasies that originate within the individual psyche inevitably clash with certain imperatives of physical and social reality; and third, because these conflicts and tensions continue to impinge upon (indeed, they constitute) the human character from birth to death, from psychological immaturity to psychological maturity.

What this means is that nothing – not maturity, not insight, neither nature nor reason – can ever entirely eradicate this tragic dimension. Even manifestly unconflicted and unproblematic rational functioning, even the attainment of subjective states of satisfaction and joy, even the highest moral judgments and acts, entail compromise and renunciation, a balancing of so-called anti-social instincts and tendencies with opposing inclinations and imperatives. Civilization would not *be* civilization without its discontents.

For Mahler and the other post-Freudian developmental theorists, the tragic story is less about impulses and instincts than about the boundaries and limitations of both one's own and the other's powers, of splits and ruptures both within and outside the self. But for these theorists, as for Freud, the end-point of development cannot be understood as a unitary or perfected state but rather as a complex integration of divergent or opposing needs and tendencies. The most fundamental tensions for Mahler are between symbiotic and narcissistic needs and longings on the one hand, innate individuation strivings on the other, and (on the third hand) certain imperatives and limitations inherent in inter-personal relationships.

Yet – and this is important – for all this pessimism, there is nonethe-less also a triumphant or transcendent dimension in these theories, much more so in the post-Freudian theories than in Freudian texts. This tran-scendent dimension is not a denial or an effacement of life's tragedy. Rather, this vision of the last things takes account of the fact that since we cannot (and perhaps should not) hope to disabuse ourselves of the wish for reunion with our objects, and of other impossible longings, maturity must entail an integration of both individuating *and* symbiotic tendencies. This is less a picture of man (or woman) perfected by an ascent to individuation and rationality, than one in which the end of development entails an integration of both individuation and fusion, rationality and impulse, and – in a limited and partial, somewhat illusory yet vital way – of self and object.

As was discussed in Chapters 2 and 3, the story of development as told by Mahler and the others is not just of a movement out of symbiosis towards autonomy and self-reliance. Rather, as I have explained, these theories also include the postulate that, on a usually unconscious level, all of us always are struggling with the longing for reunion, and that even if one has developed to a higher, more securely individuated state, as one must, one still seeks out relationships in which this desire for oneness can be integrated with the imperative of separateness. The end state of devel-opment, thus, is both autonomy and (perhaps an even higher end) the capacity to engage in certain types of limited and partial experiences of reunion with one's objects, but without losing the sense of separate and distinctive identity which one has struggled to achieve. Significantly, Fairbairn calls his "end" of development, not "independence" but "mature dependence."

In Chapters 2 and 3 I discussed the several varieties and intensities of "reunion-in-separateness" which Anglo-American post-Freudian psycho-analysts have cited as indexes of mature integration. Of these, surely the one currently emphasized most is "mature intimacy." Both the "regres-sion in the service of the ego" of falling-in-love, and the more diffuse and ongoing "relationship" are seen to entail simultaneous and/or sequential integrations of dependency, "regression," and permeability of ego boundaries on the one hand, and the intrapsychic sense of separateness and autonomy, on the other.

In short, this psychoanalytic vision of the ends of development differs significantly from the other developmentalisms discussed in this chapter. The question I wish to pose at this point is, what does this indicate about its cultural inheritance? Given psychoanalysis's more tempered and "ambivalent" view, its lack of a simple prospectivism *vis-à-vis* either individuals or society, does this mean that psychoanalytic developmental psychology is not a legatee of the Biblical historical narrative?

Kessen, White, and Kaplan have drawn our attention to the ways in which developmental psychology is continuous with a pervasive Judaeo-Christian historical design. They have made a crucially important point about the cultural patterning of contemporary psychological theory. What I have argued in this chapter is that not all psychological developmentalisms are exactly alike, and that therefore there is more work to be done to explore the genealogy of the different branches of the Biblical-historical family tree. Specifically, I would suggest that psychoanalytic developmental psychology, like cognitive-developmental psychology and other developmental theories, is heir to the Biblical template of history. However, it is heir to *a different tradition* of Biblical interpretation than has been highlighted by Kessen et al. Moreover, this tradition of Biblical interpretation underwent its own process of secularization, culminating not in Enlightenment doctrines and positivist theories but rather in the high-Romantic movement of the late eighteenth and early nineteenth centuries. In short, psychoanalytic developmental psychology also is heir to Biblical history, but it is not wholly derived from the Enlightenment secularization of that narrative and its vision of redemption. Rather, it seems to have drawn more extensively upon a different version of that history, one that was secularized into Romantic doctrines and has entered psychoanalytic thought mainly via that route.

High Romanticism, which I discuss at length in Chapter 7, was a counter-Enlightenment movement which developed its own distinctive naturalistic version of the Judaeo-Christian narrative. That version, in turn, draws more elaborately on Neoplatonized Biblical history than do Enlightenment, positivist, or evolutionist systems.

Towards a cultural genealogy of psychoanalytic developmental psychology

I have suggested that the post-Freudian narrative – insofar as it depicts maturity as the self's capacity for a reunion with its object at a higher level that preserves the self's sense of its individuated distinctiveness from the object – is less an Enlightenment vision than a high Romantic one. By high Romantic thought I refer to that movement initiated among English and German artists and intellectuals during the last decade of the eighteenth century and the first two decades of the nineteenth. Those who participated in the Romantic movement – including the poets Blake, Wordsworth, Coleridge, and Hölderlin and the philosophers Fichte, Schelling, and Hegel – were individuals who were especially attuned to what they perceived to be the costs and losses of the Enlightenment, and to the mixed blessings of scientific and industrial progress. They felt that rationalism and empiricism provided an inadequate vision of reality and that the secularized prospectivist vision embedded in these philosophical positions offered an impoverished depiction of human potential. They became particularly disillusioned with the veneration of reason when the French Revolution (that brainchild of the Enlightenment) failed to fulfill what they had perceived to be its initial salvationist promise.

Thus disappointed, the Romantics sought to construct new, naturalistic modes of salvation, as the literary critic M.H. Abrams amply demonstrated in his study of Romanticism and its sources, *Natural Supernaturalism*. They appreciated that earlier hopes for millenarian perfection (first anticipated in literal religious doctrines, and then evoked by Enlightenment doctrines of progress) could not be sustained in the old way in the post-Enlightenment world. They knew they could not return to the old religious cosmology – that this had to be a system of *worldly* salvation, which had both its beginning and its end, to quote Wordsworth, "in the very world which is the world of all of us, the place in which, in the end, We find our happiness, or not at all."[41] Therefore they attempted to transmute the Biblical narrative, to divest it of explicitly theological terms such as the soul (or even, for the most part, God), inserting in its place the mind or self.

The Biblical narrative which they thus transformed, however, was not the straightforward Providential historical account cited by Kessen, White, et al., but rather a distinctive version of that account. The Romantics, in other words, drew upon a tradition of Biblical exegesis which combined the linear design of Biblical history with Neoplatonist

[41] *The Prelude*, ed. J. C. Maxwell (London: Penguin Classics, 1988), X, p. 442.

mystical themes. From the age of Plotinus (third century AD) onwards, such Christian mystical narratives had been elaborated by numerous and diverse religious thinkers. With the advent of the Reformation, mystical themes and patterns came to be integrated into certain Protestant sectarian doctrines as well. Thus Christian mysticism began to take a form which was more "worldly" and, eventually, more "interiorized" (seen as pertaining to the inner life of the individual spirit or soul, sometimes even negating the literal interpretation of the narrative as the external history of mankind). It is mainly in these Protestant incarnations that the Romantics seem to have come into contact with Neoplatonized Biblical history, and then secularized and interiorized it still further and more definitively.

It is interesting to note that in the case of psychoanalytic developmental psychology, as in that of the other developmental theories I have discussed, we can trace a series of cultural transformations in which a Judaeo-Christian narrative was made more worldly (and in some cases interiorized) in the form of Protestant doctrines and then was fully secularized in eighteenth- and nineteenth-century movements in philosophy, arts, and letters. In the case of non-psychoanalytic (social and psychological) developmentalisms there is a stronger inheritance from Enlightenment and nineteenth-century positivist/evolutionist doctrines, whereas in the case of contemporary psychoanalytic developmental psychology there is a stronger inheritance from Romantic doctrines.

This is not to say that it is quite this clear-cut, of course: both Freudian psychoanalysis and the post-Freudian developmental narrative evince, in different ways and to different degrees, Enlightenment as well as Romantic patterns and values. And cognitive-developmental and organismic paradigms bear the imprint of both "inner light" Christian mysticism (via rationalism) and Romantic dialectics. Thus Benjamin Nelson appears to have been correct when he wrote of the "various blendings of Protestant conscience, character, and culture,"[42] both literally religious and secularized, which have come to comprise so many different folk- and high-cultural discourses in Euro-American society. In any case, we need a more complex depiction of the religious and cultural genealogy of

---

[42] "Self-Images and Systems of Spiritual Direction in the History of European Civilization," in S. Z. Klausner (ed.), *The Quest for Self-Control* (New York: Free Press, 1965).

developmentalisms than is currently available.[43] It is in the interest of exploring this greater complexity that I offer my own research on the lineage of the Anglo-American psychoanalytic developmental narrative. In the following three chapters, I sketch out this lineage along the lines that I have suggested in this chapter.

[43] As I have noted, there are a number of scholars who have linked psychoanalytic theory to Romanticism. For example, Louis A. Sass, drawing upon Abrams and other literary theorists, makes similar connections in several of his essays, including "The Self and Its Vicissitudes: an 'Archaeological' Study of the Psychoanalytic Avant-Garde," *Social Research,* vol. 55, no. 4, Winter 1988, pp. 551–697, and "Psychoanalysis, Romanticism, and the Nature of Aesthetic Consciousness with Reflections on Modernism and Postmodernism," in Margery B. Franklin and Bernard Kaplan (eds.), *Development and the Arts: Critical Perspectives* (Hillsdale, NJ: Lawrence Erlbaum Associates, 1994).

5

The Christian mystical narrative: Neoplatonism and Christian mysticism

> God – we read – is outside of none, present unperceived to all; we break away from Him, or rather from ourselves; what we turn from we cannot reach; ... to find ourselves is to know our source. [A]ll living apart from Him is but a shadow, a mimicry.
>
> Plotinus, *Enneads* (trans. Stephen MacKenna, 1962) pp. 621–2.

In Chapter 4, some basic features of Biblical history were discussed: the Biblical narrative is linear and finite; it has a well-defined plot and sequence of events or episodes; it is prospectivist and eschatological (concerned with and oriented towards the "last things"); and its key players are God, mankind, and the individual soul.

There exists a long-standing tradition of Biblical exegesis in which Biblical history is interpreted in mystical terms. Mystical themes and doctrines have influenced many different aspects of Christian (and Jewish[1]) theology, from the most "orthodox" and "objective" to the most dissenting and esoteric versions of the Christian vision.

As a generic term, mysticism tends to be defined as a seeking after and experience of proximity to God, with a corresponding retreat from or eradication of worldly and material contingencies. Andrew Louth, for example, suggests that mysticism "can be characterized as a search for and experience of immediacy with God."[2] Roland Robertson, a sociologist of religion, defines "religious mysticism" as "that orientation which seeks the experiential obliteration of this-worldly contingencies *in relation to* the supremacy of an other-worldly realm."[3] Max Weber

---

[1] On the Kabbala and the Zohar, see Gershem Scholem, *Major Trends in Jewish Mysticism* (New York: Schocken Books, 1954); *Kabbalah* (New York: New American Library, 1974); and *Zohar* (New York: Schocken Books, 1963); see also M.H. Abrams, *Natural Supernaturalism* (New York: W.W. Norton, 1973), especially pp. 155–8.

[2] *The Origins of Christian Mysticism* (Oxford: Clarendon Press, 1981), p. xv.

[3] "On the Analysis of Mysticism: Pre-Weberian, Weberian and Post-Weberian Perspectives," *Sociological Analysis*, vol. 36, no. 3, 1975, pp. 241–66, p. 253.

emphasized the contemplative mystic's "flight from the world ... In contrast to asceticism, contemplation is primarily the quest to achieve rest in god and in him alone."[4] Weber contrasted mysticism to the other ideal-typical religious orientation, asceticism. He defined asceticism as "God-willed *action*," explaining that "active asceticism operates within the world."[5] He postulated that asceticism tended to be more "inner-worldly" – i.e., to focus attention and value on worldly life and activity – while mysticism tended to focus attention and value on the "other-worldly" realm. However, he did acknowledge that there could exist otherworldly asceticism (e.g., in medieval monasteries) and innerworldly mysticism (which is further discussed in subsequent chapters, particularly Chapter 6).[6]

The Judaeo-Christian tradition is not, by definition or necessity, a mystical one. Louth asserts that "mysticism is not a religious phenomenon peculiar to Christianity, and it is disputed whether it is essential to Christianity at all."[7] Nevertheless, strong mystical currents have existed in both mainstream and "marginal" Christian thought and practice from

---

[4] *The Sociology of Religion*, trans. Ephraim Fischoff (Boston: Beacon Press, 1963), p. 169.

[5] "Religious Rejections of the World and Their Directions," in Hans Gerth and C. Wright Mills (eds.) *From Max Weber: Essays in Sociology* (New York: Oxford University Press. 1958), p. 325.

[6] Weber was interested in formulating typologies which, while respecting the particulars of different situations and traditions, ultimately could be used for comparative purposes and to discover certain universals. Others interested in the phenomenon of mysticism have perhaps been more attuned to different types or aspects of mysticism which may be specific to particular cultural traditions and contexts. Such scholars of comparative mysticism tend to agree that mysticisms share some common elements, and that the experience of mystical union *may* be the same universally but that not all mystical traditions are alike, and that (in the words of Rudolph Otto) "it is false to maintain that mysticism is always just mysticism, is always and everywhere one and the same quantity. Rather, there are within mysticism many varieties of expression."(*Mysticism East and West* [New York: Macmillan, 1970], p. 14.) See also Otto, *The Idea of the Holy* (New York: Oxford University Press, 1958). See also R.C. Zaehner, *Mysticism: Sacred and Profane* (London: Oxford University Press, 1969) on monistic vs. theistic mysticism; W.T. Stace, *Mysticism and Philosophy* (Philadelphia: J.B. Lippincott, 1960); R.T. Wallis, *Neoplatonism* (New York: Charles Scribner's Sons, 1972); W.R. Inge, *Christian Mysticism* (London: Methuen, 1948).

In this context, it is important to note that Rudolph Otto (*Mysticism*, p. 320) and Evelyn Underhill underscore Western (it is not clear whether they mean Greek as well as Christian) mysticism's more "activistic" orientation – i.e., even after mystical union, "the highest forms of Divine Union impel the self to some sort of active, rather than of passive life" (Underhill, *Mysticism: A Study in the Nature and Development of Man's Spiritual Consciousness* [New York: New American Library, 1974], p. 172). Thus, from the very beginning Christianity injected a "worldly" element into its mystical tradition, as I note later in this chapter. The question of whether Plotinian mysticism (also a "Western" – i.e., Greek – tradition) evinces a similarly "activistic" orientation (at least as compared to much "Eastern" mysticism) is more ambiguous (see footnotes 9 and 13). On the distinctiveness of Christianity's activism, see p. 127, footnote 52.

[7] Louth, *Origins*, p. xv.

the beginning.[8] Christian mysticism is considered to have developed mainly by means of the infusion into Christianity of a distinctive Western pagan mystical tradition (though one with strong "Eastern" undertones[9]), Neoplatonism.[10]

The Plotinian narrative

Neoplatonism is both an actual system of mystical practice and a system of speculative philosophy concerning the nature of the world, man, and God. In spite of its name, this philosophical system took shape not in the writings of Plato but in those of the pagan philosopher Plotinus. Plotinus was probably a Greek, born in Alexandria c. AD 204; he died in AD 270. He viewed his system as a continuation of Plato's philosophy; from this self-perception comes its name. However, "though almost all its elements existed in dispersion in the work of earlier thinkers," states E.R. Dodds, "the system which [Neoplatonism] taught seems to have been, *qua* system, the creation of a single mind."[11] Commentators[12] note innovation and originality in his system as well as mixtures of Platonic, Aristotelian, Stoic, and possibly Eastern (Persian, Near Eastern, possibly even Hindu)[13] doctrines. Whatever the exact origins of his system, or the extent of its originality, in Plotinian doctrines "we find the supreme exponent of an abiding element in what we might call 'mystical philosophy.'"[14] Or, to put it in M.H. Abrams' words, "[t]he philosophical history of this way of thinking has in the main been a long series of footnotes to Plotinus."[15]

[8] There are mystical elements in the Gospels, probably of Greek (Platonic) origin.

[9] Zaehner (*Mysticism: Sacred and Profane*) has commented on the striking affinities between Neoplatonism and Hindu mysticism/Vedanta. There seems to be no consensus as to what these parallels indicate about the sources of Plotinian mysticism (see footnote 13).

[10] See, e.g., Thomas Michael Tomasic, "Neoplatonism and the Mysticism of William of St. Thierry," in Paul Szarmach (ed.), *An Introduction to the Medieval Mystics of Europe* (Albany: State University of New York Press, 1984), p. 53.

[11] E.R. Dodds, *Select Passages Illustrating Neoplatonism* (New York: Macmillan, 1923), p. 7.

[12] Including Dodds, ibid.; Louth, *Origins*; Wallis, *Neoplatonism*.

[13] R. T. Wallis considers the question, raised by various commentators, of the possibility of Neoplatonism's "Oriental" sources. He concludes that Neoplatonism does not "involve abandonment of the Greek tradition of rational, critical thought," although it is also true that "from their earliest days Greek philosophy and science had drawn freely on the ideas of the Near East." He further acknowledges that "Indian thought bears sufficient resemblance to Plotinus's introspective mysticism to be taken seriously as a possible source." (R.C. Zaehner has noted the parallels between Vedanta and Neoplatonism.) But he concludes that "though parallels between Greek and Indian thought deserve serious study, Neoplatonism must be treated as a development of the preceding Greek tradition" (*Neoplatonism*, pp. 13–15).

[14] Louth, *Origins*, p. 36.

[15] Abrams, *Natural Supernaturalism*, p. 146.

Plotinus' disciples – including Porphyry (AD 232–304), Proclus (AD 412–490), and Iamblicus – were responsible for the written transmission of his doctrines. These were set down most completely in the *Enneads*, a collection of treatises written by Plotinus and published after his death by Porphyry. Thereafter Neoplatonist themes began to show up in the writings of early Christian mystics, including Augustine (AD 354–430), Dionysius the Areopagite (writing between AD 475 and 525), and others. As was noted above, it is possible to detect Neoplatonist themes in virtually all subsequent Judaeo-Christian mystical writings.

The Plotinian system posits a first principle, the One, which is synonymous with the Good.

The Good is that on which all else depends, towards which all Existences aspire as to their source and their need, while itself is without need, sufficient to itself.[16]

It is the character of every good to unify that which participates in it and all unification is good; and the Good is identical with the One.[17]

All existing entities emanate from, or flow out of, this primal undifferentiated unity, through a series of stages and hypostases, which are at different degrees of distance from the One:

Seeking nothing, possessing nothing, lacking nothing, the One is perfect and, in our metaphor, has overflowed, and its exuberance has produced the new ...[18]

The first emanation from the One is *nous* (mind or spirit, the source of what Plato called "ideas" or ideal forms). The second emanation is the soul, the individual life-principle or movement-principle of all beings (not only persons: stars also have souls, and the world has a world soul). The soul is ambiguous or "two-faced" because it can turn away from the *nous* and the One – towards matter (bodily existence) – as well as towards the Absolute.[19]

---

[16] Plotinus, *The Enneads*, trans. Stephen MacKenna (London: Faber and Faber, 1962), I.8.2, p. 93. There have been two translations of Plotinus' *Enneads* completed during the twentieth century. The first was done by Stephen MacKenna, the second (published in 1988 by Harvard University Press) by A.H. Armstrong. After having compared these two and also having examined several other translations of selected passages of the *Enneads*, I have chosen to use the MacKenna translation here.

[17] Proclus, *Inst. Theol.* 13; quoted in E.R. Dodds, *Select Passages Illustrating Neoplatonism*, p. 55. See also Plotinus, *Enneads* VI.9.1.

[18] Plotinus, *Enneads*, V.2.2, p. 16.

[19] See Paul Tillich, *A History of Christian Thought from its Judaic and Hellenistic Origins to Existentiatism*, ed. Carl E. Braten (New York: Touchstone, 1968), pp. 51–5. More detailed and precise works on Plotinian philosophy include Wallis, *Neoplatonism*, and Louth, *Origins*.

At the farthest point from the One is matter, which is associated with evil because of its distance from the Absolute, its "absolute deficiency" of Goodness, and its consequent status as "non-being":

Evil is not in any and every lack; it is in absolute lack. What falls in some degree short of the Good is not Evil; considered in its own kind it might even be perfect, but where there is utter dearth, there we have Essential Evil, void of all share in the Good; this is the case with Matter ... Matter has not even existence whereby to have some part in Good ... The truth would be that it has Non-Being.[20]

The individual human soul also participates in this dynamic:[21]

The Soul that breaks away from this source of its reality, in so far as it is not perfect or primal, is, as it were, a secondary, an image, to the loyal Soul. By its falling-away – and to the extent of the fall – it is stripped of Determination, becomes wholly indeterminate, sees darkness. Looking to what repels vision, as we look when we are said to see darkness, it has taken Matter into itself.[22]

The soul in its nature loves God and longs to be at one with him in the noble love of a daughter for a noble father; but coming to human birth and lured by the courtships of this sphere, she takes up with another love, a mortal, leaves her father and falls.[23]

The wayward soul is propelled by a self-assertive, willful tendency to turn away from the One and towards the material world, endeavoring to be self-sufficient and thereby also becoming a manifestation of evil:[24]

What can it be that has brought the souls to forget the father, God, and, though members of the Divine and entirely of that world, to ignore at once themselves and It?

The evil that has overtaken them has its source in self-will, in the entry into the sphere of process, and in the primal differentiation with the desire for self-ownership ... [T]he souls...no longer discern either the divinity or their own nature.[25]

Along with this movement of outflowing, or emanation, there is also an opposing process of "epistrophe," a movement of return to the One:

All things revert in respect of their Being to that Principle whence they proceed...All desire is of Good ... Thus all things proceed in a circuit, from their

---

[20] *Enneads*, I. 8.5, pp. 69–70.
[21] Elmer O'Brien points out that Plotinus was not the first to posit such a correspondence between the individual soul and the entire world: the most extensive treatments before Plotinus are found in the Stoics, Poseidonius, and Philo (*The Essential Plotinus* [New York: New American Library, 1964], Introduction, pp. 24–5).
[22] *Enneads*, I.8.4, p. 69.
[23] Ibid., VI.9.9, p. 623.
[24] Dodds points out that there is an ambiguity in Plotinus: "Sometimes evil is equated with matter, sometimes with the instinct of self-assertion which divides the particular soul from other souls and from God" (*Select Passages*, Introduction, p. 18).
[25] *Enneads*, V.1.1, p. 369.

causes to their causes again. There are greater circuits and less, in that some revert to their immediate priors, others to the superior causes, and even to the Beginning of all things. For out of the Beginning all things are, and towards it all revert.[26]

All entities revert back towards the source, striving to be reunited with it; the soul moves back towards the One by means of a "turning inward," a turning away from material existence, to contemplate the Good:

Since Evil is here, 'haunting this world by necessary law,' and it is the soul's design to escape from Evil, we must escape hence.[27]

Life here, with the things of earth, is a sinking, a defeat, a failing of the wing ... But one day coming to hate her shame, she puts away the evil of earth, once more seeks the father, and finds her peace.[28]

[T]he soul takes another life as it draws nearer to God and gains participation in Him; thus restored it feels that the dispenser of true life is There to see, that now we have nothing to look for but, far otherwise, that we must put aside all else and rest in This alone, This become, This alone, all the earthly environment done away, in haste to be free, impatient of any bond holding us to the baser, so that with our being entire we may cling about This, no part in us remaining but through it we have touch with God.[29]

The resulting experience of mystical union – a joyous feeling of becoming one with the Divine – is achieved via self-discipline:

There are those that have not attained to see. From none is that Principle absent and yet from all: present, it remains absent save to those fit to receive, disciplined into some accordance, able to touch it closely by their likeness and by that kindred power within themselves through which, remaining as it was when it came to them from the Supreme, they are enabled to see in so far as God may at all be seen.[30]

It is likened to a *joining of the lover with his beloved* (such earthly, fleshly love is seen to be but a poor "mimicry" of the true union with the Good):

Those to whom all this experience is strange may understand by way of our earthly longings and the joy we have in winning what we most desire – remembering always that here what we love is perishable, hurtful, that our loving is of mimicries and turns away because all was a mistake, our good was not here, this was not what we sought; There only is our veritable love and There we may unite with it, not holding it in some fleshly embrace but possessing it in its verity.[31]

[26] Proclus, *Inst. Theol.*, 31,33 (trans. Dodds, in Dodds, *Select Passages*, p. 27).
[27] *Enneads*, I.2.1, p. 41.
[28] Ibid., VI.9.9, p. 623.
[29] Ibid.
[30] Ibid., VI.9.4, p. 618.
[31] Ibid., VI.9.9, p. 623.

It is also described in terms of the soul's coming to know its own true source and identity – its highest and *"true self"* – as of the One, in identity with the Absolute (this is a recognition and experience of the soul's "transcendent source" in the One, rather than of its literal identity with it or with the rest of the intelligible world[32]):

We have not been cut away; we are not separate, what though the body-nature has closed about us to press us to itself; we breathe and hold our ground because the Supreme does not give and pass but gives on for ever, so long as it remains what it is.

Our being is the fuller for our turning Thither; this is our prosperity; to hold aloof is loneliness and lessening; Here is the soul's peace, outside of evil, refuge taken in the place clean of wrong; here it has its Act, its true knowing; here it is immune, here is living, the true; that of today, all living apart from Him, is but a shadow, a mimicry. Life in the Supreme is the native activity of the Intellect; in virtue of that silent converse it brings forth gods, brings forth beauty, brings forth righteousness, brings forth all moral good; for of all these the soul is pregnant when it has been filled with God; This state is its first and final, because from God it comes, its good lies There, and, *once turned to God again, it is what it was* [italics added]. Life here, with the things of earth, is a sinking, a defeat, a failing of the wing ...

Thus we have all the vision that may be *of Him and of ourselves* [italics added]; but it is of a self wrought to splendour, brimmed with the Intellectual light, become that very light, pure, buoyant, unburdened, raised to godhood or, better, knowing its Godhood, all aflame then ...[33]

Two features of this reunion of the individual soul with the One should be noted: First, it is not that the soul literally must travel to some other location (e.g., Heaven) to contemplate and join the One. Rather, as Plotinus states, "The One is not in some place, depriving all the rest of its presence. It is present to all those who can touch it and absent only to those who cannot":[34]

But in the looking beware of throwing outward; this Principle does not lie away somewhere leaving the rest void; to those of power to reach, it is present; to the inept, absent ...

In sum, we must withdraw from all the extern, pointed wholly inwards; no leaning to the outer; the total of things ignored ... the self put out of mind in the contemplation of the Supreme ...

---

[32] Wallis, *Neoplatonism*, makes this point on pp. 88–9.
[33] *Enneads*, VI.9.9, pp. 622–3.
[34] Ibid., VI.9.4, p. 618.

God – we read – is outside of none, present unperceived to all; we break away from Him, or rather from ourselves; what we turn from we cannot reach; astray ourselves, we cannot go in search of another ... to find ourselves is to know our source.[35]

Secondly, this experience of mystical fusion and identity with the One does not result in the actual abolition of the individual soul. Nevertheless, such merging is experienced subjectively by the individual during such moments:

In our self-seeing There, the self is seen as belonging to that order, or rather we are merged into that self in us which has the quality of that order. It is a knowing of the self restored to its purity. No doubt we should not speak of seeing: but we cannot help talking in dualities, seen and seer, instead of, boldly, the achievement of unity. In this seeing, we neither hold an object nor trace distinction; there is no two. The man is changed, no longer himself nor self-belonging; he is merged with the Supreme.[36]

This metaphysical vision of atemporal eternal recurrence is strikingly different from that of linear Biblical history, with its finite, right-angled prospectivist plot and personal, anthropomorphic God. Nevertheless, Christian and Jewish thinkers as diverse as Augustine, Dionysius the Areopagite, the Kabbalists, John Duns Scotus, Dante, Maimonedes, Spinoza, Pico della Mirandola, Giordano Bruno, and many others all incorporated elements of the Neoplatonist system into their theological and spiritual doctrines.[37]

The Neoplatonized Christian narrative

Although many different strains of Judaeo-Christian spiritual thought were fed by the Neoplatonist tradition, in one way or another they all dealt with the problem of how to combine two such different

---

[35] Ibid., VI.9.7, p. 621.

[36] Ibid., VI.9.10, p. 624.

[37] E.R. Dodds (*Select Passages*, pp. 22–3, fn 5, citing M. Picavet of the Ecole des hautes études) traces the genealogy of Neoplatonic influence: "three main channels of tradition may be distinguished: from Ammonius Saccas through Origen; from Plotinus through Augustine; and from Proclus to Dionysius the Areopagite. By these and other avenues Neoplatonism entered into and formed the thought of the Byzantine theologians and of such Western thinkers as John the Scot and Anselm. At the same time...it profoundly affected the Arabian and Jewish philosophers of the Middle Ages: mediated by Averroism, a fresh stream of Neoplatonic influence reaches down to the later scholastics and beyond them to Malebranche; mediated by Ibn Gabriol Maimonedes, it is carried over to Spinoza. Finally, Neoplatonism was kept alive in the Byzantine Empire by Psellus and his successors, and by them handed on to Pletho and Bessarion, and so to Pico della Mirandola, and other humanists of the Renaissance."

metaphysical systems. The Bible, after all, tells the story of mankind's progression through linear and finite history, orchestrated by an anthropomorphic God, while Plotinus in his *Enneads* posits a recurring circular process in which the Absolute is envisioned as an impersonal first principle.

Below I note some of the enduring themes that were born of this interpenetration of the two traditions. In the following enumeration of some common principles shared by various esoteric systems (all of those systems heirs to Neoplatonic mysticism) I highlight four "tensions" between the Biblical and Neoplatonist visions.[38] These tensions are discussed in terms of four major categories: the shape of the narrative; the nature of the Divinity and of the soul's relationship to it; the value accorded to selfhood and earthly life; and the nature of salvation.

The shape of the narrative: the Neoplatonic circle of emanation and return versus the linear Biblical historical progression[39]

In many Neoplatonized Judaeo-Christian narratives, the linear, once-and-for-all progression of history is retained, but it takes on a circular aspect. The fall is conceived to involve not just a fall from innocence and grace into sin, but also a fall out of an original unity (as in Plotinus' One or Absolute). The end of history is attained when the soul is returned to God (including an experience of reunion and a recognition that the soul's true nature is as part of, or like, the Absolute), at which point the movement of history stops.

In keeping with both Plotinian doctrines and with the Biblical exegetical tradition of psychohistorical parallelism, "the design of a temporal and finite great circle is applied not only to the world and all mankind, but also to the life of each redeemed individual."[40]

---

[38] These are comments about general tendencies, culled from several standard secondary sources (mainly Abrams, *Natural Supernaturalism*; Tillich, *History of Christian Thought*; and Underhill, *Mysticism*) and supplemented by my own observations. I draw most heavily on the discussion of these features in Abrams' *Natural Supernaturalism*. However, in contrast to his presentation (he employs declarative descriptions such as "the great circle is made temporal and finite" or "God becomes an impersonal first principle"), in the present discussion these are articulated as "tensions" since other scholars such as Tillich note that not all mystical Christian doctrines resolved these pagan strains on the Biblical narrative in the same way.

[39] Abrams, *Natural Supernaturalism*, p. 151.

[40] Ibid., p. 152.

> *The personal, anthropomorphic God who is the creator of all*
> *things versus the Absolute as an impersonal first principle from*
> *which all things emanate*

Abrams notes that, in the tradition of Biblical exegesis which makes use of Neoplatonist doctrines, "God" becomes read as an impersonal first principle.[41] Tillich, however, says of Dionysius the Areopagite (whom he describes as "the mediator of Neoplatonism and Christianity and the father of most of Christian mysticism"[42]) that his system was received by the West because God is given a "personalistic" element, taking on an anthropomorphic aspect.[43] In either case, there is a blending of Biblical and Plotinian themes in three features of the mystical Christian narrative. First, in Neoplatonist doctrines, all entities – including the individual soul or self – originate in and emanate out of an undifferentiated unity. The Biblical creation of the world thus comes to be interpreted *as an emanation out of an undifferentiated unity into a world of multiplicity and diversity.*

Second, a consequence of this is that *the fall becomes associated with separation, division, selfhood, and self-consciousness*[44] (self-consciousness being in this sense a false consciousness, since the true self is that which knows it is part of the One, not separate or differentiated). In Christianity, the fall of man into mortal life, evil, sin, and suffering is indicative of (and a consequence of) his loss of God's grace. Neoplatonist mysticism adds another dimension: the fall comes to be seen as separation and division (in Neoplatonist terms, as a turning-away from the One and towards matter, as the soul's self-assertion and "forgetting" of its true source and identity). When these two spiritual visions are combined,

the fall of man is conceived to be primarily a falling-out-of and falling-away-from the one into a position of remoteness and a condition of alienation from the source. Consonantly, the original human sin is identified as self-centeredness or selfhood.[45]

In this context, there seems to be some blurring of the creation and the fall: the world is fallen even before it is created, because as a differentiated material creation it is already separated and "turned-away" from God. At least some Christian theologians make use of Plotinus' ideas about separation from the One in two different ways: Tillich notes that

---

[41]   Ibid., p. 151.
[42]   Tillich, *History of Christian Thought*, p. 91.
[43]   Ibid., p. 97.
[44]   Abrams, *Natural Supernaturalism*, p. 151.
[45]   Ibid.

for Origen (one of the first and most influential of those who married Neoplatonism to Christianity) there is an element of fallenness to all creation: for him "the fall precedes creation, just as the fall follows creation:

Origen has two myths of the fall. The one is transcendent; mythologically speaking, it is not in space. It is the eternal transition from union with God to separation from God. The other is the immanent, inner-historical fall. The transcendent fall becomes actual through special acts on the historical plane ... the bodily and social [material and self-conscious] existence strengthens sin ... Sin, therefore, has a double relation to creation: With respect to the creation of free and equal spirits, creation precedes the fall; with respect to the bodily world, creation follows the fall.[46]

Thus in the Christian mystical narrative there exists a complex of meaning involving the creation, fall, separation, self-consciousness, and sin.

Third, in the state of alienation, *there is a longing on the part of the soul to return to the source, to union with and likeness to (in Christianity, an anthropomorphized) God.* This longing propels the soul back to unity.[47]

> *The extremely negative valence accorded to emanation and "selfhood" in Neoplatonism versus the more "world-affirming" and "individualistic" Judaeo-Christianity*

There is a tension in Christian Neoplatonism between world-affirming and world-negating elements.[48] There are at least three ways in which the valuation and importance accorded to selfhood and earthly life influences Christian forms of Neoplatonic mysticism:

First, there is the *Judaeo-Christian valuation of the individual and earthly life*: While selfhood, "self-assertion" (i.e., in the Plotinian sense of the Soul's turning away from the One and towards material existence), and material existence are regarded as evil, or as manifestations of evil, in Plotinian doctrines, the Judaeo-Christian tradition has always affirmed the value, meaning, and importance of individual selfhood and of at least

---

[46] Tillich, *History of Christian Thought*, p. 61.
[47] Abrams, *Natural Supernaturalism*, p. 152.
[48] Paul Tillich describes this tension in relation to Saint Augustine: "[His philosophy] had the same tension in itself as we met in the Christian Neo-Platonism in Dionysius, that is, both affirmation and negation of the world. Christianity affirms creation and sanctifies existence through the historical appearance of the divine in Christ. Neo-Platonism negates creation, it has no real creation ... Augustine was divided; insofar as he was a Christian, with his roots in the Old Testament, he valued family and sex, to the extent that sex was kept within the family. Being influenced by Neo-Platonism and the ancient negativity toward the world, he denied sex and praised asceticism. This conflict went on through the whole history of the church" (*History of Christian Thought*, p. 110).

some aspects of earthly life. This tendency became much more marked in subsequent transformations of the narrative – Protestant, Romantic, psychoanalytic – as we shall see in Chapters 6, 7, and 8.

Second, there is the *felix culpa*: Both the soul's fall/separation from God (its falling away from God), and the subsequent corruption and estrangement inherent in worldly life itself, are seen to have been valuable and perhaps necessary evils in the service of a greater good (the Incarnation and ultimately the Redemption). In an essay on the genealogy of the idea of the *felix culpa* ("fortunate fall") in Christian doctrine, the intellectual historian A.O. Lovejoy traced back to the Church Fathers the notion that the fall was actually a good and fortuitous event because only after a fall could there be a redemption:

St. Ambrose, for example (4th c.), had flatly asserted that Adam's sin "had brought more benefit to us than harm" (*amplius nobis profuit culpa quam nocuit*), and had even permitted himself the more generalized and hazardous apophthegm that "sin is more fruitful than innocence" (*fructuosior culpa quam innocentia*). God knew that Adam would fall, *in order that* he might be redeemed by Christ (*ut redemertur a Christo*). *Felix ruina, quae reparatur in melius!*[49]

Lovejoy also quotes Saint Augustine (among others) on this notion of the *felix culpa* (the "fortunate fall"):

Although those things that are evil, in so far as they are evil, are not good; nevertheless it is good that there should be not only goods but evils as well. For unless this – namely, that there be also evils – were a good, men would under no circumstances fall away from the omnipotent Good.[50]

Like many other Christian theologians before and after him, Augustine had assimilated to the Biblical idea of the fall the Neoplatonic idea of a fall out of unity (the notion of fall as separation and division). Thus in Augustine's and other Christian mystical narratives, the

---

[49] Quoted in Lovejoy, "Milton and the Paradox of the Fortunate Fall," in *Essays in the History of Ideas* (Baltimore: Johns Hopkins Press, 1948), pp. 277–95, p. 288.

[50] Augustine, *Confessions,* ch. 96 (MPL, 40.276), quoted in Lovejoy, "Milton," p. 290. Lovejoy also notes that, in suggesting that evil itself was part of God's design (along with later Christian mystics) "was here manifestly skating on rather thin ice" (since the idea of a *felix culpa* makes it sound as if sin and evil may serve a positive function, and might even be part of God's design – an idea not acceptable in this religious tradition). Lovejoy concludes his essay by suggesting that for Christian writers until and including Milton, "the only solution was to keep the two themes [the fall as deplorable and the fall as fortuitous] separate," i.e., to not include any consideration of the fall as a *felix culpa* in the initial description of it in the narrative of Biblical history, but only to include such an appraisal of it at the point where the "happy consummation" of history is described (p. 295). (In Chapter 6 we shall see that Boehme attempted a different solution – thereby skating on still thinner ice – a solution which was most influential for subsequent secularizations of this narrative.)

Neoplatonic elements of the fall – separation and self-assertion (turning away from the One) – also take on this affirmative cast, if only in the sense that, given the linear Biblical view of history, such a fall out of unity is seen to be a necessary step on the way to salvation.

Finally, there is a third way in which individual selfhood and earthly life are accorded more importance and value in Christianity and Christian mysticism than in Neoplatonism. This is the *"activistic" element of Christian mysticism*: even when the individual attains an experience of contact and union with the Divine (the *unio mystica*, or the "inner light"), he or she then turns back to the world and works to improve the lot of those around him or her. This activistic orientation of "Western"[51] mysticism has been noted by Rudolf Otto, Max Weber, Benjamin Nelson, Evelyn Underhill, and others. Underhill asserted that:

In the mystics of the West, the highest forms of Divine Union impel the self to some sort of active, rather than of passive life: and this is now recognized by the best authorities as the true distinction between Christian and non-Christian mysticism.[52]

She quotes St. Teresa:

You may think, my daughters, that the soul in this state [of ecstasy, of union with the Divine] should be so absorbed that she can occupy herself with nothing, but you deceive yourselves ... She turns with greater ease and ardour to all that which belongs to the service of God.

And, as Otto says of Meister Eckhart, one of the greatest Christian mystics,

The world, which is for Eckhart also full of sorrow, as merely creature (*siecut est in se*), becomes, when it is found again in God, a piece of joy and of spontaneous action in all good works.[53]

The ends of the spiritual trajectory – the inner light and salvation

The individual mystic may achieve illumination, which is considered to be a foretaste of the salvation that awaits mankind. Such illumination is experienced in terms of a reunion of the soul with the Absolute. It is often described in terms of a *unio mystica*, a mystical "marriage" of God and

---

51 One wonders whether they mean "Western" or "Christian." Plotinus is "Western," too, yet in this sense (i.e., its "world-negating" aspects) his philosophy seems to have more in common with, e.g., Hinduism.

52 Underhill, *Mysticism*, p. 172. Some scholars (e.g., Toynbee) have suggested that Mahāyāna Buddhism evinces an activism similar to that of Christianity. However, as R.C. Zaehner (citing Conze's essay in the same volume) affirms, "in the Mahāyāna, the

the soul; sexual and marital metaphors frequently are employed.[54] This *unio* also is described in terms of a rebirth within the soul of the spark of God, i.e., a re-joining of the soul to the Divine (as in Neoplatonism). Finally, this rebirth also entails an illumination in the sense of an intuition of Divine knowledge: knowledge of God, of one's relationship to him, and of one's "true self" as being part of him.

This re-joining of the individual soul to God, and the rebirth within that soul of God's spark, is often called the "inner light." One can hear the echoes of Plotinus in Meister Eckhart's doctrine that

The creature, including man, has reality only in union with eternal reality. The creature has nothing in separation from God. The point in which the creature returns to God is the soul. Through the soul what is separated from God returns to him. The depths of the soul in which this happens Eckhart called the "spark," or the innermost center of the soul.[55]

For some groups, e.g., the Franciscans, the inner light is at the basis of all knowledge, and hence all knowledge is Divine in its source.[56]

For the individual mystic, the experience of the inner light offers a foretaste of more permanent redemption to come – it is a precursor to the anticipated collective redemption of the race. In the case of the individual, contact with the inner light renders him or her transfigured, whether only for an instant or on a more permanent basis. When the transformation is more permanent, the individual still remains in the earthly realm, ardently impelled to grapple with this unredeemed and

sublime idea of the Boddhisattva who, 'destined to become a Buddha, nevertheless, in order to help suffering creatures, selflessly postpones his entrance into the bliss of *Nirvāna* and his escape from this world of birth and death' (p. 209) is somewhat vitiated by the opposite and more fundamental truth that 'in actual reality there are no Buddhas, no Boddhisattvas, no perfections, no stages, and no paradises' (p. 306)." (R.C. Zaehner, "Conclusion," in R.C. Zaehner, ed., *The Concise Encyclopedia of Living Faiths* [Boston: Beacon Press, 1976], pp. 413–17, p. 415. Zaehner and Conze emphasize the "dominant monist philosophy" of both Buddhism and Hinduism, stressing that the core Buddhist aim remains the "'extinction of the self' and 'the dying out of separate individuality.'" (Ibid.)

53 Otto, *Mysticism East and West*, p. 320.
54 Abrams, *Natural Supernaturalism*; Benjamin Nelson, "Self-Images and Systems of Spiritual Direction in the History of European Civilization," in S. Z. Klausner (ed.), *The Quest for Self-Control* (New York: Free Press, 1965); George Williams, "Popularized German Mysticism as a Factor in the Rise of Anabaptist Communism," in Hrsg von G. Muller and W. Zeller, *Glaube, Geist, Geschichte: Festschrift für Ernst Benz* (Leiden: E.J. Brill, 1967).
55 Tillich, *History of Christian Thought*, p. 202.
56 Ibid., p. 185. Tillich wrote that "[t]he term 'inner light' ... comes from the Augustinian-Franciscan tradition in medieval theology, which was renewed by the sectarian movements in the Reformation period, and underlies much of Protestant theology in America. The inner light is the light which everybody has within himself because he belongs to God, and in virtue of which he is able to receive the divine Word when it is spoken to

differentiated world. This is in keeping with the "activistic" orientation of Christianity described above.

Thus we observe in Christian mysticism a blending of the Biblical prospectivist vision of salvation – the redemption of the soul (and in the future, of all mankind) thanks to God's grace – with the Neoplatonist doctrine that salvation entails both a reunion with the One and an apprehension that one's true nature is "of the One which is the Good." The end of the spiritual trajectory is conceived as a divine marital union, an apprehension of the true self, and the source of all knowledge. As is discussed in Chapters 7 and 8, all three of these metaphors became secularized and "literalized" in the writings of Enlightenment, Romantic, and psychoanalytic thinkers.

Elements of the Christian mystical narrative can be found in a very large and diverse group of writings, both esoteric and orthodox, from the Middle Ages through the Renaissance. They do not appear only in devotional and esoteric writings,[57] but also have been incorporated "into the doctrinal categories of many bulwarks of Western orthodoxy, including Augustine, Aquinas, and Dante."[58] In the following chapter, I explore the persistence and modification of these elements in the doctrines of one of the greatest and most influential Protestant mystics, Jacob Boehme.

---

[57] Benjamin Nelson wrote: "There is a vast literature reporting early Christian and medieval efforts to experience the vision of God and to enjoy Him in mystical union. Thanks to Dean Inge (1899), ... Evelyn Underhill (1933)...and others, we are now able to trace the development of philosophies and techniques of meditation in the successive works of such celebrated masters of the contemplative life as the pseudo-Dionysius the Areopagite (ca. 500), Johannes Climacus (d. 649), Richard (d. 1173) and Hugo (d. 1141) of St. Victor, St. Bernard of Clairvaux (d. 1153), St. Bonaventura (d. 1274), Meister Eckhart (d. 1327), Thomas à Kempis (d. 1471), [and] the anonymous author of the *Theologica Deutsch* (ca. 1350) which left its mark on Luther" ("Self-Images," p. 65).

[58] Abrams, *Natural Supernaturalism*, p. 153.

6

Jacob Boehme: Towards worldly mysticism

Jacob Boehme is the first German philosopher; the content of his philosophy is truly German. What characterizes Boehme and makes him noteworthy is the Protestant principle, to place the intellectual world in one's own mind, and to contemplate and know and feel all that formerly was beyond in one's own self-consciousness.

> G.W.F. Hegel, quoted by David Walsh in *The Mysticism of Innerworldly Fulfillment: A Study of Jacob Boehme*, 1983, p. 6

The picture that emerges from these investigations is not of a world increasingly separating itself from God, but of a world progressively absorbing the divine substance into itself.

> David Walsh, Ibid., p. 9

As an illustration of themes and tendencies inherent in the Christian mystical narrative of salvation, the work of Jacob Boehme is both exemplary and innovative. Boehme is widely considered to be both one of the "fathers" of Protestant mysticism and one of its greatest exemplars.[1] His work perpetuates tendencies initiated in the interpenetration of Neoplatonist and Biblical themes. These themes include: the linear and finite, temporalized circle; God conceived as a first principle from which all entities emanate; the association of the creation and the fall with emanation, self-assertion, and self-consciousness; the soul's (and mankind's)

---

[1] See David Walsh, *The Mysticism of Innerworldly Fulfillment: A Study of Jacob Boehme* (Gainesville, FL: University Presses of Florida, 1983); Abrams, *Natural Supernaturalism* (New York: W. W. Norton, 1973), pp. 51, 160–2; Robert F. Brown, *The Later Philosophy of Schelling: The Influence of Boehme on the Works of 1809–1815* (Lewisburg: Associated University Presses, 1977); Winfried Zeller, Preface to Jacob Boehme, *The Way to Christ*, trans. Peter Erb (New York: Paulist Press, 1978); John Joseph Stoudt, Introduction to *The Way to Christ*, ed. J. J. Stoudt (New York: Harper and Brothers, 1947), p. xix; W.R. Inge, *Christian Mysticism* (London: Methuen, 1948); Stephen Hobhouse, Editor's Introduction to Hans Martensen, *Jacob Boehme: Studies in his Life and Teaching*, trans. T. Rhys Evans (New York: Harper and Brothers, 1949).

redemption or "illumination" conceived as a reunion with God and/or as the soul's recognition and appreciation of its true identity as "of God"; and psychohistorical parallelism (mankind and the individual soul conceived as a microcosm of the universe, and whose structure and dynamics are the same as God's).

At the same time, Behmenist doctrines embody some of the "Protestant" tendencies that were noted in Chapter 3. For example, there is emphasis on the individual's personal relationship with God, leading in some types of Protestantism (including Boehme's) to a quest for an intimate experience of the Divine Presence.[2] There is also an intensified emphasis upon the narrative of Biblical (or Neoplatonized Biblical) history as a narrative of the inner life, as the developmental trajectory of the individual soul. In some cases, as M.H. Abrams points out, radical Protestants (though not Boehme) actually came to "annul" the literal meaning of scripture as external history;[3] in other radical Protestant narratives (e.g., Boehme's), even though the literal meaning also was retained, this interiorized level of exegesis became increasingly elaborated and important. A third "Protestant" feature is that the narrative evinces a more positive valence and importance accorded to earthly life, including what Charles Taylor calls "ordinary life,"[4] especially work and family. (In Chapter 5 I noted that Christianity in general gave a more positive valence to certain trappings of earthly life than did Neoplatonism; Protestantism, in turn, promotes this tendency more so than does Catholic theology.) Corresponding to this worldliness is a fourth "Protestant" tendency. This is the belief that the "Kingdom of God" (the end of Biblical history) can be achieved on earth, whether externally, in terms of a genuine metamorphosis of man and society (e.g.,

---

[2] This was of course Luther's aim but, as Paul Tillich (*History of Christian Thought from its Judaic and Hellenistic Origins to Existentialism*, ed. Carl E. Braten [New York: Touchstone, 1968]) explains it, Luther emphasized man's experience of an unbridgeable distance between himself and God and therefore the need for *faith*. Many generations of Protestants after him have felt that on this score (man's desire for an experience of intimate connection to God) Luther, or at least the Protestant orthodoxy that succeeded him, did not go far enough.

[3] Abrams uses as an example the radical inner light Protestant sect of Gerrard Winstanley, "leader of a radical splinter group during the Puritan Revolution" (*Natural Supernaturalism*, pp. 51–2). See also Rufus M. Jones, *Mysticism and Democracy in the English Commonwealth* (New York: Octagon, 1965), p. 164.

[4] Following many other scholars, Charles Taylor notes that "With the Reformation, we find a modern, Christian-inspired sense that ordinary life was...the very centre of the good life. The crucial issue was how it was led, whether worshipfully and in the fear of God or not. But the life of the God-fearing was lived out in marriage and their calling ... I believe that this affirmation of ordinary life...has become one of the most powerful ideas in modern civilization" (*Sources of the Self* [Cambridge, MA: Harvard University Press, 1989], p. 14).

the utopian aspirations of the Puritan Revolution and of various other sectarian groups) and/or internally, in the form of certain types of spiritual experiences that the individual can attain even while living a secular, worldly life. Boehme, as we shall see, helped to elaborate the Christian mystical narrative in such a way as to strengthen the interpretation of salvation as a transformation of this world and/or of the mind, rather than as an ascent to some otherworldly Heaven.

Boehme's system as worldly mysticism

The cultural legacy of Protestantism – including both its worldliness and its emphasis on individual autonomy, personal conscience, and inner life – is often considered only in terms of its anti-mystical, "disenchanted" aspects.[5] To a great extent, this characterization derives from Max Weber's argument that worldly asceticism is Protestantism's dominant ethos, particularly in Anglo-American culture areas. But only rarely does one find references in sociological literature to the fact that it was not only ascetic elements in Christianity and Protestantism that became more worldly, and eventually were divested altogether of explicitly theological vocabulary and connotations. Mystical strains in Christianity also have survived the secularization of our civilization, even furnishing "constitutive premises" (to echo Abrams' phrase) of some aspects of the modern, secular world view.

Thus, as sociologists of religion Benjamin Nelson[6] and Roland Robertson[7] have suggested, it is necessary to modify Weber's formulation, or at least to accord more importance to other, not-exclusively-ascetic dimensions of some Protestant sects and denominations. Nelson

---

[5] Borrowing a phrase from Friedrich Schiller, Weber wrote of the "disenchantment" of the world, the increasingly "rationalized," anti-magical orientation which has come to permeate most spheres of modern life (Weber, "Science as a Vocation," in *From Max Weber: Essays in Sociology*, eds. Hans Gerth and C. Wright Mills [New York: Oxford University Press, 1976]); he argued that there were certain tendencies in Protestantism – above all, the "innerworldly ascetic" orientation of Calvinism (see Max Weber, *The Protestant Ethic and the Spirit of Capitalism* [New York: Charles Scribner's Sons, 1958]) – which complemented and helped to promote the emergence of this "disenchanted" modernity. Atwood D. Gaines ("Cultural Definitions, Behavior, and the Person in American Psychiatry," in A. J. Marsella and G. M. White, eds., *Cultural Conceptions of Mental Health and Therapy* [Dordrecht: D. Reidel, 1982]) also emphasizes this aspect of Protestantism and its influence on Northern European culture.

[6] Benjamin Nelson, "Self-Images and Systems of Spiritual Direction in the History of European Civilization," in S. Z. Klausner (ed.), *The Quest for Self-Control* (New York: Free Press, 1965) and "Max Weber, Ernst Troeltsch, Georg Jellinek as Comparative Historical Sociologists," *Sociological Analysis*, vol. 36, no. 3, 1975, pp. 229–40.

[7] Roland Robertson, "On the Analysis of Mysticism: Pre-Weberian, Weberian and Post-Weberian Perspectives," *Sociological Analysis*, vol. 36, no. 3, 1975, pp. 241–66.

questioned Weber's classification of Protestantism, within the latter's typology of religious orientations, as predominantly "ascetic" as opposed to "mystical." Weber, argued Nelson, "did not … sufficiently stress the significance of innerworldly mysticism as contrasted with otherworldly mysticisms."[8] Nelson further proposed that many "Protestant variants of conscience, character, and culture" actually represent blendings, in varying proportions, of these two somewhat opposed tendencies.

This is a complex issue, one which I dealt with at greater length in Chapters 2 and 4. At this point I wish to underscore only that Nelson has made us aware that the cultural legacy of the Protestant Reformation goes well beyond worldly asceticism. Certain mystically tinged "Protestant variants" – specifically, the doctrines of various Protestant sects, beginning during the sixteenth century[9] – evince an assimilation of the older, Neoplatonized Christian narrative of salvation into the newer Protestant trends towards greater spiritual investment in worldly life and stronger emphasis on the "interiorization" of the narrative (an interpretation of it as pertaining to the spiritual history of the individual soul, as well as, or even rather than, the external history of the entire race). Boehme's doctrines, then, participate in the general secularization process of the past five centuries while simultaneously preserving key symbols and values of the Christian mystical narrative.

I highlight the persistence of worldly mysticism to make explicit, at this point, a major argument of this study: with the advent of the disenchantment of the (Euro-American) world, this spiritual tradition, and these symbols and patterns, did not simply fade away. Rather, as I attempt to demonstrate in this chapter and in the two that follow it, they have been preserved in different but still-recognizable forms.

A standard way of explaining the parallels between the successive prepsychoanalytic narrative patterns (i.e., the Neoplatonized Christian, Behmenist, and Romantic versions) has been to view them as earlier anticipations of an only recently illuminated reality. But rather than interpreting Plotinus or Boehme or the Romantics as anticipating, in increasingly more veridical ways, the discovery of psychoanalytic "truth," it seems at least as plausible to suggest a revision of this interpretation, as was explained in Chapter 1. Rather than characterizing secularization as a progressive elimination of theological and cultural

---

[8] Nelson, "Self-Images."

[9] See George Williams, *The Radical Reformation* (Philadelphia: Westminster Press, 1962); George Williams, "Popularized German Mysticism as a Factor in the Rise of Anabaptist Communism," in Hrsg von G. Muller and W. Zeller, *Glaube, Geist, Geschichte: Festschrift fur Ernst Benz* (Leiden: E.J. Brill, 1967); Tillich, *History of Christian Thought*; Nelson, "Self-Images."

elements from our *Weltanschauung* and self-understanding, we need to recognize how secular frameworks continue to preserve a legacy of culturally constituted religious themes and symbols.

Boehme's doctrine is pivotal in this process of cultural transmutation. Boehme is widely considered to be one of the greatest Western mystics of any era.[10] In addition, he was an innovator, who combined and recombined diverse older doctrines. He extended certain preexisting tendencies, making them more explicit than before; he also contributed influential ideas which appear to have been his own (i.e., his construction of the problem of evil and its justification). Finally, Boehme is an important figure in the history of the worldly transformations of Christian mysticism because his work so strongly influenced subsequent thinkers, both religious and secular (I briefly discuss the transmission of his ideas to subsequent thinkers at the end of this chapter).

Boehme's life in historical context[11]

Jacob Boehme (1575–1624) was a Silesian cobbler. Like many other educated[12] young commoners and noblemen in that part of Europe, he became dissatisfied with the orthodox Lutheran faith in which he had been raised. He found Calvinism likewise inadequate and disturbing as a religious creed, particularly its doctrine of predestination with its implication that "God himself might be the origin of evil if wickedness has been predestined by him."[13] What Boehme also found disturbing in both Lutheran and Calvinist doctrines was their (relative) emphasis on man's distance from God;[14] therefore he sought a form of faith and spiritual

---

[10] See, e.g., Evelyn Underhill, *Mysticism: A Study in the Nature and Development of Man's Spiritual Consciousness* (New York: New American Library, 1974).

[11] Much of the information in this section is taken from Walsh, *Mysticism of Innerworldly Fulfillment*; this book and other sources are cited where appropriate. See also Will-Erich Peuckert, *Das Leben Jacob Böhmes* (vol. 10, *Samtliche Schriften,* ed. W.-E. Peuckert [Stuttgart: Fr. Frommanns Verlag, 1961]); Alexandre Koyré, *La Philosophie de Jacob Boehme* (Paris: Vrin, 1929); Brown, *The Later Philosophy of Schelling*; Arlene A. Miller (Guinsberg), "Jacob Boehme: From Orthodoxy to Enlightenment" (unpublished Ph.D. dissertation, Stanford University, 1971); J.J. Stoudt, *From Sunrise to Eternity: A Study in Jacob Boehme's Life and Thought* (Philadelphia: University of Pennsylvania Press, 1957).

[12] Until the twentieth century, those who wrote about Boehme depicted him as uneducated and not well read in spiritual and other cultural areas, but according to the more recent biographers it appears that this was not the case.

[13] Walsh, *Mysticism of Innerwordly Fulfillment,* p. 42. Boehme later resolved this concern by positing a distinctive explanation of the nature and necessity of evil and conflict. See especially pp. 144–5 of this chapter.

[14] Luther did not intend the Reformation to be a mystical movement, in spite of the fact

practice that could lead the true believer to a greater sense of unity with the Divine. Like many other dissenters from Lutheran orthodoxy, he felt that the Church of his day had rigidified and failed in its original mission. He desired a form of Christianity that would both emphasize the "subjective" side of religion (i.e., would be more experiential and "immediate") and be a speculative theodicy – two aspects of spiritual life that were neglected by Luther and/or the orthodox reformers.[15]

Other cultural and social trends also were a source of dissatisfaction and dismay for Boehme and for others like him. According to David Walsh, "he was acquainted with the discoveries of Copernicus." This new world view as well as other "developments in modern science with which he had become familiar" meant that for Boehme "the question of the divine presence and manifestation within the material universe had become particularly acute."[16] In other words, developments in science and cosmology rendered older ways of thought and belief problematic, and Boehme's doctrines may be seen as a response to the challenges posed by these cultural changes to Biblical and mystical world views.[17]

that he had been influenced by German mystics such as Tauler and the anonymous author of the *Theologia Germanica* (not to mention Saint Paul and Saint Augustine, both of whom had mystical elements in their doctrines). Paul Tillich (*History of Christian Thought*, p. 240) wrote: "Luther and the other Reformers placed the main emphasis on the distance of God from man ... This feeling of distance...is the normal relationship of man to God." This distance could be – and must be – traversed by the individual's faith, but not by a quest for mystical experience. See also Peter C. Erb, Introduction to Boehme, *The Way to Christ* (1978); Arlene A. Miller, "The Theologies of Luther and Boehme in the Light of their *Genesis* Commentaries," *Harvard Theological Review* vol. 63, 1970, pp. 261–303.

15 Walsh, *Mysticism of Innerwordly Fulfillment*, pp. 39–40; "Now although Lutheranism had severely shaken the old orthodoxy, it had itself become, in Boehme's time, an orthodoxy just as rigid" (Clifford Bax, introduction to Boehme, *The Signature of All Things*, trans. William Law [New York: E.P. Dutton, 1912], p. viii); "Protestant orthodoxy insisted on the acceptance of closely worded doctrinal statements of faith. To its enemies it was seen as a dry, intolerant defense of a single denomination's position ... From its beginnings Lutheran Orthodoxy was opposed by men who were primarily interested in the practice of piety: personal renewal, individual growth in holiness and religious experience" (Erb, Introduction to Boehme, *The Way to Christ* [1978], p. 5). See also Tillich, *History of Christian Thought*, Part I, chs. 5 and 6 ("The Theology of the Protestant Reformers" and "The Development of Protestant Theology") and Part II, ch. 1 ("Oscillating Emphases in Orthodoxy, Pietism and Rationalism").

16 Walsh, *Mysticism of Innerworldly Fulfillment*, p. 43.

17 In a recent intellectual biography, Andrew Weeks plays down the interpretation, offered by various scholars, that Boehme's doctrines embodied a response on the part of a particularly sensitive individual to the cultural crises and spiritual instabilities that characterized the early modern period. Instead, Weeks brings to the foreground "Boehme's proximate sources of inspiration" (p. 7) – i.e., local political and doctrinal disputes that took place in Middle Europe during Boehme's lifetime. However, Weeks also acknowledges the mystical-esoteric sources and the deeper existential concerns that I have noted in this section. (Andrew Weeks, *Boehme: An Intellectual Biography of the Seventeenth-Century Philosopher and Mystic* [Albany, NY: State University of New York Press, 1991].)

Hence Boehme can be seen as one in a long line of Christian mystics, as well as someone acutely sensitive to his particular historical situation. In this latter context, he was attempting to come to terms both with the religious and cultural orthodoxy with which he was dissatisfied, and with the increasingly secularized and materialistic *Weltanschauung* initiated by the scientific revolution.

Boehme also was heir to, and his doctrines participate in, some more "empowering" dimensions of this cultural and religious atmosphere: he was beneficiary to the Renaissance's (and, in a different way, the Reformation's) glorification of man and his powers,[18] as well as to the greater worldly comfort which burgeoning scientific advancements were beginning to afford. These developments, then, also played a role in leading thought, including religion, in a more worldly direction.

The Behmenist narrative

Boehme was a mystic who considered himself to be first and foremost a Christian. Many currents, many predecessor mystical doctrines, appear to have influenced his particular system.[19] Although he did not break away from the Church, his work was banned by the Lutheran pastor of Görlitz (in Silesia) in 1613, after he wrote *The Aurora* (*Morganrothe im Aufgang*), and he was forbidden to write any more. But after seven years of compliance with this interdiction he felt compelled to resume and produced a series of treatises including *The Threefold Life of Man* (1620), *Answers to the Forty Questions of the Soul* (1620), *Six Theosophic Points* (1620), *De Signatura Rerum* (1622), *Mysterium Magnum* (1623), and numerous others, before his death in 1624.

What Boehme constructed in these works was both a system of mystical practice and a speculative theodicy, i.e., an attempt to explain the nature of God, the universe, man, and their relation. In this sense his system is similar to that of Plotinus, which also is both a speculative theodicy and a system of mystical practice. As a speculative theodicy Boehme's

[18] Walsh, *Mysticism of Innerworldly Fulfillment*, pp. 3–5; Martensen, *Jacob Boehme*, pp. 22–4; Frances Yates, *Giordano Bruno and the Hermetic Tradition* (Chicago: University of Chicago Press, 1964); Alexandre Koyré, *Mystiques, Spirituels, Alchimistes* (Paris: A. Colin, 1955).

[19] In her dissertation ("Jacob Boehme: From Orthodoxy to Enlightenment," Stanford University, 1971) Arlene Miller (Guinsberg) attempted to trace extensively the sources and routes of transmission. One is left with an impression of how extremely difficult, if not impossible, it is to pinpoint which particular mystical traditions he had contact with, or those earlier traditions from which they in turn were derived. See also Koyré, *La Philosophie de Jacob Boehme*; Walsh, *Mysticism of Innerworldly Fulfillment*; Brown, *The Later Philosophy of Schelling*.

system is complex and full of contradictions, often obscure, and difficult if not impossible to make sense of in its every detail. Moreover, there are earlier and later, more "mature" works; some of the implications that are most germane for the present study (i.e., that have been of most interest and use to later generations of thinkers) are more fully developed in the later versions,[20] such as *The Way to Christ*, a collection of treatises written at the end of Boehme's life.[21]

In this book I am concerned only with the broad outlines of Boehme's cosmology and his recounting of Biblical history, which is complex and in some respects quite idiosyncratic. Below I highlight only those aspects of his system that perpetuate and/or transform the Neoplatonized Biblical narrative.

According to Boehme, God is a complex process which strives to manifest itself to itself, to become self-conscious. All of that which we think of as God's "Creation" is really God's self-objectification, his unfolding self-revelation:

The creation of the whole creation is nothing else but a manifestation of the all-essential, unsearchable God ... For God has not brought forth the creation, that he should be thereby perfect [which he is already, and always has been], but for his own manifestation, viz., for the great joy and glory ...[22]

God achieves this self-actualization by means of the positing, integrating, and overcoming of a series of *contraries:*

The Being of all beings is but one only Being, but in its generation it separates itself into two principles, viz. into light and darkness, into joy and sorrow, into evil and good, into love and anger, into fire and light, and out of those two beginnings [or principles] into the third beginning, viz. into the creation, to its own love-play and melody, according to the property of both eternal desires. [Note: this "third beginning" denotes the relation between the two polarized beginnings.][23]

The initial, unactualized God (the primordial aspect of God) is called the *Ungrund*, the "ungrounded," the divine ground of Being:

---

[20] Brown, *The Later Philosophy of Schelling*; see also Koyré, *La Philosophie de Jacob Boehme*.

[21] Erb, Introduction to Boehme, *The Way to Christ* (1978), p. 1.

[22] (*Signature*, XIV.1,2, p. 210). There is an ambiguity or contradiction in Boehme: on the one hand God is already perfect and needs no further process or substance to become more so. But on the other hand, as Brown points out, "the world is somehow necessary for God's self-unfolding" (Brown, *The Later Philosophy of Schelling*, pp. 64–5; see also Walsh, *Mysticism of Innerworldly Fulfillment*, pp. 83–4).

[23] (*Signature*, chapter XVI, "Concerning the Eternal Signature and Heavenly Joy; Why All Things Were Brought into Evil and Good," [8], p. 212).

One cannot say of God that he is this or that, evil or good, that he contains distinctions within himself. For he is himself nature-less, as well as affect-less and creature-less. He has no inclination to anything, since there is nothing before him to which he could incline himself, neither evil nor good. He is in himself the *Ungrund*, without any will toward nature or creature, as an eternal Nothing (*Nichts*) ... He is the one Being (*Wesen*), and there is no quality (*Qual*) in him nor anything that could incline itself toward or from him. He is the one Being (*Wesen*), and there is nothing that generates or produces him. He is the Nothing and the All (*Alles*), and is a single will, in which the world and the whole creation lie, in him all is equally eternal without beginning, in the same weight, measure and limit (*Ziel*). He is neither light nor darkness, neither love nor anger, but the eternal One. Therefore Moses says: the Lord alone is God (Deuteronomy 6:4).[24]

In eternity, i.e., in the Unground out of nature, there is nothing but a stillness without being; there is nothing either that can give anything; it is an eternal rest which has not parallel, a groundlessness without beginning and end. Nor is there any limit or place, nor any seeking or finding, or anything in which there were a possibility ... It has no essential principle."[25]

This primordial aspect of God strives to realize itself ("... the nothing is a craving after something...which makes something out of nothing, that is, merely a will"[26]). Initially, the tendency of the *Ungrund* towards self-realization (towards self-objectification and, ultimately, self-consciousness) is manifest in the positing of two opposing tendencies: Will (prototype of the subject and of "light" and "goodness")[27] and Desire (which gives rise to the object, and is the prototype of God's "fire" or "wrath" and of "darkness").[28] From these two initial opposing centers

---

[24] *Von der Gnaden-Wahl*, in vol. VI, *Samtliche Schriften*, 1:3, trans. and quoted by David Walsh, *The Mysticism of Innerworldly Fulfillment*, p. 69.

[25] *Menschwerdung*, II.i.8 – quoted by John Joseph Stoudt in the Introduction to his translation of *The Way to Christ*, (1947), p. xxvi.

[26] *Mysterium Pansophicum*, 1, quoted in Brown, *The Later Philosophy of Schelling*, p. 55 fn 9.

[27] Brown explains that "will is the aspiration to reveal itself, and this in turn begets a desire for self-consciousness" (Ibid., p. 55). Boehme wrote: "will conceives within itself the desire to manifest itself to itself" (*Mysterium Magnum*, i.22.4, quoted in Franz Hartmann, *The Life and Doctrines of Jacob Boehme* [London: Kegan Paul, Trench, Trubner and Co., 1891], p. 61).

[28] Brown explains: "desire is the longing for an object of self-revelation. From this first polarity [of will and desire] derive the two centres in God" (*The Later Philosophy of Schelling*, pp. 55–6).
   "First, there is the eternal liberty, which hath the will, and is itself the will: now every will hath a seeking to do, or to desire something; and herein it beholdeth itself, and seeth in the eternity what itself is; and so finding nothing but itself, it desireth itself" (Boehme, *Forty Questions of the Soul*, 1:13, 1:22, quoted in Brown, *The Later Philosophy of Schelling*, p. 51).
   Initially, "fire" is not yet "darkness" but rather is the primordial force without which nothing is generated: "Whatever is to come to anything must have fire" (Boehme, source unknown, quoted by Evelyn Underhill, Introduction to *The Confessions of Jacob Boehme*, ed. W. Scott Palmer [New York: Alfred A. Knopf, 1920]).

(and the emergence of a third principle which interrelates them[29]), are generated pairs of opposites: one pole of such pairs is known as "darkness," "evil," "wrath," and "conflict," and the other is known as "light," "love," "wisdom." These two poles[30] (which undergo their own evolutions, internally and in relation to one another) are in inescapable conflict, and this conflict is necessary: in order for God to attain his full realization, the "darkness" and the "light" must be integrated with each other and in this way, the darkness/evil pole transcended by the light/goodness pole. Without such a dynamic process whereby contraries are generated, integrated, and overcome, God could not be actualized, because it is only in relation to its opposite or objectification that an entity can come to know itself and thereby realize itself.[31] The natural world is really a manifestation of God's striving to realize himself by means of his self-objectification (i.e., he must become an object to himself and then reunite with his objectified form to form a complex unity).

Without dialectics [*Wiederwärtigkeit*] no thing can become manifest to itself. If nothing resists it, then it continually proceeds from itself; it does not return into itself again. But if it does not return to itself again, into that from which it originated, then it knows nothing of its original state. If natural life has not dialectic, and it were limitless, then it would never ask for the ground from which it came. The hidden God then would remain unknown to the natural life. Furthermore, were there no dialectic in life then there would be neither sensitivity, nor activity, nor understanding, nor knowledge. For a thing having but one will has no divisibility. If it does not comprehend a contrary will which makes it drive to action, it remains passive. For one thing knows nothing more than one: and even though it itself is good, it knows neither evil nor good, for it has nothing within itself to make it perceptible. Thus also can we philosophize concern-

---

[29] As Brown points out, "This triad gives the model for realization of self-consciousness: a principle of consciousness, a medium for self-objectification, and a bond between the subjective and objective poles of the self" (*The Later Philosophy of Schelling*, p. 56). At this stage of the process, however, true self-consciousness and self-objectification have not yet been achieved.

[30] Brown (*The Later Philosophy of Schelling*, pp. 38–40) emphasizes the important point that "The terms *good* (expressed in nature as *Sanftmuth* or gentleness) and *evil* (expressed as *Grimmigkeit* or "fury") are chiefly metaphysical in import, rather than moral or psychological. Despite Boehme's misleading statements, good and evil are not themselves qualities, but are the two basic modalities of the qualities [i.e., the most basic constituents of all things]. *Sanftmuth* is the modality of stillness and peace. *Grimmigkeit* is sheer power, an intensely active force which is both productive and destructive, since it is the source of both life and evil. Boehme claims to see these qualities, in the two modalities of good and evil, as the bases of all the phenomena of the world."

[31] Boehme commentator Robert Brown states: "God not only requires a contrary in which to objectify himself, but in his self-objectification he is a synthesis of opposites. Something is disclosed for what it is only in the presence of its opposite. God is revealed as the good precisely by his eternal victory over the potentially destructive powers of nonbeing that he contains within himself" (*The Later Philosophy of Schelling*, p. 63).

ing God's Will, saying: Had the hidden God, who is merely one Essence and Will, not led Himself by His Will out of Himself, had he not brought Himself out of eternal comprehension in the *tempermento* into a differentiation of wills, and had He not led the same differentiation into a subjectivation of a natural and creaturely life, and did this same differentiation not stand in strife in life, how then would the hidden Will of God, which in itself is single, become manifest to itself? How can there be knowledge of self in an undivided, ego-centric will?"[32]

This basic dynamic is initiated in God's being, but all entities in the universe (having all been generated out of the original Absolute ground of Being/*Ungrund*) participate in the same process. The structure of man, too, is isomorphic with the structure of God. In addition to being a microcosmos and microtheos, Man is the key participant in the process of God's self-realization. This is because, according to Boehme, it is man's salvation – via his own self-realization – which enables the culmination of God's self-unfolding. Only by means of his own spiritual rebirth can a man help direct the world towards this more thoroughgoing transformation:

God has ordained [man] in the understanding to his own dominion: He has the ability to change nature, and to turn the evil into good, provided that first he has changed himself, otherwise he cannot ...[33]

There is an external-historical reason for man's central role in this Divine unfolding: in Boehme's interpretation of Biblical history (a bizarre and idiosyncratic one), the earth and human beings were created precisely for the purpose of rectifying a preexisting "fall" in the realm of the angels (the fall of Lucifer, who turned away from the light towards evil and thereby upset the balance of contraries which is necessary for God's full self-manifestation). Man's task is to restore to this ongoing process of creation (i.e., God's self-revelation into a complex self-conscious entity) the harmony and balance which have been disrupted. Unfortunately, man too has fallen (Adam's fall[34]) and so the balance of

---

[32] *The Way to Christ*, trans. John Joseph Stoudt, Seventh Treatise; ch. 1: "Of Divine Contemplation," pp. 8–10, p. 163. Here is a similar passage from another text: "[God's] holy life would not be revealed without nature, except in an eternal stillness, in which there can be nothing without the expressing and comprehending. God's holiness and love would not be revealed; if it is to be or become revealed there must be something to which love and grace are necessary, and which is dissimilar to love and grace. Now this is the will of nature, which stands in opposition (*Wiederwärtigkeit*) in its life: to this love and grace are necessary, so that its painfulness might be changed into joy" (Boehme, *Gnaden-Wahl*, IX:12; cited in and trans. by Walsh, *Mysticism of Innerworldly Fulfillment*, p. 77).

[33] Boehme, *Signature*, VIII.26, p. 83.

[34] Actually, Adam also falls twice in Boehme's distinctive rendering of Biblical history: His first fall "can be identified with [the] desire in Adam to know all creatures in their individuality in nature and not in their spiritual unity in God" (Walsh, p. 98) (clearly there

contraries on earth is disrupted as well. Therefore, in the human realm, evil and "darkness" (and conflict itself – the "strife" of opposing contraries) are problematic in a way that they were not before these several falls occurred (first the fall of Lucifer, and then the fall of Adam who had been created to set right the disharmony generated by Lucifer's turning towards the darkness and embracing evil):

Immediately when the knowledge of the life of individualities became manifest, then nature held life and caught in dissimilarity, and established her rule. This is why life became painful and why the inner divine ground of the good will and substance became extinguished, that is, inoperative in the sphere of creaturehood. For life's will broke away from life and entered into perceptibility, as unity into manifoldness, striving against the unity, against the eternal rest and the one good. When this happened then the divine ground – as the second principle wherein the divine Power with the exhaled Will of God has imagined itself into the life of images as the counter-image of God ... – became distorted in the false will. For the cause of movement within divine Essentiality had changed itself into earthliness in which good and evil stand in strife. Therefore the second principle, God's Kingdom, was extinguished. In its place there arose the third kingdom in its own figuration as the source of the stars and the four elements, from which the godly became coarse and animal, and the senses false and earthy. Life thus lost the *tempermentum*, or eternal rest, and by its own desire made itself dark, painful, gruff, hard and rough.[35]

Man's trajectory towards salvation (which is instrumental in God's own self-actualization, yet at the same time made possible by God's mercy and grace[36]) therefore must entail the revelation that there is no progression towards salvation without the strife of contraries. Humans must recognize that (in the words of Evelyn Underhill) the outer world "is both evil and good, both terrible and lovely, since in it love and wrath strive together":

are echoes of Plotinus here). His second fall (the more familiar one) is an outcome of the temptation of Eve and the eating of the apple from the Tree of Good and Evil. See Walsh, *Mysticism of Innerworldly Fulfillment*, pp. 98–101.

[35] *The Way to Christ*, trans. Stoudt, Seventh Treatise, ch. 2, 6–9, p. 173.
On the spiritual rebirth of man, Boehme writes: "As the eternal birth is in itself, so is also the process with the restoration after the Fall...there is not the least tittle of difference betwixt them; for all things originally arise out of the eternal birth, and all must have one restoration in one and the same manner" (*Signature*, VII.72, p. 75).

[36] "God's great Love again came to the aid of this captive life and immediately after this degeneration breathed into the internal *Ens*, into the extinguished essence of the divine quality, and gave life or a counter-image, as a new source-spring of divine unity, love and rest, into the distorted divine *Ens*...so that it might extinguish its own painfulness and restlessness in its ego-centric center" (*The Way to Christ*, trans. Stoudt, Seventh Treatise, ch. 2, 11, p. 174).

Evil, as a counter-will, activates the good, the true will, to seek its own essential state again, to press in upon God, to make the good desirous of good. For something that is good only in itself, having no source, wants nothing, seeks nothing, since it knows nothing better within itself or for itself after which it might be inclined.[37]

For God's anger works thus in the love, so that the love (as the eternal One and Good) might become separate, sensible, and perceptible; for in conflict (*Streite*) and opposition (*Wiederwillen*) the Groundless (*Ungrund*), as the eternal One that is outside of nature and creature, becomes revealed.[38]

Many commentators have remarked that Boehme's narrative is both literal history and allegory. He seems to have intended its meaning literally (at least on one level), prophesying that a real millennium (the "*Lilien-Zeit*" or "*Rosen-Zeit*"[39]) is close at hand. But subsequent generations of thinkers have emphasized the allegorical element in Boehme's system. They have highlighted his contention that heaven and hell are not actual locations, and that indeed salvation is not an episode of literal history. On such a reading, heaven and hell are viewed as *states of mind*, and salvation as an internal rather than an external event.[40] A famous passage by Boehme underscores this dimension of his doctrine, which has had so much meaning for later thinkers:

Men have always been of the opinion that heaven is many hundred, nay, many thousand, miles distant from the face of the earth, and that God dwells only in heaven. Now observe: if thou fixest thy thoughts concerning heaven, and wouldst willingly conceive in thy mind what it is and where it is and how it is, thou needst not to cast thy thoughts many thousand miles off, for that place, that heaven, is not thy heaven.

And though indeed that is united with thy heaven as one body, and so together is but the one body of God, yet thou art not become a creature in that very place which is above many hundred thousand miles off, but thou art in the heaven of this world, which contains also in it such a Deep as is not of any human numbering. The true heaven is everywhere, even in that very place where thou standest and goest; and so when thy spirit presses through the astral and the fleshly,

---

[37] *Way to Christ*, trans. Stoudt, Chapter One: "Of Divine Contemplation" [13], p.164.

[38] *Mysterium Magnum*, LXXI:14, trans. by and quoted in Walsh, *Mysticism of Innerworldly Fulfillment*, p. 52.

[39] Walsh, Ibid., p. 104; Ernst Benz, *The Mystical Sources of German Romantic Philosophy*, trans. Blair R. Reynolds and Eunice M. Paul (Allison Park, PA: Pickwick Publications, 1983), pp. 10–11.

[40] For example, William Inge insisted that Boehme did not anticipate "a golden age on this earth." Indeed, for Inge, Boehme is "most interesting as marking the transition from the purely subjective type of mysticism to Symbolism [i.e., allegory]" (Inge, *Christian Mysticism*, pp. 277–86).

and apprehends the innermost moving of God, then it is clearly in heaven.[41]

Boehme (unlike, e.g., Plotinus) also maintains that there is an "external" heaven:

But that there is assuredly a pure glorious heaven in all the three movings aloft above the deep of this world, in which God's Being together with that of the holy angels springs up very purely, brightly, beauteously, and joyfully, is undeniable. And he is not born of God that denies it.[42]

Nevertheless, in his doctrine, the heaven and hell within, and those that are far away, are essentially one ("Thou must know that this world in its innermost unfolds its properties and powers in union with the heaven aloft above us; and so there is one Heart, one Being, one Will, one God, all in all"[43]). As much as they are literal locations, they also are states of mind, and the history of salvation is read as the subjective history of the individual soul.

Finally, although the stages of God's self-unfolding are depicted as if in temporal sequence, the process actually is supposed to be a simultaneous, not a temporal, one. Creation is ongoing.[44] The soul cannot be saved until it recognizes its part in this process of Divine self-unfolding, and thereby also recognizes the fallenness and falseness of temporal existence and experiences the rebirth of God within itself.

Key features of the Behmenist narrative

Below are summarized three features of the Behmenist narrative which exemplify and/or extend the Neoplatonized Christian narrative discussed in Chapter 5. These are the spiral narrative; the constructive role of "evil" or "wrath" in God's (and man's) self-actualization; and the end of the spiral trajectory: salvation as a complex unity.

---

[41] Boehme, *Confessions*, pp. 15, 22–3. See also "Of Heaven and Hell" in "A Dialogue Between A Scholar and His Master Concerning the Supersensual Life," in *Signature*, pp. 259–75.

[42] Boehme, *Confessions*, p. 23.
   M.H. Abrams points out that, perhaps even as early as the mid-seventeenth century, some radical Protestant mystics (e.g., radical Inner Light Puritans of England, who probably had had contact with Boehme's doctrines in the form of translations by the English theologian William Law), "systematically invalidate the literal sense" of Biblical history (*Natural Supernaturalism*, pp. 51–5). See also Erwin Paul Rudolph, *William Law* (Boston: Twayne Publishers, 1980).

[43] Boehme,*Confessions*, pp. 23–4.

[44] Newton P. Stallknecht, *Strange Seas of Thought: Studies in William Wordsworth's Philosophy of Man and Nature* (Durham: Duke University Press, 1945), p. 102.

The spiral narrative

The Neoplatonized Biblical narrative takes the form of what Abrams called a "temporalized circle," a fall out of unity and a movement back to unity. For Boehme the path to salvation takes a somewhat different form: it is not a simple circular return to unity with God, as it was for Plotinus and earlier Christian mystics. Rather, it has a spiral shape. Insofar as God (and, paralleling God, the individual soul) actualizes himself in a form that is more complex and full than was his initial manifestation, the circular narrative of emanation and return to unity now has taken on a *spiral* aspect: the end is higher than the initial ground of Absolute Being (*Ungrund*). The entire process is necessary in order for this higher end – the unfolding of God in his complexity and fullness via the overcoming of contraries – to be attained. As noted above, Boehme did not intend this to be a temporal narrative, and tried to maintain that God is no less perfect as *Ungrund* than as fully realized self-consciousness. Nonetheless, there is an implication that the world – and man – are in some sense necessary for God's self-unfolding.

The constructive role of "evil" or "wrath" in God's (and man's) self-actualization

For Plotinus, evil is the privation of being and of goodness. It is present where Being is entirely absent – i.e., in matter, as well as in the self-assertive tendency of the soul to turn away from the One and towards physical life. For Boehme, "evil" (viewed as a self-assertive, dynamic, productive, and destructive force) is a "positive constituent"[45] of God. Moved to actualize himself, God generates a "dark" and evil center so that he may overcome it and thereby know himself as goodness and light. The existence of such "evil" and "wrath" is bound up with God's self-objectification, which likewise is constructive and necessary for him to become self-conscious.

The problem for man is that on earth the balance of contraries has become disrupted, leaving man prey to all the vicissitudes of evil untempered by good. In the words of Robert Brown:

Boehme says that God who is a complex of oppositions contains the ontological source of evil as a 'positive' (real) constituent in himself. God eternally overcomes this disruptive power in his own life process, whereas the same principle, when projected into the creation, becomes the source of actual evil in the creatures.[46]

[45] Brown, *The Later Philosophy of Schelling*, p. 22.
[46] Ibid., p. 22.

It is this disrupted harmony which must be restored in human life.

Thus, in Boehme, we see the emergence of the notion that, in order for the highest manifestations of Being (both God's and man's) to occur, there must be both evil and good, and both subject and object. Although this is considered to be an original innovation, it also may be seen as a further development of the idea of the *felix culpa* described in Chapter 5.

There are two corollaries of this vision of divinity and human nature. First, *the movement of God's unfolding progresses via the "strife" of contraries.* Evelyn Underhill states that for Boehme, "man must be at war with himself, if he wishes to be a heavenly citizen."[47] As Brown explains, it is only in the presence of its opposite that something can be disclosed for what it is: "God is revealed as the good precisely by his eternal victory over the potentially destructive powers of nonbeing he carries within himself."[48] Conversely, problems occur (e.g., in man's condition on earth) because the contraries do not achieve a kind of harmonious strife – because, as David Walsh explains it, "the fire or anger of god...is separated from his love and no longer tempered by the light of self-giving."[49]

Second, *self-assertion and even "estrangement" (e.g., God's self-objectification) serve a constructive purpose.* Plotinus accords to the soul's self-assertion, and to separation in general, only a negative valence. But for Boehme, these evils ultimately call forth God's self-revelation. God (and the individual soul) must estrange himself from his essence, and then reunite with himself at a higher level, forming a complex unity, in order for him to manifest himself in the fullest way (which he is impelled to do). Therefore, both self-estrangement (self-objectification), and the force which impels one to undergo this process, are constructive rather than pernicious. In the earthly temporal realm, this complex process has gotten "out of joint," but man, and only man, can set it right again by means of his participation in and understanding of this dynamic.[50]

---

[47] Introduction to Boehme, *Confessions.*
[48] Brown, *The Later Philosophy of Schelling*, p. 63.
[49] Walsh, *Mysticism of Innerworldly Fulfillment*, pp. 52–3.
[50] Walsh (*Mysticism of Innerworldly Fulfillment*, pp. 90–1) and Brown (*The Later Philosophy of Schelling*, pp. 65, 70) extend the implications of Boehme's doctrines even farther. Both point out that Boehme seems implicitly to assert that evil is somehow necessary for God's self-unfolding, and even that the creation of the ("fallen") world is necessary for the fullest, most actualized form of his self-realization. (In Brown's words, "only by a work of regeneration can God disclose his love and grace" [p. 70].) Both notions of course conflict with the basic Christian view of God, but persist in secularized versions of this narrative, as is shown in Chapters 7 and 8.

*The "end" of the spiritual trajectory: God's self-manifestation
and man's salvation entail a complex unity*

For Plotinus, salvation is a return of the soul to the One ("the flight of
the alone to the Alone"); Christian mystics married the Biblical idea of
salvation from sin to this notion of the soul's reunion with the Source.
For the individual spiritual pilgrim, this meant an experience of the
"inner light," the rebirth of the spark of God in the soul. For Boehme,
too, the end of both individual and external history entails such a rebirth.
This is a regeneration of the spirit (and of the earth) such that the soul
becomes reunited with God, thereby appreciating both its true identity as
part of God and the true nature of reality and the universe.

What is a departure from Plotinus and also from most prior Christian
mysticism[51] is Boehme's doctrine of the necessity of contraries, conflict,
objectification, and evil. Thus Boehme's answer to the "theodicy"
problem is likewise radical and innovative (and also somewhat self-
contradictory): God is not the source of evil, yet evil and "strife" are
generated by him and are necessary for his full self-realization. This is
only problematic at the level of human existence because in this fallen
world there is a disruption of the balance between evil and good (when
there is such a balance, good ultimately triumphs). And this doctrine in
turn is related to a difference between Boehme's vision of the end of the
spiritual trajectory (both God's self-unfolding and man's) and Plotinus'.
Boehme's end is a *complex* unity, not a return to the simple unity
described by Plotinus. By asserting that God's "wrath" and self-
objectification are necessary for his full manifestation – that his ultimate
aim is to become self-conscious[52] – Boehme conceptualized the end of the
spiritual trajectory as one in which God is manifest in terms of a new
complexity, a "higher" and fuller self-revelation. Since human nature is
isomorphic with the nature of God, it must manifest itself in terms of the
same process.

[51] Most commentators I have cited in this chapter suggest that this idea (what Blake later
asserted as "without contraries no progression") is one of Boehme's most striking and
influential innovations. However, it appears that there may be an earlier precedent for
this idea (although less explicitly articulated) in the idea of the *felix culpa* which was
discussed in Chapter 5. Various scholars have also noted proto-dialectical ideas in the
systems of Heraclitus, Nicholas of Cusa, and John Duns Scotus (the latter two were
pre-Protestant Christian mystics). See Inge, *Christian Mysticism*; Abrams, *Natural
Supernaturalism*.

[52] Of course, this is a different "self-consciousness" than Plotinus' sense of the term. In the
latter's usage, the self-conscious soul is characterized by shame, estrangement, and
hubris because it has turned away from the One and towards the material world. For
Boehme, self-consciousness has the connotation of a reunion, a restored (and enhanced)
integrity. Both senses of "self-consciousness" persist in modern (Romantic and psychoanalytic) usages of the concept.

In addition to this innovation regarding the nature of the end of the spiritual trajectory, Boehme also presented a different vision of the realm in which salvation will occur. When the climax of literal Biblical history occurs (and Boehme seems to have felt it was going to occur in the near future), it is *this* world that will be transformed. Earthly reality will undergo a definitive metamorphosis, and what heretofore was perceived as material reality will be transfigured, revealing its true spiritual essence:

On the last day we will not ascend from the place of this world, but will remain as in our fatherland, and go home into another world, into another principle of another quality ... This earth will be like a crystalline sea, where all the wonders of the world will be seen, all entirely transparent, and the radiance of God will be the light within it.[53]

Perhaps an even more radical implication of Boehme's vision of the last things is his contention that not only is heaven not located somewhere "out of this world," but its true location (along with that of hell) may be within the human mind. This is the "interiorization" of the Biblical narrative to which I referred earlier in this chapter:[54]

Understand then what heaven is: It is but the turning in of the will into the love of God. Wheresoever thou findest God manifesting himself in love, there thou findest heaven, without traveling for it so much as one foot. And by this understand also what hell is, and where it is ...

---

[53] Boehme, *Forty Questions of the Soul* XL:2,4, trans. by and quoted in Walsh, *Mysticism of Innerworldly Fulfillment.*

[54] As I have noted, most commentators hold that Boehme maintained that there is an external heaven, and that there would be an external-historical millennium in the near future which would transform the earth and our vision of it. Whether or not he intended this literal interpretation, it remains clear that the interiorized reading of both cosmology and Biblical history is strongly elaborated in Boehme's writings. Thus many see him as perhaps the most important transitional figure in the shift from a cosmological/external historical version of the Christian mystical narrative to an interiorized one.

    Of course, what Abrams calls "psychohistorical parallelism" (see Chapter 4) long predates Boehme and can be detected in both Plotinian and Christian doctrines, but with him, and with subsequent Protestant left-wing mystics, this level became more emphasized and elaborated. And if Boehme was ambiguous about the existence of a "real" heaven (in addition to the one within the self), subsequent left-wing Protestant mystics tended more and more to emphasize that heaven and hell are states of mind.

    It might be argued that Boehme's move towards interiorization is neither innovative nor distinctive because Plotinus also offered a kind of "interior" narrative, insofar as he wrote that to contemplate the One one must only look within. For Plotinus, however, such a looking inward to contemplate the One does not mean that the One is really human personality. On the contrary, his point is that the world of material existence and of individuals is coextensive with the true reality, i.e. the realm of ideas, pure forms, and (at the center of a series of concentric circles) the One. The more successfully the soul turns away from materiality and the closer it gets to its "true self" and source, the less it harbors the illusion that it is an individual personality at all – whereas for Boehme (arguably) and for subsequent thinkers, the discourse of external cosmology starts to look as if it really *is* a symbolic language of the self.

Know then, my son, that when the ground of the will yieldeth up itself to God, then it sinketh out of its own self, and out of and beyond all ground and place, that is or can be imagined, into a certain unknown deep, where God only is manifest, and where only he worketh and willeth. And then it becometh nothing to itself, as to its own working and willing; and so God worketh and willeth in it. And God dwells in this resigned will; by which the soul is sanctified, and so fitted to come into divine rest ... And then the soul is in heaven, and is a temple of the Holy Ghost, and is itself the very heaven of God, wherein he dwelleth. Lo, this is the entering of the will into heaven; and thus it cometh to pass.[55]

During his own lifetime, Boehme's writings gained him disciples among nobles and young educated men in Silesia.[56] After his death, his influence spread: his ideas were carried to mystical Protestant groups – Pietistic sects and Quakers, for example – in other parts of Germany, as well as the Netherlands and England.[57]

Beginning in the second half of the eighteenth century, there was what David Walsh has called a "second wave of Boehmean influence both in England and on the continent."[58] This "wave" fed directly into the thought of the German Idealist philosophers (Fichte, Schelling, Hegel) and English and German Romantic men of letters. There were several channels, both direct and indirect, through which these secular thinkers and artists were influenced by Behmenist doctrines. A large number of Romantics – including Schelling, Hegel, Blake, Coleridge, Novalis, and others – actually read his writings and mention him and his importance in their work. Some of these intellectuals also were exposed to Behmenist influence through their own radical Protestant (e.g., Pietistic) backgrounds or through their acquaintance with eighteenth-century mystical philosophers like Friedrich Christoph Oetinger, a German Pietist, and Louis Claude de Saint Martin, a French Freemason.[59] As we shall see in Chapter 7, the Romantics translated the Christian mystical narrative, including Boehme's innovations upon it, into a truly "naturalized," secularized form.

---

[55] Boehme, "Of Heaven and Hell," in *Of the Supersensual Life*, in *Signature*, pp. 260–1.
[56] See Arlene A. Miller (Guinsberg), "Jacob Boehme."
[57] See Miller, ibid.; Rudolph, *William Law;* Preface and Introduction to Boehme, *The Way to Christ* (trans. Peter Erb); Walsh, *Mysticism of Innerworldly Fulfillment*, pp. 23–6.
[58] Walsh, ibid., p. 26.
[59] See Benz, *Mystical Sources*; Walsh, *Mysticism of Innerworldly Fulfillment*; Brown, *The Later Philosophy of Schelling;* Abrams, *Natural Supernaturalism*.

7

Romantic thought: From worldly mysticism to natural supernaturalism

All deities reside in the human breast
        William Blake, *The Marriage of Heaven and Hell*, 1970, p. 37

Not in Utopia, subterraneous Fields,
Or some secreted Island, Heaven knows where!
But in the very world which is the world
Of all of us, the place in which, in the end,
We find our happiness, or not at all!
        William Wordsworth *The Prelude*, 1988, p. 442

Secular humanism also has its roots in Judaeo-Christian faith: it arises
from a mutation out of a form of that faith. The question can be put,
whether this is more than a matter of historical origin, whether it
doesn't also reflect a continuing dependence.
        Charles Taylor, *Sources of the Self*, 1989, p. 319

In Chapter 6, I described how Behmenist and other radical Protestant
doctrines evince a movement towards more worldly, secularized versions
of the Neoplatonized Biblical narrative. It was only in subsequent intellectual movements, however, that Christian mystical themes and patterns
became truly secularized, wholly divested of their theological connotations. In this chapter I focus mainly on one such movement – high
Romantic thought. Before exploring the Romantic narrative, I briefly set
it in context: first in the context of other secular systems that have been
influenced by Biblical history and inner light mysticism, and then in the
context of "Romanticism" itself.

At the end of Chapter 6 I briefly discussed the transmission of
Behmenist doctrines to other radical Protestant groups, and to both
laypersons and persons of high education and culture. By the end of the
1600s, the inner light began to mutate into "reason" and "autonomy,"
and the eschatological trajectory into mankind's march in the direction
of "progress." This trend was continued and widened during the

eighteenth and nineteenth centuries, when certain themes and patterns from Biblical history and mysticism were secularized both in Enlightenment ideas of progress and rational autonomy and in the subsequent Romantic protest against the Enlightenment.[1]

From prospectivist eschatology to social "progress"

After the Renaissance, and especially during the late seventeenth and eighteenth centuries, various thinkers (including Holbach, Condorcet, and other eighteenth-century philosophers) articulated a belief in "progress," in the natural movement of history towards a radical improvement of life on earth for mankind. In the eyes of many eigteenth-century intellectuals (some of whose contributions would help to furnish the ideology of the American and French Revolutions), the time of this dramatic amelioration of man's life on earth was close at hand. This improvement was now conceived as movement (either gradual or abrupt and "revolutionary") in the direction of rationality, science, and civilizational advancement, rather than as a literal millennium (although of course many Deist, rationalist, and Enlightenment thinkers still believed in God, viewing him as a real if somewhat distant First Cause and Prime Mover).

As Peter Gay has pointed out,[2] the French, English, and German

---

[1] Charles Taylor, *Sources of the Self* (Cambridge, MA: Harvard University Press, 1989), ch. 18 ("Fractured Horizons"), pp. 305–20. Taylor argues that there were "two big constellations of ideas which either immediately or over time have helped generate forms of unbelief ... [O]ne joins a lively sense of our powers of disengaged reason to an instrumental reading of nature [Deism mutating into Enlightenment – e.g., Bentham, Holbach, Condorcet]; the other focuses on our powers of creative imagination and links these to a sense of nature as an inner moral source [Pietism mutating into Kantianism but also and especially into Romanticism]." See also ch. 12 ("A Digression on Historical Explanation"), pp. 199–207.

   Similar visions of the "mutation" of theology into several different secular strains are detectable in the work of numerous scholars: Karl Lowith, *Meaning in History: The Theological Implications of the Philosophy of History* (Chicago: University of Chicago Press, 1949); Benjamin Nelson, "Self-Images and Systems of Spiritual Direction in the History of European Civilization," in S. Z. Klausner (ed.), *The Quest for Self-Control* (New York: Free Press, 1965); Abrams, *Natural Supernaturalism*; Maurice Mandelbaum, *History, Man and Reason* (Baltimore: Johns Hopkins Press, 1971); Paul Tillich, *History of Christian Thought from its Judaic and Hellenistic Origins to Existentiatism*, ed. Carl E. Braten (New York: Touchstone, 1968); Ernst Benz, *The Mystical Sources of German Romantic Philosophy*, trans. Blair R. Reynolds and Eunice M. Paul (Allison Park, PA: Pickwick Publications, 1983); Robert Nisbet, *History of the Idea of Progress* (New York: Basic Books, 1980).

[2] Peter Gay, *The Enlightenment: An Interpretation*. Vol. 2: *The Science of Freedom* (London: Weidenfeld and Nicholson, 1969); see especially pp. 98–125. See also Steven Best, *The Politics of Historical Vision: Marx, Foucault, Habermas* (New York: Guilford Press, 1995), pp. 6–11.

philosophers and men of letters associated with the Enlightenment were not as simplistically optimistic about the nature and effects of progress as is sometimes alleged. Even in the writings of the "professional optimist" Voltaire,[3] and the exuberantly hopeful Condorcet, there can be found expressions of cynicism and pessimism regarding the morally transformative powers of progress, as well as a Stoical attitude regarding the inevitability of certain forms of human suffering. But Gay also acknowledges the *philosophes'* confidence that science and reason – whatever their risks and deficiencies – were advancing as never before, and that they offered the best chances humans had for edification, improvement, and enduring well-being.[4]

Undoubtedly there were a variety of material and intellectual developments that promoted the emergence of the secular idea of progress during this period.[5] But whatever its other sources and causes, this idea of unilinear social progress seems to have been importantly conditioned by the generative metaphor of Biblical prospectivism. This connection has been highlighted by various historians of ideas,[6] as well as by the psychologists and social scientists discussed in Chapter 4.

From the inner light to rational autonomy

It is a fact worthy of further exploration that the rationalist philosophers of the Enlightenment (up to and including Immanuel Kant[7]) were versed in, and in some respects their systems grew out of, Christian mystical

---

[3] Gay, *Enlightenment*, p. 103.

[4] Ibid., p. 124. The ideal-typical Enlightenment vision of the "perfecting" (if not yet, and perhaps not ever, perfected) mind and world differs from the quasi-redemptive ends envisioned by the Romantics. The champions of science and reason had a sharp sense of who and what their enemies were: superstition, ignorance, inequality, and other malign elements. The battle might be an uphill one, but the battle lines were drawn clearly and the imperative was that the darker forces must be defeated or subdued by the light. The typically Romantic claim, by contrast, was that non-rational elements must be integrated with their "enlightened" antitheses in order for human beings to develop the potential to become more fully moral or fulfilled. If the *philosophes* tended to draw the goals of history and development in monochrome, the Romantics utilized chiaroscuro.

[5] See pp. 101–3 on Blumenberg in Chapter 4.

[6] See Taylor, *Sources,* ch. 19, "Radical Enlightenment," pp. 321–54, especially pp. 353–4. See also Benz *Mystical Sources*; Lowith, *Meaning in History*; Nisbet, *History of the Idea of Progress*; Abrams, *Natural Supernaturalism*, pp. 58–9; Ernest Tuveson, *Millennium and Utopia: A Study in the Background of the Idea of Progress* (Berkeley and Los Angeles: University of California Press, 1949); Carl Becker, "Progress," in *The Encyclopedia of the Social Sciences* (1934), vol. XII.

[7] See Robin May Schott, *Cognition and Eros: A Critique of the Kantian Paradigm* (Boston: Beacon Press, 1989), especially pp. 96–100.

doctrines. Thus it was that the inner light of God in the soul metamor-
phosed into the inner light of *reason*.[8] "The rationalists," wrote Paul
Tillich, "were all philosophers of the inner light, even though this light
later on became cut off from its divine ground." Both "the subjectivity
of Pietism [and] the doctrine of the 'inner light' in Quakerism and other
ecstatic movements, [have] the character of immediacy or autonomy
against the authority of the church. To put it more sharply, modern
rational autonomy is a child of the mystical autonomy of the doctrine of
the inner light."[9] This is not to assert that rationalism is merely de-
divinized mysticism; but it is to suggest that even in their departure from
religious doctrines, rationalistic approaches to knowledge and morality
retained certain formative assumptions about the nature and value of
knowledge and the knower, and about what is true and good.

Biblical and mystical themes are preserved not only in Enlightenment
ideas about progress and reason, but also in the Enlightenment's varied
intellectual and cultural heirs. These heirs include nineteenth-century
positivist and evolutionist systems, and various developmentalist and
rationalist strains in twentieth-century social science, including cognitive-
developmental psychology.

From worldly mysticism to high Romanticism

Ideas about progress and rational autonomy are not, however, the only
secular discourses in which Biblical and Christian mystical themes and
patterns survive. Such themes are most elaborately and painstakingly
preserved in yet another secular mutation of the inner light: high
Romantic thought.

The Romantics could not avoid being legatees of disenchanted reason,
of the transformation wrought by Enlightenment thinkers in man's view
of himself and the world. Yet they were, simultaneously, in rebellion
against that transformation. They lamented, and attempted to rectify,

---

[8] Tillich wrote: "the principles of reason develop out of an originally ecstatic experience
which produces insight. This insight can become rationalized. As the principles of reason emerge within us, the original underlying ecstasy can disappear or recede, with the
result that the Spirit becomes Reason in the largest sense of the concept ... rationalism
is the daughter of mysticism" (*History of Christian Thought*, p. 317). He adds: "There
are many reasons why rationalism was born out of mysticism both in Greek and modern culture ... [I]t happened on a large scale in the late seventeenth and eighteenth centuries. Ecstatic Protestant groups and their leaders were also the leaders of the
Enlightenment. This happened in many places ... The one term which grasps their unity
is the term 'inner light'" (ibid., p. 318). See also Nelson, "Self-Images"; Taylor, *Sources*,
pp. 366–7.

[9] Tillich, *History of Christian Thought*, p. 185.

what they perceived to be the spiritual impoverishment concomitant to the rationalist-empiricist worldview. The great English and German philosophers and men of letters who initiated the Romantic movement during the last few years of the eighteenth century, and the first decades of the nineteenth, were unified by this shared dissatisfaction with, and protest against, the Enlightenment and its social, intellectual, and political offspring.

In this chapter I explicate a generic Romantic narrative pattern and demonstrate that it is a secularized version of the Neoplatonized Biblical narrative I have traced in Chapters 5 and 6. In this pattern we can observe a continuation and intensification of the tendencies highlighted in Chapter 6 – i.e., the increasingly worldly and interiorized discourse on the soul, theodicy, and salvation that was initiated in medieval and Protestant mysticism. Before exploring the narrative, however, it is necessary to discuss the term "Romanticism" itself.

"On the discrimination of Romanticism"[10]

M.H. Abrams, one of the greatest modern critics who has written on Romanticism, highlights in it a counter-Enlightenment impulse to preserve worldly mysticism (although he doesn't use these words) in secularized form. He argues that this intention was shared by an otherwise diverse group of German and English artists and thinkers whom he groups together as "Romantics." Abrams called his classic study of Romanticism, *Natural Supernaturalism* after a phrase in Thomas Carlyle's essay, "Sartor Resartus";[11] this phrase underscores the prevalence, among the Romantics, of "the secularization of inherited theological ideas and ways of thinking."[12] Drawing upon a huge body of primary, historical, and critical sources, Abrams highlights the fact that these men of letters sought "in diverse degrees and ways, to naturalize the supernatural and to humanize the divine."[13] He asserts that they were seeking to construct new modes of theodicy and salvation, modes equivalent in emotional and cosmological import to those of religion, but minus its supernatural trappings.

---

[10] This is a slightly altered version of the title of A.O. Lovejoy's famous essay ("On the Discrimination of Romanticisms" in Lovejoy, *Essays in The History of Ideas* [Baltimore: Johns Hopkins Press, 1948], pp. 228–53), in which he challenges the validity of using this term to refer to a unitary cultural movement.

[11] Abrams quotes Carlyle's protagonist in this work as saying that "The Mythus of the Christian Religion looks not in the eighteenth century as it did in the eighth," and that therefore the "great need of the age" is "'to embody the divine Spirit of that Religion in a New Mythus.'" (*Natural Supernaturalism*, pp. 67–8).

[12] Ibid., p. 12.

[13] Ibid., p. 68.

Abrams' characterization of these artists and thinkers (including the German idealist philosophers Fichte, Schelling, and Hegel, German poets Holderlin and Novalis, and English poets such as Blake, Wordsworth, and Coleridge, among others) as "Romantics" is by no means an unorthodox or marginal perspective.[14] Nevertheless, it is necessary to point out that there have been, and continue to be, those who would take issue with various aspects of his argument. One point of view that appears to diverge from Abrams' is that of the celebrated historian of ideas, A.O. Lovejoy. In arguing that we can articulate a set of central Romantic concerns and themes, Abrams departs (at least implicitly) from Lovejoy's earlier treatment of Romanticism,[15] expounded in an essay written in 1924. Lovejoy suggested that "the word 'romantic' has come to mean so many things that, by itself, it means nothing."[16] He challenged the pervasive assumption that "Romanticism" refers to a unitary literary and philosophical movement, noting instead that

there are various historical episodes or movements to which different historians of our own or other periods have, for one reason or another, given the name ... The fact that the same name has been given by different scholars to all of these episodes is no evidence, and scarcely even establishes a presumption, that they are identical in essentials.[17]

On the contrary, he argued,

each of these so-called Romanticisms was a highly complex and usually an exceedingly unstable intellectual compound; ... and when certain of these Romanticisms have in truth significant elements in common, they are not necessarily the same elements in any two cases.[18]

Thus Lovejoy asserted that there is not a single overarching "Romanticism" but at least three different "Romanticisms," each of these three in turn analyzable into several distinguishable strains. The implication of Lovejoy's thesis is that the literary historian should not generalize about "Romanticism" as a unitary movement; this would seem to imply that a study such as *Natural Supernaturalism* is bound to misrepresent and distort these various Romanticisms and to exaggerate their thematic and stylistic affinities.

[14] See, e.g., Harold Bloom (ed.), *Romanticism and Consciousness: Essays in Criticism* (New York: W. W. Norton, 1970).

[15] That Abrams is answering Lovejoy is suggested in an essay on Wordsworth by Ernest Bernbaum, James V. Logan Jr., and Ford T. Swetnam Jr., in Frank Jordan, Jr., *The English Romantic Poets: A Review of Research and Criticism* (New York: Modern Languages Association of America, 1972), p. 105.

[16] Lovejoy, "On the Discrimination of Romanticisms," p. 232.

[17] Ibid., pp. 235–6.

[18] Ibid., p. 235.

Not all major critics of Romanticism have concurred with Lovejoy regarding the inadvisability of articulating a broader Romantic sensibility and set of common themes. For example, E.D. Hirsch (echoing another celebrated literary historian and critic, Rene Wellek[19]) has countered that while "[n]o doubt Lovejoy is right to insist that not everyone who has been called a romantic ought to be so called, I do think it makes sense to think of romanticism as a unitary and international movement."[20] Those who belonged to the Romantic movement, argues Hirsch, "shared a certain type of *Weltanschauung*." (His depiction of this Romantic *Weltanschauung* is for the most part harmonious with Abrams'.)

But even if one were to heed Lovejoy's caveat regarding the abuse of the *word* "Romanticism," perhaps his objections could be circumvented simply by using another word altogether (albeit with a more circumscribed and self-conscious application). Hirsch chose the term "Enthusiasm" to denote "the pattern of experience" depicted in the writing of two exemplary and influential Romantics, Wordsworth and Schelling. And more recently, the philosopher Charles Taylor has denoted a quasi-Romantic set of concerns and values using the term "Expressivist."[21] Both of these scholars thus have nodded to the master ("Lovejoy has done his work too well," wrote Hirsch) without bending to him. Abrams, asserting himself as a master in his own right, does not even nod: he simply retains the term "Romanticism." Other disagreements with Abrams' depiction of Romanticism have been voiced by the various critics who reviewed or responded to *Natural Supernaturalism* (which they nonetheless acknowledged to be an important book). Among the criticisms that have been voiced by his colleagues, there are two that it is relevant to consider in the context of my use of Abrams' ideas. The first is that while Abrams' reading of those he calls "Romantics" is undeniably a plausible one, *Natural Supernaturalism* is not a comprehensive depiction of central "Romantic" themes[22] (this is the inverse of Lovejoy's complaint). The second, related, challenge to Abrams' thesis is that it is

---

[19] Rene Wellek, "The Concept of 'Romanticism' in Literary History," *Comparative Literature*, vol. 1, nos. 1–2, 1949, pp. 1–23, 147–72.

[20] E.D. Hirsch, Jr., *Wordsworth and Schelling: A Typological Study of Romanticism* (New Haven: Yale University Press, 1960), p. 2.

[21] Taylor, it seems, has attempted to make the category of Romantics still more inclusive; his intention is to highlight the counter-Enlightenment motives and visions that informed many eighteenth- and later nineteenth- (and twentieth-) century thinkers, not only those who wrote between 1790 and the early 1800s (*Sources*, ch. 21 ["The Expressivist Turn"], pp. 368–90).

[22] Wayne Booth, "M.H. Abrams: Historian as Critic, Critic as Pluralist," in *Critical Inquiry* (Spring 1976), pp. 443–4.

no more persuasive or "true" an account of the essential nature and messages of Romanticism than are any number of other (mostly still unwritten) alternative interpretations.[23]

Abrams himself gives what is for my purposes a satisfactory response to these two criticisms, and to Lovejoy's argument, when he cites his own book to clarify just what he does and does not mean by "Romanticism:"

> I don't believe that there exists an abstract entity, named "Romanticism," whose essential features are definable; or to put it another way, that we can set the necessary and sufficient conditions for the correct use of the term, "Romanticism." Instead, I use the word as an *expository convenience* [italics added] to specify, as I say on the opening pages, "some of the striking parallels, in authorial stance and persona, subject matter, ideas, values, imagery, forms of thought and imagination, and design of plot or structure" which are manifested in a great many important English and German writers, in a great variety of literary, philosophical, and historical forms, during those three or four decades after the outbreak of the French Revolution which, following common historical usage, I call the Romantic era (*Natural Supernaturalism* pp. 11–12).[24]

In other words, Abrams premises his project on the observation that a collection of distinctive themes and patterns is present in the work of a large group of important artists and philosophers. This observation cannot be invalidated by the observations (1) that other central themes and concerns also may be detected in Romantic works, or (2) that these Romantic works are not only similar but also diverge from one another along equally significant thematic and stylistic lines.[25]

On the basis of these considerations, I retain the term "Romantic" in this chapter, using it, as Abrams does, to denote the "striking parallels" of theme and plot structure that obtain across a large and otherwise varied assortment of writings by English and German men of letters who wrote at the cusp of the eighteenth and nineteenth centuries. In particular, I focus on what he refers to as a distinctive "plot structure." This generic narrative depicts the development of the mind, self, or "subject"

---

[23] Ibid., pp. 439–40.
[24] M.H. Abrams, "Rationality and Imagination in Cultural History: A Reply to Wayne Booth," *Critical Inquiry* (Spring, 1976), pp. 447–64, 450–1.
[25] One implication of Abrams' characterization of Romanticism is that even certain thinkers who are not generally considered Romantics by literary scholars are, according to this usage, admissable into that category. I am thinking specifically of Friedrich Schiller, to whom Abrams frequently refers without ever acknowledging that Schiller is not, by a narrow definition, a Romantic, but rather is usually situated within high classicism. Yet in some of his important writings he did utilize the narrative pattern that Abrams describes, and in these same writings expressed some characteristically Romantic responses to the limitations of Enlightenment thought and the "failure" of the French Revolution.

from an original state of undifferentiation to a final, higher state of complex unity with nature or the "object."

In addition to this general depiction of Romanticism, Abrams (not as systematically as this)[26] puts forward several other propositions that I also make use of in the remainder of this chapter (and discuss in more detail in the following section). First, this Romantic narrative pattern is essentially a secularization of Christian mysticism (Neoplatonized Biblical history), especially those forms of the Neoplatonized Biblical narrative that developed in areas with strong radical Protestant traditions (i.e., England and Germany). Second, the Romantics were more often than not quite aware of their desire to translate the sacred into the secular in an effort to preserve certain religious themes and values. Abrams suggests that

> While the assimilation of Biblical and theological elements to secular or pagan frames of reference began with the establishment of Christianity, and ... was immensely accelerated from the Renaissance through the eighteenth century, what is exceptional in this period beginning in the 1790s is the scope of this undertaking, and the deliberateness with which it was often carried on.[27]

Finally, Abrams alleges that there were several concerns that motivated these artists and philosophers to undertake such a project at this point in history: First, he seems to suggest that there was simply a desire to preserve a viable theodicy – a way of making meaning of suffering and "evil," and of holding out the hope of some sort of salvation, however different from the literal religious one. Secondly, this Romantic narrative, and Romantic discourse in general, were intended as a protest against and critique of the Enlightenment and the industrial and social revolutions that attended and followed it. As I have noted, Enlightenment ideas and doctrines also had assimilated Biblical history and even mysticism to a more secular world view. But the Romantics tended to be very dissatisfied with these eighteenth-century renderings of Judaeo-Christian doctrines. They felt that Enlightenment doctrines depleted the spiritual and moral life of man more than they preserved it. Thirdly, Abrams highlights a pivotal historical event to which the Romantics were responding: the French Revolution. He suggests that for these English and German intellectuals,[28] the course taken by the

---

[26] It is not only Abrams who proposes these ideas: in his book he draws upon a huge body of secondary as well as primary sources. Some major scholars who have concurred with some or all of his premises and conclusions are Ernst Benz, Maurice Mandelbaum, E.D. Hirsch, Newton Stallknecht, Robert Brown, and many contributors to Bloom's volume.

[27] Abrams, *Natural Supernaturalism*, p. 66.

[28] Many of them had Pietistic or nonconforming backgrounds, and had studied esoteric (e.g., Behmenist) doctrines; more generally, as Abrams points out, they came from culture areas that had long-standing traditions of "radical Protestant revolt."

Revolution in France – its rapid descent into violence and tyranny – was experienced as a bitter disappointment. Their quasi-millenarian hopes dashed at a time when most of them were quite young, they were moved to radically re-think the nature of human beings, the world, their relation, and mankind's prospects for redemption.

In the following section I discuss these propositions about Romanticism and Romantics in more detail, integrating Abrams' work with the writings of other scholars. I then explicate some central features of the generic Romantic narrative – what Abrams calls the "circuitous journey" – and explore how it both preserves and departs from Neoplatonist and Behmenist Biblical history.

Romanticism as "natural supernaturalism"

The Romantic period in art and philosophy is considered by historians and critics to have been characterized by a profound dissatisfaction with, and revolt against, certain dominant social and intellectual trends of the eighteenth century. When, for example, literary historian Peter Coveney suggests that the work of Rousseau, Coleridge, and others embodied a rebellion against the "materialist, rationalist, perfectionist and essentially secular eighteenth century," he is referring to the rationalism of the *philosophes* (and Kant's less-than-successful attempt to overcome its limitations), the empiricist psychology of John Locke, and Newton's mechanistic view of the universe.[29] Some scholars, including critic E.D. Hirsch and the intellectual historian Maurice Mandelbaum,[30] emphasize that the post-Kantian philosophers in Germany felt that the Kantian paradigm was inadequate not only from an epistemological standpoint, but also from a spiritual one. In the eyes of Fichte, Schelling, and Hegel, Kant's system – itself an attempt to mediate and dissolve the gulf between empiricism and rationalism – was inadequate because it contained its own version of an unbridgeable gulf between the human mind and the natural world. This is often viewed by philosophers as a purely epistemological issue. To consider it solely on this level, however, is to overlook the deeper spiritual meaning that rendered Kantian epistemology problematic for the idealist philosophers who immediately followed him. Mandelbaum commented on the compelling attraction of more "unitary" (monistic) systems for many German (and English) intel-

---

[29] Peter Coveney, *The Image of Childhood: The Individual and Society – A Study of the Theme in English Literature* (Harmondsworth: Penguin, 1967), p. 40.
[30] Hirsch, *Wordsworth and Schelling*; Mandelbaum, *History, Man and Reason.*

lectuals of the day, as well as the "metaphysical pathos" induced by certain limitations within the Kantian system:

There were grave difficulties with the Kantian system, which [the German idealists] believed ... only a new monistic metaphysics could overcome; one must also take into account the appeal which the doctrine of divine immanence exerted upon German thought at the time. One finds that doctrine in Lessing, Herder, Goethe, and Novalis, as well as in Fichte, Schelling, and Hegel. However, it would be impossible to espouse such a view and yet remain within the framework of the Kantian system ... In short, Kant's system *made it impossible to find any form of ultimate unity within experience, either between man and nature or within man himself* [italics added].

It was against such a view that Kant's idealist successors revolted. Behind all of their variant technical arguments, each in his own way sought that higher unity which was part of the metaphysical pathos of the times, and each sought it in an idealist form of the doctrine of divine immanence.[31]

Another, related, source of disillusionment was the industrial revolution: its accelerating scientific and technological advances were accompanied by a growing sense, in some quarters, that such "progress" also entailed great social and humanitarian costs. The final source of a sense of moral and spiritual impoverishment among many intellectuals was the failure of the French Revolution, that brainchild of the Enlightenment, to fulfill its initial "salvationist" promise. Particularly among intellectuals in Protestant nations, the French Revolution had raised both secular and spiritual aspirations: its rationalistic and this-worldly utopian vision, inspired by eighteenth-century Enlightenment thought, was experienced through the prospectivist and millenarian lens through which both secular and religious experience were still being filtered. Thus its failure (like that of the Puritan Revolution before it) was a bitter blow, one that was construed spiritually as well as politically.

Sparked by this most decisive disappointment, many English and German artists and thinkers (some of whom had been sympathizers with the Revolution and had even participated in its early utopian projects) were motivated to reconstruct what, heretofore, had been an overtly religious vision of the meaning of life and the justification for suffering.

These highly educated and sophisticated young men appreciated that earlier hopes for millenarian perfection – first anticipated in literal

---

[31] Mandelbaum, *History, Man and Reason*, p. 31. This is sometimes viewed by philosophers as an epistemological problem, internal to the history of philosophy; but we must not forget that it also has a spiritual root, a source in explicitly religious concerns. As I have discussed, the Christian mystical tradition is based on the desire to have a closer relationship and contact with the Divine, and it explains all the *malaises* of mankind – evil, immorality, suffering – in terms of estrangement, separation, and division.

religious doctrines and the worldly revolutions they inspired (e.g., the Puritan Revolution of 1648), then evoked by optimistic Enlightenment doctrines of reason and progress, and finally engendered by the initial phases of the French Revolution – could not be sustained in the old way in the post-Enlightenment world. They knew that they could not return to the old religious cosmology, that this had to be a system of worldly salvation that had both its beginning and its end, to quote Wordsworth, "in the very world which is the world of all of us, the place in which, in the end, We find our happiness, or not at all." In the words of Abrams, they sought

[to] salvage traditional experience and values by accommodating them to premises tenable to a later age...to save the overview of human history and destiny, the experiential paradigms, and the cardinal values of their religious heritage, by reconstituting them in a way that would make them intellectually acceptable, as well as emotionally pertinent, for the time being.

Some of these intellectuals saw themselves as attempting to restore to secular thinking a dynamic and holistic vision which mechanism and empiricism could not provide.[32] Others felt they were "refining" the older dogmas and myths into a more systematic, "scientific" truth.[33] In either case, the religious themes, patterns, and images that they simultaneously preserved and transformed were drawn from an older cultural reservoir.

Why did these thinkers look to *mystical* themes and patterns in their efforts to articulate a counter-discourse to Enlightenment ideals? For Coleridge, mystical traditions were appealing because he perceived them to embody "deeper feeling and stronger imagination than belong to most of those to whom reasoning and fluent expression have been as a trade learnt in boyhood."[34] He found in Boehme and George Fox (the founder of the Quaker movement) "fulness [*sic*] of heart" as well as of intellect; "they contributed," he wrote, "to keep alive the *heart* in the *head*."[35] To keep alive the heart was deemed by him, and by other Romantics, as more than just an optional supplement to rational-empirical knowledge. Rather, Coleridge insisted, there was no true knowledge without the inclusion of a spiritual (and affective) dimension: "My opinion is that deep thinking is attainable only by a man of deep feeling; and that all truth is a species of revelation."[36]

[32] The English Romantic poets, particularly Coleridge and Blake, exemplify this motive.
[33] An example of this project is Hegel's philosophical system.
[34] Samuel Taylor Coleridge, ch. IX, *Biographia Literaria* (Oxford: Oxford University Press, 1975), p. 97.
[35] Ibid., p. 98.
[36] Quoted in Newton P. Stallknecht, *Strange Seas of Thought: Studies in William Wordsworth's Philosophy of Man and Nature* (Durham: Duke University Press, 1945), p. 28.

In short, neither sensory knowledge, nor reason, nor man's attempt to institutionalize reason with the French Revolution, had proved sufficient to satisfy the spiritual requirements that had shaped our culture for two millennia.

The secularization of the Christian mystical narrative

Thus were the Romantics at odds with many aspects of the world in which they lived. They were disillusioned with the rational-empirical world view, with the emerging social and economic arrangements of modernity, and finally by the failure of the French Revolution to implement the millenarian hopes and ideals with which they had endowed it. But, Abrams writes, "though Romantic writers soon lost confidence in a millennium brought about by means of violent revolution, they did not abandon the form of their earlier vision." Instead, there occurred "a widespread shift in the bases of hope from political revolution to the powers inherent in human consciousness."[37] Henceforth the "mind"[38] – both individual and collective – would become the locus of a developmental progression towards a renewed and redeemed man.

Therefore they attempted to translate the design of Biblical history into a narrative in which the key participants were not God and the soul, but rather (individual and collective) man and the natural world. Man's "fallenness" – the human condition – now was conceived in terms of an estrangement of self and nature, or subject and object. This estrangement is embodied both in an inner division in man's selfhood (between the rationally civilized and the primitively "natural" or instinctual) and in an experienced separation between the perceiving subject and the objects of his perception.

As has been discussed, explicitly theological versions of the Christian mystical narrative all depicted the present fallen mortal human condition in terms of the severance of the soul from its unity with God (and, in Behmenist terms, also the estrangement of God from his self-objectifications, a condition mirrored by the condition of man) and followed the soul's passage towards an apocalyptic reunion with him. In the naturalized Romantic narrative, it is the individual and/or collective human mind (not God or the soul), initially undifferentiated and unself-

---

[37] Abrams, *Natural Supernaturalism,* p. 65.

[38] We have seen that this has some precedent in the Behmenist doctrine, in which the structure of man's consciousness is seen to be isomorphic with that of God. Nevertheless, the Romantic relegation of God to the background, and of the human mind to the foreground, is the definitive one.

conscious, which undergoes a painful series of ruptures and losses. Through such ruptures the mind grows and develops its powers, ultimately achieving a reunion with the nature from which it has been severed – but this reunion is at a higher level than the initial unity.

For some (e.g., the German idealist philosophers), both subject and object are generated out of an initial undifferentiated One. For others (e.g., William Wordsworth), the starting point of the trajectory is a state in which mind and nature are "fitted" together and then become rent asunder.[39] But in both cases, the end and *telos* of the journey is a rejoining of the estranged elements at a higher level, a level at which their individuated distinctiveness is preserved in the form of what Samuel Taylor Coleridge called "multeity-in-unity."[40]

This basic Romantic narrative pattern recurs throughout the literature and poetry of the likes of Schiller, Schelling, Fichte, Hegel, Hölderlin, Novalis, Kleist, Blake, Keats, Shelley, Coleridge, Wordsworth, and others.[41] In the remainder of this chapter I explore this generic Romantic narrative first in terms of its departure from, and then in terms of its continuities with, Plotinian and Behmenist doctrines. First I highlight three changes in the narrative which evince its radical transposition from religious to secular terms.[42] Then, in the section following this one, I discuss four characteristics of the Romantic narrative in terms of their continuities with the Neoplatonized Biblical narrative as it was presented in Chapters 5 and 6.

First and foremost, *God is eliminated or relegated to a position of relative unimportance.* The Neoplatonized Christian narrative depicts the severance of the soul from its unity with God and follows its passage towards a single, apocalyptic reunion with him. The Behmenist narrative posits a developmental trajectory in which God is the original subject of the narrative (splitting himself so that he may become an object of his own consciousness); the individual soul participates in the same process: the human being is a microtheos and microcosmos. In these explicitly religious frameworks, God is, in Abrams' words, "utterly prepotent as the creator and controller of [the soul and the natural world] and as the

---

[39] Abrams, *Natural Supernaturalism*, p. 281.

[40] Quoted in Abrams, *Natural Supernaturalism*, pp. 185–6, 268–9 (no specific Coleridge text cited).

[41] Abrams provides a multitude of examples of the prevalence of this pattern in Romantic and quasi-Romantic writings. See also Stallknecht, *Strange Seas*; Hirsch, *Wordsworth and Schelling*; Brown, *Later Philosophy of Schelling*; Benz, *Mystical Sources*.

[42] The following three points are a selective summary of Abrams' ideas in his section on "Forms of Romantic Imagination," pp. 169–95 of *Natural Supernaturalism*. Additional material is derived from pp. 113–14 and pp. 448–57 (on the Romantic "crisis") and pp. 91–2. Commentary on the Behmenist narrative is my own.

end, telos, of all natural process and human endeavor."[43] In an attempt to construct a post-Enlightenment, post-French Revolution, version of salvation, Romantic thought introduces an important modification into this system:

the tendency in innovative Romantic thought ... is greatly to diminish, and at the extreme to eliminate, the role of God, leaving as the prime agencies man and the world, mind and nature, the ego and the non-ego, the self and the non-self, spirit and the other, or (in the favorite antithesis of post-Kantian philosophers) subject and object.[44]

"Thou art a Man God is no More," wrote William Blake, "Thy own humanity learn to adore."[45] William Wordsworth's long semiautobiographical poem, *The Prelude*, provides an example of this innovation. This work chronicles the development of the mind (of the individual, of the poet, of the race) from an originally innocent sense of unity with nature, through a crisis of disillusionment, self-consciousness, and alienation, culminating in a higher level of unity. In this developmental narrative, God is still present, but he has been relegated to the background; his role is somewhat analogous to that of the present Queen of England, i.e., he is "a purely formal reminder of his former self."[46]

The second radical change, a corollary of the first, is that *the subject, self, or mind appropriates the powers of God and the dynamics of his self-unfolding.*[47] In Chapter 6 I noted a tendency on the part of Boehme to "internalize" or "psychologize" the Christian mystical narrative. However, in his and most other Protestant mystical doctrines, the conventional interpretation of Biblical narrative also is retained, i.e., Biblical history is also read as the history and destiny of the world and the human race. Boehme's innovation is his assertion that Biblical history, in the final analysis, is the history of the unfolding and self-actualization of God; the history of individual human souls runs parallel to God's history because man is a microcosmos and microtheos.

For the Romantics, this historical narrative is transmuted into the story of the unfolding and realization of the mind or self. This is first and foremost a phenomenon that occurs at the level of the individual. Even where there remains a parallelism between the story of the self and the

---

[43] Abrams, *Natural Supernaturalism*, p. 91.
[44] Ibid.
[45] William Blake, *The Everlasting Gospel*, in *The Poetry and Prose of William Blake*, ed. David Erdman (Garden City, NY: Doubleday, 1970), p. 511.
[46] Abrams, *Natural Supernaturalism*, p. 90.
[47] In addition to Abrams and Benz, Stallknecht also describes this transmutation (*Strange Seas*, pp. 26–9).

story of the race, it is these interior changes that will effect larger, "external" civilizational changes. The individual mind or self is the source and agent of both this history and its more far-reaching effects.[48] The powers heretofore ascribed to God are still operative in Romantic narratives, but now they are located entirely in the mind, rather than originating in an external supernatural force.

Ernst Benz highlights this transition from supernaturalism to naturalism, from the unfolding of God to the unfolding of the human personality, when he asserts that

[i]dealistic philosophy progresses from the basis of classical ontology to the discovery of the human personality as the center of all knowledge and action. The absolute, seen by philosophers of preceding centuries as in a transcendent hereafter far away from us, becomes real in the consciousness of man, in the mind conscious of itself, in the Self.[49]

The mind or self, in reuniting with its estranged essence (nature or the object world), becomes self-conscious and thus self-realized. This is the same as or similar to Boehme's narrative, only now it is mainly about the self, and not at all (or much less importantly) about God.

Explicitly theological versions of the Christian mystical narrative depict the present "fallen" mortal human condition in terms of the severance of the soul from its unity with God (who remains the first cause and prime mover of history), and follow its passage towards an apocalyptic reunion with him. In Romantic narratives, the tragedy of the human condition no longer is perceived to be the rupture between the soul and God, but rather the estrangement between the mind and nature. Sin and pernicious division – heretofore the literal "fall" – are initiated by, and a function of, this moral and epistemological alienation. The highest stage of being and knowing is one in which the mind or subject reappropriates its object and comes to be "at home with itself in its

---

[48] For Wordsworth, the developed artist possesses both the power and the ethical imperative to help move other human beings towards this capacity: "Once we have felt this [sense of unity], it becomes not so much our duty as our deep-seated and intense desire to help further the development of an independent, spiritual resourcefulness in our fellow men and in ourselves" (Stallknecht, *Strange Seas*, p. 22). And Schiller suggested that civilization (again, cast in the mold of the artist or aesthetically developed individual) must go through a similar spiritual trajectory – beyond the civilized "barbarism" of cold reason and aestheticism-for-its-own-sake towards a stage in which feeling and reason are integrated and provide a moral vision to guide both the individual and mankind (*On The Aesthetic Education of Man: In a Series of Letters,* ed. Elizabeth M. Wilkinson and L.A. Willoughby [Oxford: Oxford University Press, 1982]). Thus, in both these senses, this trajectory is not only about the development of the individual mind but also about mankind.

[49] Benz, *Mystical Sources,* ch. 2 ("The Mystical Sources of Some Fundamental Ideas of German Idealism"), p. 21.

otherness" (Hegel), or in which mind and nature fit together exquisitely as they once did before (Wordsworth). In this reunited state, the developed mind is all the better for what it has become over the course of its arduous journey back home.

The third transformation notable in the Romantic narrative is that *"this world" becomes the sole locus of development and redemption.* Both Neoplatonist and Biblical designs locate the redemptive "end" of the spiritual trajectory in some realm other than the mortal, natural world. For the Romantics, however, "the aim of our life in this world can be nothing else than to enhance the quality of that life itself."[50] Our fulfillment, our "redemption," is to be found (to invoke the famous Wordsworth lines)

> Not in Utopia, subterraneous Fields,
> Or some secreted Island, Heaven knows where!
> But in the very world which is the world
> Of all of us, the place in which, in the end,
> We find our happiness, or not at all.[51]

What is transformed in "this world" is, first and foremost, human consciousness. I discuss the nature of this transformation later in this chapter. For now I shall only note that while this notion of what Abrams calls "apocalypse by imagination or cognition"[52] (i.e., a sweeping change in the way one perceives the world, oneself, and their relation) is by no means brand new with the Romantics, it is now for the first time used to denote an unambiguously psychological state. Plotinus speaks of reunion as a change of consciousness, and Boehme also speaks of salvation in this way. But for Plotinus the change of consciousness (the soul's turning back to contemplate the One) entails a concurrent turning away from material life – indeed, from one's false, earthly self. For Boehme, man's radical change of consciousness does take place on this earth (though the earth is thereby transfigured), but it is parallel to God's self-actualization, not a replacement of it. For the Romantics, all deities *really do* reside within the human breast – salvation has become not only an entirely this-worldly affair, but also an interiorized, psychologized one.

I have noted that many Romantics still did have hopes for salvation at the level of external history – an achievement to be effected largely through the accomplishments of poets and philosophers like themselves. But it was always artistic imagination, or philosophic cognition, that

---

[50] Abrams, *Natural Supernaturalism*, p. 183.
[51] *The Prelude* (London: Penguin Classics, 1988), X, 724–8, p. 442.
[52] Ibid., p. 374.

would promote – or were promoting – this amelioration of human life on earth.

Key features of the Romantic narrative

Above I described the narrative in terms of how it became more secularized. Below is a summary of four prominent structural features which this Romantic narrative retained from the religious narrative. Through an examination of these features, we can see how the Christian mystical narrative was translated and transformed into "natural supernaturalism":

The Romantic spiral

In Chapter 5, I described how the Neoplatonist circle of emanation and return became assimilated to the temporal, finite, linear prospectivist design of Biblical history. The result was a single, temporalized circle. In Chapter 6, I noted that Boehme made a crucial additional alteration in the Plotinian design: the circle became a spiral. The end is higher than the beginning, because the *Ungrund* is God as potentiality, while the *telos* of mystical history is the fully actualized God.

The Romantics adopted this spiral design. As Robert Brown has demonstrated (and others have noted), Schelling's later philosophy is basically Boehme's "mature" doctrine made clearer, more systematic, and more explicit.[53] A number of other Romantics were acquainted with, and openly admired, Behmenist or Boehme-influenced teachings: Coleridge,[54] Blake,[55] even Hegel. But even in the writings of those who may not have had direct contact with Boehme's teachings, the basic design of the narrative (not only the proto- and actual dialectical systems explicated by Romantic philosophers but also the literary scenarios penned by Romantic poets) is a spiral that clearly resembles Boehme's, albeit now in secularized form. The mind must undergo severance from nature, resulting in a split within man himself, as well as in a sense of self-consciousness and estrangement from the object(s) he perceives. It must further undergo a difficult process of growth and development, in which the fall into self-consciousness and the strife of conflicting tendencies (both within the mind and between mind and external nature) culminate in what Abrams has called a "reversion to a higher unity."

---

[53] Robert Brown, *The Later Philosophy of Schelling: The Influence of Boehme on the Works of 1809–1815* (Lewisburg, PA: Bucknell University Press, 1977).
[54] *Biographia Literaria*, ch. IX.
[55] Abrams, *Natural Supernaturalism*, p. 55; see also Leopold Damrosch, *Symbol and Truth in Blake's Myth* (Princeton: Princeton University Press, 1980).

Rupture, division, opposition, and differentiation are now seen as necessary precursors to a desired end-state characterized by "an organized unity in which all individuation and diversity survive, in Coleridge's terms, as distinctions without division."[56]

There are many examples of such a basic narrative structure in the writings of Romantic philosophers and men of letters. Of course, the dialectical ascent is found in the philosophy of Hegel, as well as in the proto-dialectical systems of Fichte and Schelling.[57] Blake traces the self's development from innocence to experience to a higher or "organized" innocence.[58] Yet another example of this narrative form is found in the *Bildungsroman* – the German Romantic literary genre which chronicles the development of consciousness, the progressive education of the self.[59]

In many Romantic narratives, this story of the growth of the individual mind parallels (and is seen to be a function of) mankind's history. Civilized man, who is estranged from both his "natural," instinctual self and from external nature, is considered to have reached his apex with the Age of Enlightenment. This period – characterized by the veneration of a rationalism that sharply divides subject and object, and by the fragmentation and specialization that typify emerging socio-economic arrangements – is seen to be a necessary but insufficient and ultimately problematic stage in mankind's history. In *The Aesthetic Education of Man* (written in 1793–4, at least partly in response to the violent and anti-humanistic turn taken by the French Revolution), Friedrich Schiller asks how it is, if "our Age is Enlightened ... that we can still remain barbarians?"[60] Man, he asserts, has gone from "all-unifying Nature" to "all-dividing Intellect."[61] In becoming estranged from nature, man becomes estranged from himself – from those qualities and sensibilities which culture (*Kultur*), with its emphasis on reason and specialization, has repudiated and marginalized.

> It was civilization itself which inflicted this wound upon modern man ... [With the advent of scientific and political specialization], the inner unity of human nature was severed too, and a disastrous conflict set its harmonious powers at variance.[62]

[56] Abrams, *Natural Supernaturalism*, p. 185.
[57] See Abrams, *Natural Supernaturalism*; Brown, *The Later Philosophy of Schelling*; Hirsch, *Wordsworth and Schelling*; David Walsh, *The Mysticism of Innerworldly Fulfillment: A Study of Jacob Boehme* (Gainesville, FL: University Presses of Florida, 1983).
[58] See Northrop Frye, *Fearful Symmetry: A Study of William Blake* (Princeton: Princeton University Press, 1947).
[59] See, e.g., J.W. von Goethe, *Wilhelm Meisters Lehrjahre*.
[60] Schiller, *Aesthetic Education of Man*, Eighth letter, pp. 49–51.
[61] Ibid., Sixth letter, p. 33.
[62] Ibid.

"This disorganization, which was first started within man by civilization and learning," has had problematic, even disastrous, consequences. Certain aspects of life and humanity, certain sensibilities essential to the highest forms of life and the spirit, have become marginalized, neglected, atrophied: "The dead letter takes the place of living understanding, and a good memory is a safer guide than imagination and feeling":[63]

We know that the sensibility of the psyche depends for its intensity upon the liveliness, for its scope upon the richness, of the imagination. The preponderance of the analytical faculty must, however, of necessity, deprive the imagination of its energy and warmth.[64]

Man is alienated from himself as a natural being and has lost that sense of oneness which characterized his primitive, "natural" state. He has moved from a "physical" to an "aesthetic" state:

As long as man, in that first physical state, is merely a passive recipient of the world of sense, i.e., does no more than feel, he is still completely One with that world; and just because he is himself nothing but world, there exists for him as yet no world. Only when, at the aesthetic state, he puts it outside himself, or contemplates it, does his personality differentiate itself from it, and a world becomes manifest to him because he has ceased to be One with it.[65]

Yet this second, "aesthetic" stage and its concomitants – separateness, rationality, and civilization – are in fact necessary elements of being human, and of human progress. They are essential moments in every act of perception, as they are crucial steps in the march of man's spiritual history. For the conflict between man's natural side and his rational, objectifying side furnishes the necessary motor of development:

I readily concede that, little as individuals might benefit from this fragmentation of their being, there was no other way in which the species as a whole could have progressed.[66]

Thus it must be this way. It is necessary that we develop analytical and practical faculties and that we consequently become estranged both from external nature and from certain natural aspects of ourselves, and it is necessary that there be conflict between the estranged elements. This "strife" of contraries (to invoke Boehme's phrase) is necessary to impel both the individual man and mankind towards a third state which Schiller calls "moral," a stage which is at once the result of beauty and

---

[63] Ibid., p. 35.
[64] Ibid., p. 39.
[65] Ibid., Twenty-fifth letter, p. 183; see also Twenty-fourth letter, p. 171.
[66] Ibid., Sixth letter, p. 41.

the outcome of an even higher form of knowing and being. This final stage is characterized by a mode of consciousness and activity that entails a passage from "beauty" to "truth."[67] Man's true moral and spiritual destiny is grounded in the fact that

> Nature is not meant to rule him exclusively, nor Reason to rule him conditionally. Both these systems of rule are meant to co-exist, in perfect independence of each other, and yet in perfect concord.[68]

> Since in the enjoyment of beauty, or aesthetic unity, an actual union and interchange between matter and form, passivity and activity, momentarily takes place, the compatibility of our two natures, the practicability of the infinite being realized in the finite, hence the possibility of the sublimest humanity, is thereby actually proven.[69]

In aesthetic unity (the enjoyment and/or the creation of beauty) "actual union and interchange" of subject and object also take place, as Schiller discusses in greater detail in another essay, *On Naive and Sentimental Poetry*.[70] The Fine Arts – which involve what Schiller calls the "play drive" (*Spieltrieb*) – are the key to the reintegration of man's reason with his feeling.

This vision of man's search for wholeness and integrity may be found in the work of the myriad Romantics who were influenced by Schiller's ideas and elaborated upon them. Through self-development, man – and society – may come in the end not only to regain (however fleetingly) lost unity, but also to attain something higher and more valuable. Thus the shape of the Romantic narrative trajectory is a spiral – a movement from initial unself-consciousness and "naturalness," through a necessary stage of differentiation and "rationalization," culminating finally in a higher integration of that which is natural and that which is rational, as well as of subject and object. The prototype of this higher unity may be found in the act of aesthetic perception, which is discussed later in this section.

The constructive role of individuation and conflict in the mind's growth and development

For Boehme, "evil" is a self-assertive, dynamic force which is a positive constituent of God. The generation of opposites out of God's undifferentiated unity (the *Ungrund*) – wrath as opposed to goodness/peace,

---

[67] Ibid., Twenty-fifth letter, p. 189.
[68] Ibid., Twenty-fourth letter, p. 181.
[69] Ibid., Twenty-fifth letter, p. 189.
[70] *On the Naive and Sentimental in Literature*, trans. Helen Watanabe-O'Kelly (Manchester: Carcanet New Press, 1981).

darkness as opposed to light, and subject as opposed to object – is part of the process by which God manifests himself to himself in all his glory. It is only (in the special case of fallen earthly life) because contraries cannot be reconciled, and wrath thereby overcome by goodness, that God's self-division has resulted in the pernicious estrangement of man from God, and the prevalence of suffering and evil on earth.

The Romantics substitute the self or mind for God. Thus the problem of God's (and the soul's) self-estrangement, and of man's estrangement from God, now becomes framed in terms of man's estrangement from nature. For the Romantics, the mind or subject is estranged from the natural world and from those "natural" parts of itself.

Although the narrative has been re-cast into this secularized terminology, familiar themes are detectable nonetheless. The first of these is that *"without contraries is no progression."* This is a famous phrase of Blake's: it is from his poem, "The Marriage of Heaven and Hell," which obviously echoes Boehme. Blake continued:

Attraction and Repulsion, Reason and Energy, Love and Hate, are necessary to Human existence. From these contraries spring what the religious call Good and Evil. Good is the passive that obeys Reason[.] Evil is the active springing from Energy.[71]

In order for there to be movement towards higher unity – what Blake at times called "organized innocence" – there must be a dynamic interplay of opposing forces and entities. Schelling, the German philosopher who, like Blake, was directly influenced by Boehme, also articulated this principle:

For every nature can be revealed only in its opposite – love in hatred, unity in strife. If there were no division of the principles, then unity could not manifest its omnipotence; if there were no conflict then love could not become real.[72]

Without the division of the world and of the self, "love could not become real," and neither could what the English Romantic poets called "joy." For the most intense and ecstatic emotions take their meaning only in relation to their opposites. As Shelley wrote in "To a Skylark":

> Yet if we could scorn
> Hate and pride and fear
> If we were things born
> Not to shed a tear
> I know not how thy joy we ever should come near.[73]

[71] In *Poetry and Prose*, p. 34.
[72] Quoted in Brown, *The Later Philosophy of Schelling*, p. 132.
[73] "To a Skylark," in *Shelley's Poetry and Prose*, ed. Donald H. Reiman and Sharon B. Powers (New York: W.W. Norton, 1977), p. 228.

The deepening of experience and heightening of emotion that characterize the artist's imaginative reunion with nature are possible only because pain and dejection have been experienced, and continue to be appreciated, as part of the human condition.

As a corollary of this, *the division between the self and the natural world, or between subject and object (and the corresponding division within man between his natural, instinctual self and his rational, individuated self) is a positive, as well as a negative and lamentable, situation.* Such division is valuable in its own right as a sign of progress and civilization. In the writings of Schiller which were cited above, there is such an assertion: human beings' "fragmentation" – the severance of nature from culture, subject from object – was necessary because "there was no other way in which the species as a whole could have progressed." Thus both individuation and reason (the Enlightenment ideal) are necessary and valuable, and embody progress, in spite of the "evil," suffering, and incompleteness that are attendant upon them.

But of course, for Romantics, linear "progress" in the Enlightenment mode is not enough. Rather, the fall into separation, fragmentation, and self-consciousness is a *felix culpa* because of the type of self, and ultimately the type of higher unity with nature, which thereby may be developed. It is necessary for the self to undergo the suffering entailed in the experience of division, conflict, and alienation, so that it may come to know its own identity and relation to the rest of the universe (yet again there are echoes of Boehme, and of Plotinus as well). Rupture and division, and the suffering that is their concomitant, are spurs to the development and growth of a deeper, more fully-developed self. Such a self, and the richness of experience of which it is capable, constitutes its own reward. Part of the "reward," then, is simply maturity itself; but the reward also consists of the capacity of the mature, philosophical or imaginative mind for a higher unity with its objects, a capacity which will be further described later in this section.

The Romantic crisis

In many Romantic literary narratives, there occurs a distinct episode of crisis, a moment or series of events in which the subject experiences profound disillusionment and despair, and reaches a crossroads or turning-point in terms of further development. Such crises often involve revelations of the disparity between confident, joyous expectation and a harsher, disappointing reality, between the ideal and the real. There are often intense, unexpected encounters with evil and suffering. The theme of "contraries" also may be prominent; heightened recognition of the conflicts and divisions that characterize human life engenders a sense of self-consciousness (and its complement, alienation) in the subject, who also experiences despair, or, as the English poets called it, "dejection."

It appears that this Romantic depiction of the experience of rupture and "dejection" is a secular transformation of certain aspects of the Christian mystical narrative which was described in Chapters 5 and 6. There are actually two episodes in Neoplatonized Biblical narratives which entail an awareness of the rupture between man and God, and the soul's consequent distress. The first is an episode of "external" history – the moment when Adam and Eve become aware of their sinfulness, mortality, and estrangement from God. Their subsequent existence thus becomes permeated with self-consciousness and a longing for reunion with God, a longing that cannot be fulfilled until history reaches its climax. The second type of crisis found in many Christian mystical narratives is not an event of external history but rather a moment in the life of the individual soul. This is the moment at which the already-fallen individual recognizes his or her distance from God, as well as the extent of the conflict and suffering inherent in earthly life. This dark and melancholy period may be followed by a sort of breakthrough to a higher level of knowledge and being, or even by a glimpse of the inner light of the Divine. The Romantic crisis, then, embodies a secular transformation of this much older cluster of spiritual themes. In Wordsworth's *The Prelude*, for example, the crisis of rupture and self-consciousness depicted in Book VI is symbolized both in terms of recent historical events (i.e., the French Revolution and its bloody aftermath) and in terms of the narrator's relationship to the natural landscape.[74] The Revolution, which initially had Europe "thrilled with joy" ("France standing on top of golden hours/And human nature seeming born again"),[75] is quickly revealed to possess its own destructiveness and treachery.[76] The disappointment felt by the narrator at the dashing of his millenarian political hopes is mirrored in his subsequent experience of chagrin upon discovering that, instead of being headed for the glorious peak of the mountain he is climbing, he has already begun his descent.[77] In the context of these disappointments, the narrator experiences a heightened awareness of the divisions, disparities, and oppositions that comprise the human condition. The recognition of

---

[74] Abrams, *Natural Supernaturalism*, pp. 448–62, contains an explication and interpretation of this section of *The Prelude*.

[75] *The Prelude* (1850 version), lines 339–41.

[76] Ibid., lines 414–88.

[77] Ibid., lines 580–96.

such contraries engenders a sense of self-consciousness and isolation in the subject, and, along with these emotions, the aforementioned despair and "dejection."

In a poem by Friedrich Schiller entitled "The Walk" ("Die Spaziergang"), the speaker's "moment of truth" also combines a vision of the violent, disillusioning aftermath of the French Revolution (and thus the failure of reason and culture alone to redeem the world) with a symbolic image of the landscape. In this case, the narrator believes himself to be safely ascending a well-marked path up a mountain (symbolizing the progress of civilization), but finds instead that he has abruptly come to a precipice that seemingly is at the end of the world.[78]

In both these poems, then, the achievements of civilization, individuation and rationality are revealed to contain their own evil and destructive dimensions. There is a heightened sense of the self's estrangement and isolation, and a recognition of the coexistence of evil and goodness, joy and pain, in the world. Although in both *The Prelude* and "The Walk" a higher integration or resolution of the crisis does, ultimately, occur, there are numerous Romantic poems in which it does not. For example, at the end of Coleridge's crisis-poem, "Dejection: An Ode," the narrator remains stuck in the state of dejection, although it is uncertain as to whether he is destined to remain that way.[79] Nonetheless, although in this poem Coleridge is caught at a moment of bleakness (imaginative reunion and "joy" apparently impossible), the larger vision of hope and transcendence, of crisis-resolution via the integration of opposites, still dominates his (at least during his youth), as well as other Romantics', philosophical systems.[80]

One difference between the resolution of the individual spiritual "crisis" in Christian mystical devotional literature and its resolution (insofar

[78] "And the glade opening, with a sudden glare/Lets in the blinding day! Before me, heaven/With all its far unbounded! – one blue hill/Ending the gradual world – in vapor/Where/I stand upon the mountain summit, lo/As sink its sides precipitous before me" ("The Walk," in Friedrich Schiller, *Complete Works*, trans. and ed. by Charles J. Hempel [Philadelphia: I. Kohler, 1861]). Abrams discusses this poem in *Natural Supernaturalism*, pp. 453–7.

[79] As Thomas M. Raysor and Max F. Schulz point out in their bibliographic essay on Coleridge, "[t]he outcome of 'Dejection' has...elicited considerable [critical] controversy" (in Frank Jordan, Jr. [ed.], *The English Romantic Poets: A Review of Research and Criticism* [New York: Modern Language Association of America, 1972], p. 202). Is the poet to remain stuck in his sense of estrangement and inner deadness (Of the stars, the moon, and the clouds he can only lament, early in the poem, that "I see, not feel, how beautiful they are!")? Or will his crisis, his "dark night of the soul," give way to resolution and "joy" (a word used repeatedly in the poem), in the near or distant future? See also Abrams, *Natural Supernaturalism*, pp. 275–7, 448; Humphry House, "Kublai Khan, Christabel and Dejection," in Bloom (ed.), *Romanticism and Consciousness*, pp. 304–26.

[80] See Abrams, *Natural Supernaturalism*, and House in Bloom, ibid., especially p. 324.

as it is resolved) in Romantic works has been noted by Abrams. Taking Augustine's *Confessions* as a prototype of the theological "crisis-autobiography," Abrams notes that

In Augustine's account, although his spiritual preparation has been long, the conversion is instant and absolute ... In Wordsworth's secular account of the "growth" of his mind, the process is one of gradual recovery ... and for the Christian paradigm of right-angled change into something radically new he substitutes [the typical Romantic pattern] ... in which development consists of a gradual curve back to an earlier stage, but on a higher level incorporating that which has intervened.[81]

In many Romantic narratives, then, the post-crisis development towards redemptive reunification is a gradual and progressive process, rather than an abrupt, explosive, right-angled change.

Romantic endpoints: extraordinary moments of "higher" reunion and the achievement of self-formation[82]

Of what, then, does such resolution consist? For Boehme, the end of the spiritual trajectory was conceptualized in terms of God's self-manifestation and reunion with his estranged essence at a higher, more complex level than that of the original unity. As has been discussed, the Romantics re-cast the Behmenist narrative of God's self-unfolding into different terms: instead of God being estranged from himself (and the individual soul from God), it was the mind or self that was estranged from nature (both its own natural aspects and the natural world of objects external to the subject). Correspondingly, the end of the trajectory, in Romantic terms, is not God's re-connection to his own objectified essence, but rather the self's re-connection to those natural objects and dimensions from which it has been alienated.

And, indeed, the most clear-cut ending to the spiral narrative does entail such a re-connection, a reintegration of polarities – subject and object, evil and good – at a higher level than the original unselfconscious, "innocent" unity. This is Blake's organized innocence, Hegel's spirit at home with its otherness, and Coleridge's "multeity-in-unity" – his assertion that (in Abrams' paraphrase of him) "liberty is ... to be found ... only in the communion of the individual mind with the 'earth, sea and air' of the natural world."[83]

---

[81] Abrams, *Natural Supernaturalism*, pp. 113–14.
[82] See Ibid., especially chs. 6–8.
[83] Ibid., p. 339. Abrams here refers to, and quotes, a poem by Coleridge called "Religious Musings," first written in 1794.

Such endings entail, above all, a change in *consciousness*. The Romantics took Boehme's interiorization and psychologization of the narrative even farther than radical Protestant thinkers had done. What in theological writings had been conceived as a literal coming of a new heaven and new earth now was replaced by nothing more nor less than a transformation of the inner life exclusively (although many Romantics and idealists hoped and expected, at least in their youth, that the inner transformations of individuals would have a broader social impact as well).

There are two types or aspects of this inner transformation that shall be noted here. The first of these is the actual experience of transcendence, or unity of mind and nature, which is perhaps the central Romantic aim. The second aspect of the transformation is the process of self-formation and self-overcoming itself, for this process, too – infinite and never finally achieved – was conceived as a redemptive end by Romantic thinkers. The first type of transformation entails the actual experience of illuminated "moments" – temporary experiences of oneness or transcendance or "joy." Referring to such times, Blake wrote of the "Moment in each day that Satan cannot find" which "renovates every Moment of the Day if rightly placed." Such illuminative and redemptive experiences are particularly exemplified in modes and moments of artistic creation and aesthetic perception. Coleridge wrote that the function of art is "to make the external internal, the internal external, to make nature thought and thought nature...body is but a striving to become mind."[84] This re-joining is effected via what he called the "secondary imagination,"[85] a conscious attempt to reconcile the polarities of life into a higher unity. He wrote:

Art is a mediatress between, and reconciler of, nature and man. It is, therefore, the power of humanizing nature, of infusing the thoughts and passions of man into every thing which is the object of his contemplation.[86]

As Abrams points out, Coleridge is similar to Schiller in his belief that the complex "multeity-in-unity" which is the function and effect of art is higher than the original unself-conscious unity (Blake's "innocence") of the pre-lapsarian mind (or society).

Such Romantic "moments" of illumination and transcendence are secular descendants of the Neoplatonized Christian doctrine of the inner light. The reunion, or "divine marriage," of the soul and God became the

---

[84] Coleridge, *Biographia Literaria*, vol. II, *On Poesy and Art*, p. 258.
[85] Ibid., vol. I, ch. XIII ("On the imagination, or esemplastic power"), p. 202.
[86] Ibid., vol. II, *On Poesy and Art*, p. 253.

reunion of mind and nature or subject and object; the illumination of the soul with the Divine Spark was translated into this-worldly acts of creative imagination and aesthetic perception.

In addition to extraordinary moments and experiences of reunion with nature or the object, there is another dimension that characterizes the end of the Romantic spiral trajectory. The aim of development is not only the attainment of such extraordinary moments and relationships, but also the quality of the mature mind itself. Abrams points out that the high Romantics were not the escapists or sentimentalizers they are often made out to be. "The fact is … ," he insists, "that these poets were almost obsessively occupied with the reality and rationale of the agonies of the human condition."[87] They did not ignore or deny the problem of evil; rather, they endeavored to re-frame the terms of its reality and the rationale for its existence:

Finding no longer tenable the justification of earthly suffering as a divine plan for sorting out those beings who will be translated to a better world, they undertook to justify the experience of suffering within the limits of experience itself.[88]

One consequence of this shift from otherworldly to worldly and from theological to secular was that the formation of selfhood – the growth and development of the mature mind, forged out of conflict, crisis, and suffering – came to be viewed as its own reward, an "end" of development as significant and valuable as those extraordinary moments to which the mature mind may have access. In this view, human life is characterized by an ongoing struggle of love against destructiveness, good against evil, hopefulness against despair. It is precisely this struggle that deepens and enriches the individual's attempts to strive for and hold on to the positive sides of these various polarities. It is in the course of this struggle that the self is formed. Its very formation (*Bildung*), and the quality of experience that it thereby becomes capable of, comprise life's triumph.

Moreover, as the attainment of joy and perfection is never complete, and as the ideal is always in dynamic interplay with the real, the spiral journey must be an infinite one. According to the Romantic vision, man's reach always must exceed his grasp, and in this fact consists much of the heroism of the human condition.

Thus the Romantics conceived a new spiritual, philosophical, and emotional vocabulary and introduced it into Euro-American culture. The Romantic repertory of symbols and patterns, and the sociocultural critique embedded therein (one which, admittedly, has been put to

[87] Abrams, *Natural Supernaturalism*, p. 443.
[88] Ibid., p. 444.

diverse social and political uses), thereby was made available to the highly-educated community that came into contact with Romantic and post-Romantic works of literature, philosophy, and even science.

One late nineteenth-century cultural figure who was exposed to, and made use of, Romantic motifs and structures was Sigmund Freud. As was noted in Chapters 1 and 2, Henri Ellenberger, Madeleine and Henri Vermorel, and William McGrath, among others, have provided evidence that many aspects of Freudian psychoanalysis evince a profound Romantic influence. This influence is manifest, state Vermorel and Vermorel, "not only in the person and work of Freud but also in the living aspects of psychoanalysis today."[89] Thus it was not only Freud himself who was a legatee of Romantic motifs and patterns. All educated Central Europeans and Britons of the nineteenth and early twentieth century – including those analysts whose work is the subject of this study – were exposed to Romantic discourses, just as we continue to be exposed to them today. As Abrams, Charles Taylor,[90] and others have noted, Romantic visions of the self and the meaning and value of life are still very much with us in both popular and high-cultural discourse.

It is not the purpose of this book to explore the immediate historical circumstances or personal motives surrounding the emergence of Freudian or post-Freudian theories. However, it is illuminating to note that the historian Carl Schorske has identified a strong "counterpolitical" thrust in the origins of psychoanalysis.[91] The birth of "psychological man," he argues, was rooted in intellectuals' disillusionment with the public, political sphere. Viennese society at the *fin de siècle* was plagued by a "crisis of liberal culture": it was undergoing the collapse of a liberal sociopolitical regime that had sought to institutionalize core Enlightenment values. Those who had placed their personal, political, and even professional hopes in the continuing progress of democratic reform – those whose expectations were raised in anticipation of a widening scope of freedoms and opportunities – were affected both practically and subjectively when the hegemony of liberal culture was finally thwarted by reactionary and anti-Semitic forces. The disappointment and frustration that educated middle-class intellectuals and professionals (Freud

---

[89] Madeleine Vermorel and Henri Vermorel, "Was Freud a Romantic?" *International Review of Psychoanalysis* vol. 13, 1986, pp. 15–37.

[90] Taylor, *Sources*.

[91] Carl E. Schorske, *Fin-de-Siècle Vienna: Politics and Culture* (New York: Alfred A. Knopf, 1980). See especially Introduction, pp. xvii–xxx; ch. 1, "Politics and the Psyche: Schnitzler and Hofmannsthal," pp. 3–23; ch. 4, "Politics and Patricide in Freud's *Interpretation of Dreams*," pp. 181–207. See also William J. McGrath, "Freud and the Force of History," in Toby Gelfand and John Kerr, eds., *Freud and the History of Psychoanalysis* (Hillsdale, NJ: The Analytic Press, 1992), pp. 79–97.

among them) experienced in the face of liberalism's defeat engendered a heightened awareness of those elements of human nature and social life that the forces of rationality and autonomy could not fully control. Hence the turn – evident in Viennese turn-of-the-century art and literature, as well as in the birth of the psychoanalytic movement – towards an emphasis on the irrational and the instinctual, and on the dynamics of the inner life.[92]

Like the Romantic movement, then, psychoanalysis took root during a period[93] when it had become acutely clear that there were limits to progress and rationality, particularly when it came to the successful implementation of these values in social and political life. In this atmosphere of disillusionment, thinkers and artists turned to a more complex and darkly-hued vision of human motivation, frailty, and potential. And much of the vocabulary that psychoanalysts used, and have continued to use, to elaborate this more inclusive vision, is drawn from the naturalized supernatural language – of rupture and integration, spiral development, and the dynamic interplay of conflicting forces – that is the legacy of the Romantic movement.

As was explained in Chapter 1, the purpose of this study is not to document direct transmission of these religious and Romantic patterns to psychoanalytic theorists, although it should be possible to do so. Rather, the intention is to demonstrate the strong parallels between the post-Freudian psychoanalytic developmental narrative and the cultural-genealogical lineage that includes both Neoplatonized Biblical history and high Romanticism. In the following chapter, these parallels are explored.

---

[92] This is not to deny the strong liberal-Enlightenment dimension that Freud retained in his theory. As McGrath points out, while the psychoanalytic turn resulted in part from a questioning of "the monolithic faith in reason that had long characterized Austrian liberalism" (p. 80), it also embodied a way of salvaging the liberal idea of freedom: that idea now became internalized and "psychologized" through analysis's promotion of rational understanding and the strengthened ego. ("Freud and the Force of History," in Gelfand and Kerr, *Freud and the History of Psychoanalysis*) Also, the scientistic cast of post-Darwinian naturalism, with its sober blend of pessimism and optimism, is evident in the Freudian tenet that "sex was stronger than politics ... but science can control sex." (Schorske: "Politics and Patricide," in *Fin-de-Siècle Vienna*, p. 201).

[93] It is tempting to speculate that there may be a pervasive and ongoing dialectic (sometimes sequential – as when counter-Enlightenment movements are triggered by sociopolitical disappointments – but also simultaneous) in post-Enlightenment society. This dialectic poses an emphasis on the potential of politics and scientific progress to improve the human lot, against a divergent view that (while also supporting rationality and science as crucial cornerstones of advanced society) places more emphasis on the complex and dynamic nature of the inner life, and on the internal and external splits and conflicts that characterize the human condition.

8

Personal supernaturalism: The cultural genealogy of the psychoanalytic developmental narrative

Having examined the narrative in its religious and Romantic incarnations, it is time to make explicit the correspondences between those earlier versions and post-Freudian psychoanalytic theories of the development of the self. Before exploring the homologies and thematic parallels between the psychoanalytic narrative and its predecessors, however, two crucial dissimilarities between Romanticism and psychoanalysis must be noted. First, *the psychoanalytic narrative does not glorify subjectivity in the way Romantic works do.* In Chapter 7 I noted that, in Romantic thought, the self tends to take over much of God's former primacy as the first cause and prime mover of human endeavor. In some Romantic systems – e.g., Hegel's idealist philosophy – the subject, or "spirit," is even accorded ontological primacy: it actually generates the objective world with which it ultimately is reunited. The question of how the relation of mind to reality is represented in various other Romantic works (or, for that matter, in psychoanalytic and cognitive-developmental psychology) is quite difficult, far too complex to consider here. However, it does seem fair to generalize that psychoanalytic theories – though they, too, chronicle the development of subjectivity – have a much more materialist slant than Romantic works tend to exhibit. There is no ambiguity about the ontological status and characteristics of the object world. That world exists prior to, and independently of, the emergence and evolution of the self's subjective sense of it. In the psychoanalytic narrative, the child's development of an *intrapsychic sense* of the object-world is not the same as a *literal creation* of that world. The baby "creates"[1] the object, as Winnicott would say, but only in a special and qualified sense, for the assumption is that there does exist a "real"

[1] D.W. Winnicott, *Playing and Reality.* New York: Routledge, 1989.

mother independent of the baby's developing representation of her.

Second, theological and Romantic narratives are frequently intended to be read as chronicling both individual and collective history (although, as I have noted, there is a tendency to highlight the "interior" interpretation of Biblical history more strongly in Protestant mysticism and Romanticism than in earlier Christian narratives). In contrast to such psychohistorical parallelism, *the psychoanalytic narrative chronicles the individual lifecourse only*.[2] Moreover, *psychoanalytic theories place particular emphasis on infancy and early childhood as the first, prototypic, and in many ways definitive, era of self-formation*.[3] This is not the case with either the theological or the Romantic narratives (although, in the case of Romanticism, the era of childhood is accorded a prominence, as well as certain specific characteristics, which do portend the modern framework). While the capacity for true redemptive integration of the self–other cleavage (i.e., mature intimacy) must await further maturation and gradual development, the child's earliest years are considered to be the most critical period of unity, rupture, crisis, and preliminary integration.

Given, then, that the psychoanalytic narrative unfolds in the context of a naturalistic, material universe, and chronicles the intrapsychic development of a single individual, it nonetheless manifests the following similarities to the earlier systems.

The developmental spiral

In Chapter 5 I described how the linear, temporal, finite prospectivism of Biblical history assimilated the Neoplatonic circle of emanation and return. This hybrid construct was, in turn, transformed into the spiral – first Behmenist and then Romantic – in which development and redemption are characterized by what Abrams calls a "reversion to a higher level of unity."

The post-Freudian psychoanalytic narrative is shaped very much like the Romantic trajectory of unity, rupture and division into contraries, higher unity. The emergence of the self is depicted as a process in which an undifferentiated unity (what Mahler calls symbiosis) undergoes differentiation and individuation. This developmental process is not

---

[2] One might qualify this by noting that psychoanalytic theories have sometimes been used to generalize about other cultures, or about specific groups within our own society, in implicitly or explicitly evolutionaristic terms.

[3] Some of the NeoFreudians – most notably Sullivan and Horney – softened this emphasis on early development and emphasized that the self can and does change throughout life.

pain-free, but rather highly problematic. Various aspects of human psychological birth – the self's emerging sense of its separateness, of its own potential for destructive effects on those it loves, and of the uncontrollable nature and imperfections of external reality (including other persons) – force upon the self a consciousness of its internally and externally divided state. In Mahler's theory, this dawning awareness of rupture and difference culminates in a crisis of confidence, the rapprochement period. In the theories of Winnicott and Kohut, the disillusionments, necessary losses, and painful tensions inherent in development are portrayed as being experienced and negotiated on a more extended basis (through transitional phenomena, the move from object relating to object usage, and "optimal" failures of one's self-objects). In all these theories, the self that emerges out of these travails not only begins to assert itself as separate and independent, but also starts to re-work its sense of connection to that from which it has been severed. These nascent forms of re-connection (of self and other, good and bad self- and object-representations, and, in many psychoanalytic theories, love and aggression) are more complex than the original, archaic, undifferentiated forms of unity.

Thus psychoanalytic theories of personality and emotional development are in large measure stories of how the self comes to forge new, higher-level forms of connection to the objects from which it has been (at once tragically, inevitably, and felicitously) disunited. These modes of re-connection are higher in the sense that the individual who engages in them possesses the capacity to be autonomous and self-directed, and to recognize the separateness and limitations of others (some of these forms of reunion, however, entail the partial or temporary suspension of those capabilities). They include the capacity for internalization of the object (Mahler's constancy and Kohut's transmuting internalization), verbal communication, the creative process, play, Winnicott's transitional phenomena, and Kohut's "higher-level" transformations of narcissism (in which the individual, having already developed a firmly differentiated and cohesive nuclear self, engages in various forms of life-enriching re-connections with self-objects). Finally, there is the relatively late-in-development but most "redemptive" reunion of all – the capacity for mature intimate relationship, the "divine marriage" made human.

It is often noted that the use of the spiral to describe psychological development is an emulation of the biological model of development in which there is a progression from diffuseness of functioning, to greater differentiation, to an integration of the discrete parts. Certainly it is true that Hartmann, Mahler, and others sought consciously to draw on aspects of biological and evolutionary theory in constructing their models of psychic development and functioning. However, one could still question whether there is any necessary or intrinsic reason to employ biological metaphors in describing the development of essentially non-material, intangible constructs such as the psyche, the self, and object-relations.

After Darwin, of course (and even before, as was noted in Chapter 4), there was an increasing tendency on the part of social theorists to look to scientific models in general, and the theory of evolution in particular, for metaphors to explain and construct guidelines for many aspects of social life. But in addition to this obvious link with Darwin and biology, in Chapters 5, 6, and 7, I have suggested older sources of the spiral model – specifically, Boehme and some of the esoteric traditions upon which he drew. In other words, I have demonstrated that psychological narratives which describe the development of the mind or self in terms of a spiral pattern appear to have (although via indirect rather than direct trans-mission) sacred as well as naturalistic-secular roots. This, of course, echoes the views of Kessen, White, and Kaplan about developmental psychology, views described in Chapter 4. But it puts more emphasis, especially in the case of psychodynamic theory, on the persistence of *mystical* (not merely Biblical) sources of dynamic and developmental ideas.

The self's origin in and development out of a sense of undifferentiated unity with the object world

Mahler calls this "the symbiotic origin of the human condition" and sug-gests that even in adulthood, "every human being" continues to long for this state unconsciously. Winnicott asserts that the baby's earliest com-merce with the world must entail an experience of "primary creativity," of "the infant's hallucinating and the world's presenting, with moments of illusion for the infant in which the two are taken by him to be identi-cal." He too stresses that the need for illusion, in the form of experiences such as transitional phenomena, persists throughout life. And Kohut (who likewise emphasizes that adults retain a need for such illusory con-gruence, in the form of self-objects) posits that the infant needs to begin existence with a sense of "absolute perfection," abetted by the close empathic attunement of caretakers to her (psychic as well as physical) needs.

These psychoanalytic depictions of the self's initial sense of fusion with the object world are reminiscent of several concepts from the Neo-platonized Christian and Romantic narratives:

First, *human selfhood (or the subject–object rupture) originates in and emanates out of an undifferentiated unity*. In the psychoanalytic narrative, of course, this is merely an intrapsychic representation of such a unity, rather than the theological (otherworldly) or Idealist (prior to the object-world) primal unities. Second, *the recognition of one's estrangement from the "source" is associated with self-consciousness, evil, and suffering*. In psychoanalytic models, individuation is not "evil" as it is in Neo-platonism (this is further discussed below). However, the theories of Mahler et al., like the doctrines of Boehme and the Romantics, do hold that separation-individuation is experienced subjectively as involving pain and conflict, of which some residue persists throughout life. Third, *the self manifests a perpetual yearning to return to the undivided state*. In Neoplatonized Christianity, the *circuitus spiritualis* embodies this longing to return to the unity that is God.[4] Many Romantic narratives also make reference to this sentiment, which the Germans called *Sehnsucht*, "long-ing." For Mahler and the psychoanalysts, of course, this symbiotic long-ing is only part of the "developmental" story, because the individuating trend (which is discussed below), which derives from a separate source of energy, propels the individual in an anti-symbiotic direction.

> *The assumption that individuation, "contraries" (self and object, good and bad self and object), and even aggression (for some theorists) are valuable and necessary for developmental progression*

The Plotinian odyssey accords to individuation a negative moral value: the selfhood that turns away from contemplation of unity is unambigu-ously evil. We have seen how, in Behmenist and Romantic narratives, the innovation of the spiral attributes a far more positive function than did Neoplatonism to contraries and division: ruptures and contraries are now necessary for development, for they propel the subject towards reconcil-iation with its objects on a higher level, towards an integrated unity that is morally and epistemologically superior to the original, undifferentiat-ed Oneness.

In addition to continuing the Protestant mystical and Romantic trend of according a constructive role to division and differentiation, Mahler's additional innovation – further elaborating the value of individuation – is to distinguish between *individuation* and *separation*. "Individuation" – the maturation of various cognitive and motor skills, and the develop-

---

[4] David Walsh, *The Mysticism of Innerworldly Fulfillment: A Study of Jacob Boehme* (Gainesville, FL: University Presses of Florida, 1983), p. 97.

ment of a sense of autonomy – becomes the innate thrust (a constructive facet or transformation of Freud's aggressive drive) to assume and exercise one's aptitudes and characteristics. "Separation" – while also a positive goal of development – is simply the increasingly veridical awareness of one's separateness from mother and, through that, from the world. The growth of this awareness is considered to be a necessary consequence of the maturation and development of various individuation functions, particularly cognition and locomotion. The child's increasing awareness of his separateness brings to the fore his conflicts and anxieties connected to separation-individuation: these include various levels of separation anxiety, and the rapprochement conflicts surrounding the attainment of "optimal distance" and a beginning sense of identity. It also stimulates a residual longing to return to the intrapsychic state of symbiosis "for which," Mahler contends, "deep down in the original primal unconscious ... every human being strives."[5]

By distinguishing between individuation and separation, Mahler is able to make of individuation and the "longing to return to symbiosis" two distinct psychic forces. Thus her work is in concordance with the American cultural goals and indices of successful development I described in Chapter 2: autonomy, expressiveness, individuality. (As has been discussed, these values are not without their own religious roots.) Yet by also positing a residual longing for symbiosis which motivates the healthy adult to seek love and intimacy, her model simultaneously preserves some other, equally salient ideals and concepts derived from the religious/Romantic cultural lineage.

Winnicott's depiction of the constructive role of aggression as individuating energy is strikingly reminiscent of Behmenist (and some Romantic) doctrines regarding the nature of God, the world, man, and evil. Boehme depicted *Grimmigkeit* – fury or evil – as "sheer power, an intensely active force which is both productive and destructive, since it is the source of both life and evil."[6] God, moved to actualize himself in order to ultimately realize himself at a higher level, generates this "wrathful" center within himself. It is this active, wrathful, "evil" (but not evil in the moral sense) energy that propels him to objectify himself – to create a world of differentiated objects and conflicting forces. By this process of self-estrangement and reunion with his own objectified essence at a higher level, God becomes self-conscious. He reasserts his ultimate

---

[5] Margaret Mahler, Fred Pine, and Anni Bergman, *The Psychological Birth of the Human Infant* (New York: Basic Books, 1975), p. 85.

[6] Robert Brown, *The Later Philosophy of Schelling: The Influence of Boehme on the Works of 1809–1815* (Lewisburg, PA: Bucknell University Press, 1977), pp. 38–40.

goodness and perfection at a superior, more complex level than would be the case if his wrath had never overflowed and prompted him to split into opposing entities, into subject and object. As was described in Chapter 6, man figures into Boehme's cosmology in that he is microcosmos and microtheos, as well as the key actor in God's self-realization process.

With the Romantics (specifically those who drew heavily upon Boehme – e.g., the philosopher Schelling and the poet Blake), the powers and dynamics Boehme had attributed to God came to be seen first and foremost as attributes of the human mind or subject. And in our own era Winnicott can be viewed as continuing, and further secularizing and "personalizing," this once-cosmological vision. For he, too, posits a morally neutral individuating energy[7] – a self-assertive, dynamic force that propels the subject (now simply the emerging human self) to posit that which is not itself. In the terms of modern psychology, this energy drives the subject to recognize the external world of objects and thereby also to begin to acknowledge its own separateness. Individuation, which is both a good in itself and a step on the way to more mature forms of re-connection (or at least more controlled forms of regression), is seen by Winnicott to spring out of aggressive energies which in the words of Adam Phillips "invite opposition." "When the Me and the Not-Me are being established," Winnicott wrote, "it is the aggressive component that more surely drives the individual to a need for a Not-Me or an object that is felt to be external."[8]

Similarly to Boehme, who held that God's wrath only became destructive and morally evil when the balance of contraries on earth was upset (preventing God's self-realization and the achievement of salvation), Winnicott holds that it is only when aggression is "unmodified by relationship"[9] that it becomes truly destructive and pathogenic. If the development of the self goes felicitously, in other words, aggression serves the end of (and indeed is essential for) the self's reaching higher and more constructive forms of consciousness and relationship.

---

[7] Melanie Klein gave this aggressive drive a more "cruel" cast; nonetheless, her developmental vision also emphasizes the necessity of integrating aggression (for Klein, this is evinced by "envy" and phantasies of destruction of gratifying objects) with more constructive affects (concern, love, and the desire for "reparation" of one's sadistic impulses). And it, too, bears the imprint of the Behmenist–Romantic trajectory. In order to become a more fully human and moral being, the self must attain a sense of the wholeness of itself and others that can only emerge out of the tempering of aggression, a tempering that is linked to the overcoming of fragmentation ("splitting") and estrangement.

[8] "Aggression in Relation to Emotional Development," *Collected Papers*, pp. 204–18, p. 215

[9] Adam Phillips, *Winnicott* (Cambridge, MA: Harvard University Press, 1988), p. 105.

The rapprochement crisis

Although the parallels are not exact, Mahler's rapprochement crisis shares some basic and significant characteristics with the Biblical fall and the Romantic crisis of dejection.

In Biblical history, the initial and decisive rupture (apart from the creation) occurs when man is cast out of the Garden of Eden and knows sin, evil, suffering, and mortality. This fate is not to be redeemed until the Last Judgement, which is yet to come. Under the influence of Neoplatonist doctrines, this fall from innocence and paradise became a fall-out-of-unity, a fall-into-separate-selfhood, as well.

As was discussed in Chapter 7, there are actually two episodes of Christian mystical narratives that entail an awareness of the rupture between man and God, and the soul's consequent distress. The first is an episode of "external" history: Adam and Eve, eating of the Tree of Knowledge, become aware of their creatureliness and are born into sin, mortality, and suffering (the Biblical dimension), as well as separateness, self-consciousness, and shame (the Neoplatonist dimension). This awareness permeates all subsequent existence, leading to the yearning and "*Sehnsucht*" described above. The second type of episode of Neoplatonized Christian narratives is not an event of external history, but rather of the history of the individual soul-as-spiritual-pilgrim. In many Christian mystical narratives, there are depictions of a period during which the (already-fallen) individual recognizes with heightened intensity and despair his isolation and distance from God, and the evils and disturbing contradictions of this world. Characterized by a despairing and melancholy mood, this period is a necessary prelude to the individual's deeper revelation of his or her own true nature and to a final (though perhaps transitory) sense of reunion with the divine. Boehme wrote of his own crisis:

For I discovered that there was good and evil in all things, in the elements as well as in creatures, and that it went as well with the godless as with the devout in this world, and also that the barbaric nations had the best countries and that fortune aided them even more than the devout.

I became on that account completely melancholy (*ganz melancholich*) and deeply depressed (*hoch betrubet*), and no Scripture could console me although they were well known to me. For the devil would definitely not be shaken off and he frequently drummed pagan thoughts into me, of which I will be silent here.

In such depression (*Trubsal*), however, I very earnestly raised my spirit (for I understood little or nothing of what it was) up to God...and would not let go until he blessed me, that is, until he enlightened me with his Holy Spirit so that I might understand his will and be freed from my sadness (*Traurigkeit*).[10]

[10] Boehme, *Morganrothe im Aufgang* (in vol. I, *Samtliche Schriften*), XIX: 8–10 (translated by David Walsh, quoted in Walsh, *Mysticism of Innerworldly Fulfillment*, p. 42).

I have suggested that the Romantic crisis is a condensation of both types of Christian mystical episodes or moments of "rupture" (the original fall/separation and the moment of acute recognition of one's separateness and the world's evil), both of which ultimately propel the individual back towards reunion and redemption. As was described in Chapter 7, the Romantic literary scenario also involves a crisis of rupture and self-consciousness, an episode in which the subject experiences a new and heightened sense of estrangement from the natural world. In Wordsworth's *Prelude* and Schiller's "The Walk" this is precipitated both by an experience in which the narrator sees the extent of evil and suffering in the world, and by a consequent shattering of his hope for human perfectibility. (Images of the unsatisfactory outcome of the French Revolution are sometimes used to convey this sense of disillusionment.) This crisis underscores the need to come to terms with, and transcend, human limitation and the existence of contraries – evil coexisting with good, pain with joy, the ideal with the real, and so on.

Mahler's rapprochement subphase is characterized by a similar sense of rupture and disillusionment. It follows a period of elation, optimism, and relative confidence in one's own powers and invulnerability. For a brief time the toddler both "walks alone" (enjoying many of the pleasures and satisfactions of his emerging individuated powers) and is intrapsychically connected to mother and the world in a reassuring way. But with the dawning of the rapprochement era, this confident belief that one is climbing ever higher (to borrow Wordsworth's image) and that one's path is secure (to paraphrase Schiller) is irrevocably undermined. The child experiences for the first time how decisive and limiting his separateness is, and how vulnerable and alone this makes him. In addition to experiencing conflicts over this newly recognized separation between self and other, "contrary" images of the other (and of the self) also begin to be a problem for him (although "splitting" of the object-world persists past the rapprochement period).

In that it details the struggle for separate-selfhood and autonomy, Mahler's emphasis on the rapprochement subphase is very much in accord with the strain in American culture that valorizes separateness and individuality. What I have suggested above is that it is also a continuation of the spiritual/Romantic depiction of a moment or period during which man's "rupture" is experienced as particularly painful and in need of redemption and reintegration.

Redemption: constancy, authenticity, creativity, intimacy

M.H. Abrams has described how the apocalyptic/millenarian outlook, so deeply ingrained in the Biblical design of history, was accorded different meanings over time. Although initially the "coming of a new heaven and a new earth" was believed to be imminent, the failure of such an event to materialize meant that certain modifications had to be made in the way Biblical history was read. Such re-interpretation entailed a belief that the millennium would occur gradually, by means of progressive amelioration of the condition of mankind. Another strategy on the part of "Biblical exegetes" was to "[postpone] the millennium to an indefinite future and [interpret] the prophecies of an earthly kingdom as metaphors for a present and entirely spiritual change in the true believer."[11] I have described how Boehme's doctrine, and other radical Protestant mystical narratives, are regarded as being particularly significant landmarks in the interiorization of Biblical history, strengthening and intensifying earlier psychohistorical strains.

But as we have seen, the development of a more explicitly interiorized version of the narrative did not eradicate hopes for other, "external" forms of the millennium, both sacred and secular. First the abortive Puritan Revolution, and then the French Revolution, recapitulated early Christianity's raised and dashed hopes for a drastic, revolutionary change in the condition of mankind. Romantic literature may be understood as a turning-inward, a looking to the powers of the mind to effect salvation, once the expectation that such salvation could be effected from without had been so graphically violated.

"To put the matter with the sharpness of drastic simplification," asserts Abrams, "faith in apocalypse by revelation had been replaced by faith in apocalypse by revolution, and this now gave way to faith in apocalypse by imagination or cognition."[12] Whether these "naturalized" versions of apocalypse were thought to be attained at brief moments during the course of everyday life (e.g., the artistic "apocalypse by imagination" described by William Blake as "Moments in each Day that Satan cannot find," which "renovate every Moment of the Day if rightly placed"), or envisioned as truly sweeping changes in the condition of man's understanding of, and relation to, the objective world and history (e.g., the "cognitive" millennialism of Hegel), the basic idea is that of "reversion to a higher unity." The (individual and/or collective) subject, mind, or self achieves a relation to the natural world such that their respective

[11] M. H. Abrams, *Natural Supernaturalism* (New York: W. W. Norton, 1973), p. 373.
[12] Ibid., p. 374.

differentiations are preserved, but minus the pain and incompleteness of knowledge associated with separateness, division, and fragmentation.

The idea of "apocalypse by imagination" is still very much alive. In *Natural Supernaturalism* Abrams demonstrates its pervasiveness in the work of mid-twentieth-century poets. In addition, it is evident in both popular and psychological discourse on creativity. In her book, *On Not Being Able to Paint*, psychoanalyst Joanna Field (Marion Milner) says of the creative process,

It is surely through the arts that we deliberately restore the split and bring subject and object together into a particular kind of new unity ... [T]he experience of the inner and the outer coinciding...is consciously brought about in the arts, through the conscious acceptance of the as-if-ness of the experience and the conscious manipulation of a malleable material.[13]

This is a "conscious," disciplined reuniting of subject and object. It is a form of reunion that is deemed developmentally superior not only to symbiosis but also to a rigid autonomy that does not include the capacity for such controlled regressions. Field considers creativity to be both a temporarily transcendental process and a more enduringly therapeutic, personality-transforming one. Winnicott and Kohut also envision creativity as a key developmental end. By "creativity" they mean not only artistic creation strictly defined, but also a broader range of experiences and activities.

In addition to the creative process, Anglo-American psychoanalytic models of personality development evince other ideals of selfhood that are heir to the spiritual/Romantic model of redemptive reunion: constancy and transmuting internalization, authenticity (self-direction), and "apocalypse-by-intimacy."

As the rapprochement struggle is resolved, the toddler begins to develop a form of integration that Mahler calls "constancy." Mahler's "libidinal object constancy," and what Kohut calls "transmuting internalizations," can be understood, on the one hand, as evidence of increased *independence* from the environment (a salient American folk-goal, as we have seen), since they involve the internalization of certain mothering functions. But on the other hand, such internalization can be viewed as a *reunion* of self and other on a more sophisticated level: the child becomes able to tolerate actual separateness from the other, and to assume other functions heretofore performed by the caretaker, precisely because he has "taken in" a representation of the other, and made it a part of his self. For Mahler, constancy also entails another kind of

[13] Joanna Field, *On Not Being Able to Paint* (Los Angeles: J.P. Tarcher, 1957), p. 131.

synthesis – of contrasting "good" and "bad" images of the other and the self. Finally, constancy (and Kohut's transmuting internalization as well) helps the individual to cope with other forms of loss, disappointment, and frustration encountered throughout life. The dynamic underlying all these aspects of constancy thus involves the ability to reconcile and transcend split and estranged elements whose divisions and differentiations are associated with loss and limitation.

Such achievements of "constancy" *vis-à-vis* emotional objects can be seen as a process of growth and progressive "education" about the world of human relationships. The individual psyche gradually attains a more veridical knowledge and acceptance of others, the self, and the potentials and limits inherent in their re-connection. This painful-but-growth-promoting process can be considered a form of redemption in the Romantic sense that one's increasing knowledge constitutes its own reward. In addition to preserving the Romantic ideal of the *Bildung* – a celebration of the enhanced vision and enriched existence that maturity brings – some object-relational and self-psychological theories[14] also evince the survival of the notion that a strengthened or revived apprehension of one's "true self" constitutes a developmental end. This, of course, harkens back all the way to Plotinus – although, as was discussed in Chapter 2, the inner light has been completely divested of its identity with the Divine, and is now nothing but one's own unique and "authentic" self.

In addition to constancy and authenticity, there exists in current psychoanalytic theories a further goal of emotional development, one that has more "apocalyptic" connotations than does constancy *per se* and which harkens back to the Judaeo-Christian mystical idea of the "Divine Marriage." In fact, it makes of this spiritual symbol a literal human occurrence. I speak here of "intimacy," or what Mahler called "the ability to make commitments [and] form warm, intimate relationships."[15] As has been described, mature intimate love is seen to involve an integration of self and other, and of oneness and separateness, such that the "symbiotic longing" is somewhat mitigated and yet the ego functions and sense of individuality are, for the most part, retained. Mahler's associates[16] have theorized that love revives feelings from the symbiotic phase,

---

[14] This is less an explicit Mahlerian end than a Winnicottian and Kohutian one. See Chapters 2 and 3.

[15] "Analyst Focuses on Life's Early Years," *New York Times*, March 13, 1984.

[16] Martin Bergmann, "Psychoanalytic Observations on the Capacity to Love," in John B. McDevitt and Calvin Settlage (eds.), *Separation-Individuation: Essays in Honor of Margaret Mahler* (New York: International Universities Press, 1971); see also Louise Kaplan, *Oneness and Separateness: From Infant to Individual* (New York: Touchstone/Simon and Schuster, 1979).

but that the mature relationship is a "higher union" than the original symbiotic merger. Such a higher union can, at times, provide a subjective sense of "salvation" from the awareness of one's separate-selfhood, an awareness that can be a source of dejection as well as pride.

Another influential contemporary American analyst, Otto Kernberg, has voiced similar and complementary views in his essay, "Boundaries and Structure in Love Relations." More or less in line with other contemporary Anglo-American psychoanalysts, Kernberg asserts that the "normal capacity for falling and remaining in love" entails "the general capacity for a normal integration of genitality with the capacity for tenderness," (a "classical" Freudian definition) and "a stable, deep object relation with a person of the other sex (Balint, 1948)."[17]

Writing of sexual passion, which he considers to be "a fundamental [though not the only] quality of love," Kernberg contrasts the regressive merger of psychopathology (an attempt to enact the "lower" unity of symbiosis or pathological narcissism) with the benign and enriching crossing of self-boundaries of which only the individuated and internally "integrated" self is capable:

The most important boundaries crossed in sexual passion are those of the self. In contrast to regressive merger phenomena which blur self–nonself differentiation, concurring with the crossing of boundaries of the self – a step in the direction of identification with structures beyond the self – is the persistent experience of a discrete self. Crossing the boundaries of self, thus defined, is the basis for the subjective experience of transcendence. Psychotic identifications (Jacobson, 1964) with their dissolution of the self–object boundaries interfere with the capacity for passion thus defined; madness, in other words, is not in continuity with passion.[18]

The constructively regressive dimensions of mature love also are highlighted by Kohut, though he is not as explicit as Kernberg on the distinction between pathological and healthy passion. As was noted in Chapter 3, Kohut writes that "there is no mature love in which the love object is not also a self-object ... [T]here is no love relationship without mutual (self-esteem enhancing) mirroring and idealization."[19]

Yet another analyst, object-relations theorist Michael Balint, writes of adult love as including a "*unio mystica*," the temporary (regressive) attainment of what Balint considers to be "the aim of all human striving":

---

[17] Kernberg, "Boundaries and Structure in Love Relations," in *Internal World and External Reality: Object Relations Theory Applied* (New York: Jason Aronson, 1980), pp. 278–9.
[18] Ibid., pp. 289–90.
[19] Heinz Kohut, *The Restoration of the Self* (New York: International Universities Press, 1977), p. 122 fn 12.

the aim of all human striving is to establish – or, probably, re-establish – an all-embracing harmony with one's environment, to be able to love in peace.[20]

For Balint, as for Mahler and Kernberg, the individual must first have developed a sufficiently realistic and enduring sense of her own separateness and differentiation in order to achieve this aim. She must be able to appreciate her object's individuality and distinctive needs in order to perform what Balint terms "the work of conquest," thereby inducing the object "to tolerate being taken for granted for a brief period, that is, to have only identical interests."[21] In this way, says Balint, the "primary harmonious mix-up" (a regression to the pre-individuated state of the human psyche) may be achieved for a brief time in the form of an orgasm and/or a "harmonious partnership." The linkage of this type of experience with Christian mysticism is quite explicit (albeit apparently reflexive and unself-conscious) in Balint: as noted above, he actually calls it the *"unio mystica."*

Of course, as was discussed in Chapter 7, the Romantics harbored a lofty set of ambitions regarding how the human imaginative reunion with the world could renovate the human condition. In this their hopes far surpassed those of psychoanalysts. Milner, Winnicott, and the others, even at their most lyrical, have been much more modest in their appraisal of the potential of the mature self and its relatedness to literally transfigure the world. In Romanticism, the sense of disjunction between the subjective experience of higher reunion and the reality of separation is perhaps less definitive and absolute than is the case in psychoanalysis, which is more explicitly materialist in its metaphysical assumptions. But, as I have shown in this chapter, the pattern of the post-Freudian psychoanalytic developmental narrative preserves Romantic (and, through them, Christian mystical) concerns and sensibilities and does so to a far greater degree than do non-psychoanalytic developmental theories. In Chapter 9 I consider some possible implications of this genealogical linkage for our appraisal of psychoanalytic theory's strengths and virtues as well as of its limitations.

---

[20] *The Basic Fault: Therapeutic Aspects of Regression* (New York: Brunner/Mazel, 1979), p. 65.
[21] Ibid., pp. 74–5.

9

Conclusion

In this study I have followed the peregrinations of the generative metaphor of theodicy/*Bildung*. That cosmopolitan Judaeo-Christian trope now resides in secular Anglo-American society under the name of the developmental narrative of the self. It is in liaison there with its own distant cultural cousin, the ideal person of Anglo-American ethnopsychology. The narrative has traveled a long way from its point of origin and over the course of its journey has become much changed in aspect, yet it still carries the mark of its ancient heritage. Its lineage is most tellingly revealed in the way it constructs the dilemmas of human existence, the way in which it bears the stamp of an inherited spiritual problematic of ultimate concern.

Such an understanding of the roots and nature of psychoanalytic developmental theories builds upon and further develops broader philosophical challenges to those theories' objectivist and naturalist status. By highlighting their cultural character and spiritual aspect, as well as pointing out their intimate entanglement with social practice, I have intended this work to be a contribution to the more general project of reconsidering the meanings, uses, value, and limitations of psychoanalysis and developmental theory in contemporary society. What are the implications of my analysis, which brings the metaphoricity and theodicy-like character of the developmental trope to the foreground? Does such an understanding of psychoanalysis and development have consequences for how we should appraise the value and usefulness of such theories? In this final chapter I briefly consider several possible ways to approach these questions. First, however, I explore the narrative's persistence and compelling quality in terms of its linkage to theodicy and counter-Enlightenment discourses.

Psychoanalytic developmental psychology as theodicy and counter-Enlightenment discourse

I have argued that contemporary Anglo-American psychoanalytic developmental theories are cast and elaborated in terms of a generative metaphor that has an ancient and culturally distinctive source: the Judaeo-Christian mystical narrative of the history of the soul. This narrative pattern has been progressively secularized and interiorized: the entire trajectory now is seen to take place in this world, over the course of an "ordinary" life. Moreover, it is now told as the story of the development of the individual personality – not of the history of the race, or the world. In place of the Plotinian distaste for individuation and individuality, and Christian mystics' ambivalence regarding them, psychoanalytic developmental psychology imbues individuation (in the Mahlerian rather than the Jungian sense) with an unambiguously positive value; it is made an end of development in itself. As for that other end of development, exemplified in the capacity for intimate relationship, it too has been modified over the course of time and disenchantment. The essentially rationalist and materialist view of the world in which psychoanalytic theory participates dictates that the forms of "redemption" still permitted us by psychoanalysis – intimacy, authenticity, the creative process, and, in a more subtle sense, internalization itself – are more modest, more truncated, certainly less enduring and absolute than the traditional religious forms. In no sense do they constitute a remaking of the human condition, and in no sense, except a most subjective and transient one, do psychoanalytic forms of redemption constitute a remaking of the world. Yet in these forms of worldly redemption the inherited spiritual code lives on. That code supplies the rhetoric that molds and authorizes every variant of psychoanalysis's quintessentially modern vision of the possibilities and limitations that contour the course of individual life.

I have argued that the linkage of contemporary developmentalist discourse to this ancient spiritual template is not merely a formal one. Like its forebears, the psychoanalytic narrative remains a narrative of ultimate concern, spelling out the terms of the meaning of life and the sources of suffering. Thus the psychoanalytic story too, like the Judaeo-Christian mystical narrative (and like non-mystical Biblical history), is a theodicy. Weber asserted that as religions began to be more rationalized, they addressed the problem of evil and suffering in a more systematic and explicit way. The world's great religious traditions, including Judaeo-Christianity, emerged out of this rationalizing tendency. M.H. Abrams recognized that within the overarching category of Biblical theodicy there was a subcategory, which he called "the Christian theodicy of the private life,

in the long lineage of Augustine's *Confessions*, [which] transfers the locus of primary concern with evil from the providential history of mankind to the providential history of the individual self, and justifies the experience of wrong-doing, suffering, and loss as a necessary means toward the greater good of personal redemption.[1]

He added that the Romantics transformed this into "a secular theodicy – a theodicy without an operative *theos*." He actually suggested calling this form of Romantic narrative a "biodicy," implying that it served the same meaning-making function, and preserved the same structures of meaning, as the explicitly theological versions.

The Romantic narrative thus eschewed "God" and the "soul" and, in a complex transposition that has precedent in Boehme's system, substituted "mind" for both of these. The ultimate problems of existence no longer were conceived in terms of the soul's estrangement from God, but rather in terms of man's estrangement from nature. Man is estranged, so the narrative goes, both from those "natural" (uncivilized, instinctual) aspects of himself and, perhaps even more crucially and fundamentally, from "nature" as the entire world external to himself – the "object[s]" from which he, the subject, has been severed.

If Freud ultimately was more interested in the first of these forms of rupture (although his psychoanalysis did include consideration of both types of severance), the post-Freudian object-relations theorists, and ego and self psychologists, have been far more concerned with the second type. And this second type, as we have seen, is a relatively faithful secular transformation of the Neoplatonized Christian narrative of fall/rupture and redemption. Psychoanalytic developmental psychology, then, also is a "biodicy." It is a meaningful account, and to some degree a justification, of the suffering and "evil" inevitably encountered over the course of a human being's psychological development. The evils – separation, loss, disappointment, frustration, imperfection, and reactive or innate destructiveness – are viewed as necessary aspects of and/or con-comitants to the twin ends of the developmental trajectory. The first of these is *individuation*, that process by which one develops autonomy and authenticity, and gains a more veridical apprehension of reality and truth (in themselves pinnacles of developmental progress and therefore valuable goods of human existence). The second, still-higher end – the utopia, or at least the fleeting paradise of ordinary life – is *intimacy* (and

---

[1] *Natural Supernaturalism* (New York: W.W. Norton, 1973), p. 95.

the structurally similar capacities for play, healthy narcissism, and creativity). It, too, can only be attained if one has first traveled the long and difficult path towards individuation, towards what Mahler called the "consolidation of individuality and the beginnings of emotional object constancy."

Put most baldly, then, the psychoanalytic narrative of self-development is a theodicy, no less than the *Bildungsroman*, *The Phenomenology of Spirit*, or even *The Way to Christ*. It is not simply analogous to a theodicy – i.e., serving the same function as one. It is, in fact, a literal heir to a particular tradition. It is the latest issue in a succession of generations of a template that lends meaning and structure both to life's travails and to the hope (however truncated and diminished it has become in this disenchanted age) of some form of redemption from them.

It is as if the cosmos represented in our religious doctrine – the literal "heavens and the earth" – has been re-located to the arena of ordinary life, and has shrunken to the scale of the self, its development, and its relationships. Heaven and hell are in the human breast; this is the place where we find meaning and fulfillment in our lives, "where we find our happiness, or not at all." In this perception of modernization as entailing an "interiorization of all human realities" I echo the observation of the psychiatrist and philosopher J.H. van den Berg. He wrote that Luther played an important part in the "personification of religion," and that Romantics such as Schleiermacher articulated a further and more radical development in this direction in asserting that "we have only understanding of God insofar as we are God ourselves, which means insofar as we have God within ourselves." Thus was accomplished the completion of "the transference of faith to the inner life." By the end of the nineteenth century, argues van den Berg, "faith threatened to become a quality belonging entirely and only to the inner life."[2] It was at this point, he contends, that modern psychology (and psychoanalysis in particular) – the "science" of this newly interiorized reality – was born.

It is not difficult to understand why the theodicy metaphor was and continues to be invoked to constitute the narrative pattern utilized in psychoanalytic developmental psychology: The "ordinary-life" arena of the self and its relationships is the contemporary repository of once-theological concerns about the meaning of life and the nature and sources of fulfillment. But Neoplatonized Biblical history is not the only theodicy available to psychologists. There is also straightforward Biblical history, in which the fall is less explicitly associated with separation, and

---

[2] J.H. van den Berg, *The Changing Nature of Man: Introduction to a Historical Psychology* (New York: W.W. Norton, 1983), pp. 228–9.

in which, correspondingly, salvation does not entail reunion but simply the perfection of life. As has been discussed, even the idea of progress itself – so central to all scientific paradigms – draws some of its meaning and its authority from the design of Biblical history. Thus non-psychoanalytic paradigms of psychological understanding (both developmentalist and non-developmentalist) are theodicies, too, in various ways and to varying degrees. Yet, as was discussed in Chapter 4, psychoanalytic developmental psychology is different from other developmentalisms, and from other modern visions of human progress. A brief exploration of how it diverges from them makes it clear that it is not only a secular theodicy, but that it also carries an additional meaning or set of connotations.

First, psychoanalysis covers a distinctive territory: the psyche or self, the emotions, and the "irrational." More than this, psychoanalysis is a distinctive *way* of conceptualizing and analyzing the human mind as a whole. It conceives of humans as possessing enduring and relatively coherent "personalities" which, in turn, are governed by complex and conflicting "motives" that can only be understood in terms of their "dynamics," their "depth." Finally (and perhaps subsuming the other two features), psychoanalytic psychology conceives of the human condition and the lifecourse as fraught with inevitable suffering, frustration, and loss, and furnishes a framework by which at least some of these vicissitudes are given a rationale and endowed with meaning. A corollary implication is that it is essential to explicate these dimensions of human existence and to understand their role in determining individual and social activities. For apologists of psychoanalytic thinking, there is something highly attractive and compelling about including such concepts in our endeavors to describe and account for human phenomena. Psychoanalysis is considered valuable because it recognizes and explores processes that other forms of social understanding overlook, dismiss, or deny – processes that seem important and "real," and need to be included among the available forms of psychological and social explanation.

On the basis of this characterization of the nature of psychoanalysis and of a part of its allure, I would suggest that the contemporary psychoanalytic narrative of development thus has incorporated not only the Christian mystical theodicy, but also the counter-Enlightenment connotations and values that Romanticism added to that theodicy. In other words, beyond its affinities with Neoplatonized Biblical history, this developmental narrative carries an additional set of meanings and connotations. It embodies another layer of cultural significance, acquired via the translation of the mystical narrative into high Romanticism.

Some of the concerns described above – the irrational, the affective, the life and growth of the self – are characteristically Romantic preoccupations and themes. Also Romantic, and perhaps even more fundamental, is the fact that psychoanalytic modes of explanation embody a distinctive way of conceiving of experience, and of the human condition and the potentials for its renovation. The psychoanalytic mode of understanding is pitched as a challenge or supplement to purely materialist and rational-empiricist systems of social explanation (albeit a supplement that does not finally undermine the world view and metaphysic that underlie those systems). In this respect psychoanalytic views of development are heir to the Romantic protest against the inadequacy of disenchanted Enlightenment discourses.

The Romantics insisted that Enlightenment philosophies (such philosophies' own use of Biblical and even mystical metaphors notwithstanding) provided an inadequate, spiritually and morally impoverished means of making sense of the human condition. They looked backward, to Christian mysticism, and translated it into secular terms. These artists and thinkers were attempting to preserve the central spiritual and moral discourses of two millennia, while at the same time making them relevant and applicable to the concerns of their own age. In so doing, they not only developed literary narratives and philosophical systems that were more elaborately faithful to Christian mysticism than were those of the Enlightenment; they also used these narratives to tell the story of their own era. In other words, the fall was not only a fall into sin, suffering, and separation. It also symbolized the necessary movement towards autonomy and rationality, towards the civilized position mankind (and intellectuals in particular) had reached with the advent of the Enlightenment. But the necessary sufferings and losses inherent in the achievements of civilization could be redeemed, both by the enriched quality of the mature mind itself, and by that mind's capacity for an actual healing of the severance, for a higher reunion with the world and with itself.

The Romantic movement can be fruitfully understood as having introduced into European educated culture a new vocabulary for designating certain domains and modes of experience, meaning, and value. Its critique of Enlightenment and other modern European social and intellectual trends constituted an insertion of naturalistic, non-theological versions of worldly mystical Christian doctrines into Euro-American intellectual and cultural discourse. This repertory of symbols and patterns, and the sociocultural critique embodied therein (one that has been put to diverse uses, from the most reactionary to the most revolutionary), thereby was made available to the educated community that was exposed to themes and imagery found in Romantic and post-Romantic works of literature, philosophy, and even science. Thus, as has been discussed, it is in the form of this translation into Romantic literature, philosophy, and biology – a "high culture" in which all educated Central Europeans and Britons of the late nineteenth and early twentieth centuries were immersed – that the Neoplatonized Christian history of the individual soul flowed into psychoanalysis's model of the psyche and its development. Analysts' invocation of the generative metaphor of the Romantic spiral imbued psychoanalysis with dimensions and connotations that challenge or supplement more purely rationalist and empiricist models of the mind and social life.

This study was not intended to be an inquiry into the biographies or personal sensibilities of either psychoanalytic theorists or those who employ or espouse such theories. But whether or not specific psychoanalytic theorists considered themselves or could be interpreted as "crypto-Romantics," these psychoanalytic modes of explanation – particularly the set of theories I have examined – clearly may be viewed as carriers of this counter-Enlightenment set of connotations. Romantic thinkers and artists perceived a shallowness and a spiritual impoverishment in much of emerging modernity. In their view, disenchanted visions of nature, self, and history were inadequate (such visions' bright teleologies notwithstanding) to offer hope of a moral and existential integration that took full and sophisticated account of the inescapability of suffering and tragedy (an inescapability made all the more poignant and concrete by the Romantics' own experience of the French Revolution). Just as the Romantic spiral was conceived to provide a more adequate spiritual account, so psychoanalytic theories too embody a perpetuation of this tragic-hopeful sense in the midst of later-modern social life.

Thus psychoanalytic developmental theories offer a disenchanted version of Judaeo-Christian culture's most profound and pervasive tradition of commentary regarding the suffering and imperfection inherent in physical and social life; they embody, as well, a discourse on the limitations and vicissitudes of modernity's emphasis on rationality and autonomy. The theories can be seen as efforts to preserve (as well as evidence that such preservation is inevitable), through transmutation, an inherited spiritual dialectic of severance and integration, suffering and redemption. Surely their linkage to this venerable and (in the West) ubiquitous tradition of spiritual reflection is one source of these theories' continuing attraction, and arguably of their value. To understand the theories in these terms renders more comprehensible the widespread resonance of the trope, as well as its continued visibility on the cultural landscape even in the face of its most recent exile, from American medical schools' psychiatry departments.

But it is possible to appreciate these theories' wisdom – their relative sophistication and depth – yet still recognize their symbolic nature. Neither the inherited shape of the narrative nor the secular character it has lately assumed is fully or incontrovertibly dictated by the relative indeterminacy of existence (inescapable though some forms of suffering and social conflict themselves may be). Armed with this enhanced awareness of the theories' contingent aspects, we are thus afforded greater latitude to critically appraise the values and social relations that these theories express and are used to enact. Such critical self-consciousness might lead us to explore new metaphors and new types of theories, as was suggested in Chapter 1. At the very least, it can prompt us to use the theories we already have in more ironic, more playful or "resistant," and less reifying ways.[3]

Furthermore, the light I have shed on the trope's genealogy also can serve to render more visible the special pressures and demands that shape human existence in contemporary societies influenced by post-Protestant and post-Romantic culture. As has been discussed, there has been an absorption of "divine substance" into our constructions of self and world. Secularization has entailed the transfer of images of fulfillment, and depictions of the routes to it, from religious discourses to naturalistic and, increasingly, to personal and interpersonal ones. Viewed in this genealogical context, the psychoanalytic narrative comes to appear as a partially contingent scripting of a narrative of ultimate concern in which psyche and object-world have replaced soul and God as the key players.

And indeed, do we not today invest human selfhood, relationships, and productive and creative activity with heavenly hopes, with a spiritual and moral ultimacy once sought mainly through otherworldly pursuits? Psychoanalysis, of course, explicitly seeks to disabuse its patrons of just such idealized, such unrealistic, expectations. Yet at another, more subtle level it can be seen to unself-consciously perpetuate analogously intense and insistent expectations of self, relationship, and ordinary life.[4] Granted, it is not psychoanalysis alone that is the origin of this attitude – although surely it has strengthened, elaborated upon, and "normalized" it – but rather modernity itself. Arguably from late-medieval times,

---

[3] See this chapter, pp. 207–8.
[4] Philip Rieff makes a similar point in "The American Transference: From Calvin to Freud," in *The Feeling Intellect: Selected Writings* (Chicago: University of Chicago Press, 1990), pp. 10–14.

and certainly since the Renaissance and Reformation, this trend has prevailed. The Puritan ethic deemed the world consequential as a place in which we find *evidence* of salvation through the self's activity; since then, this world increasingly has become "the place in which, in the end, we find our happiness, or not at all." With those words Wordsworth spoke of a redemptive reunion of mind and nature, a salvation most readily available to the artist. Nowadays our more common and democratized utopias are self-realization and human relationship; and our hell, too, is other people.

It may even be worth asking whether – in making the drama of the self and relationships the central source and locus of ultimate meaning and fulfillment, in imbuing it with hopes and expectations that once were directed to God and the hereafter – post-Freudian psychoanalysis (along with its dilute variants) doesn't further exacerbate that strain of modernity that incites us to ask too much of ordinary life, of ourselves and others. Perhaps we (Americans particularly, along with the many others we influence) now use the personal and interpersonal spheres to play out a moral imperative of "normalcy" and fulfillment to a far greater degree than this terrible and ambiguous world can accommodate.

Human science and social order

For better and for worse, however, the absorption into worldly life of the once-otherworldly quest for reunion with the divine would seem an irreversible fact of contemporary existence. It is clear that the psychoanalytic narrative is used as a theodicy (or, more properly, a "biodicy") in contemporary American life, both in professional practice and in everyday talk. Psychological theories, especially psychodynamic ones and their variants, are employed to make sense of the distress and imperfection that we encounter in our own lives and in the lives of those whom we interpret and endeavor to help.

At the same time, psychoanalytic discourse on the self, its development, and its pathologies carries other meanings and uses besides that of being a theodicy. In addition to their indisputable theodicy-function, the human sciences and helping professions are woven into the fabric of modern social, political, and economic life in many other ways as well. We do not look to psychological and psychiatric discourses only to enhance comfort and provide healing. They also dictate how we should appraise ourselves and others, and how we should behave with our children, parents, siblings, and spouses. Beyond this, they furnish standards according to which we evaluate, measure, and legitimize or marginalize persons in many different formal and informal situations. We ask these theories (and those professionals who are authorized to employ them) to tell us whom we should hire, whom we should trust, whom to convict and whom to absolve. Thus one of the clearest certainties of contemporary life is that psychology, psychiatry, and even psychoanalytic modes of understanding, will continue to occupy a space of authority and power in social relations (from the most public to the most private) and cultural consciousness in the years to come.

Therefore it is of both epistemological and sociological interest to consider whether the epistemic status and social legitimacy of the psychoanalytic developmental trope need to be reconsidered, once that trope's metaphoricity, cultural sources, and value-suffused character have been probed. So the question must be posed: what are the implications of the fact that it is a symbolic language, a metaphorical trope with deep cultural and religious roots? Does this delegitimize psychoanalytic developmental psychology as a language of psychological and psychiatric explanation?

There are a number of possible responses to this question. One will see different morals in this genealogical story depending upon whether one is an objectivist, a pragmatist, an interpretivist, or a poststructuralist. The objectivist, for example, might celebrate this study as yet another nail in the coffin of a prescientific theory that is well lost to those who would advance objective psychological and psychiatric knowledge. On such a reading, what has been shown here is that psychoanalysis and developmental theory are more poetry than science, more theology than truth.[5] The best course of action, on this view, would be to disabuse psychology of this sort of premodern residue, the better to strive towards naturalistic knowledge of the social and psychological realms (these days, it is widely held that the most valid and scientific forms of such knowledge detail the biological "bases" of experience and behavior). The caveat I would offer about this approach, powerful (in every sense) as it is, concerns the problematic epistemic status of objectivism itself. In Chapter 1 I noted that the oppositions assumed by the objectivist – between natural object and metaphor, between empirical essence and interpreted construction – have been seriously problematized, with many if not most major twentieth-century philosophical currents flowing against this sort of thoroughgoing objectivism. Thus it would seem naive

---

[5] Of course, there are those who are engaged in attempts to preserve psychoanalytic theory by making it more "scientific" — i.e., through modification of it based on empirical research findings. In such cases, the epistemological critique of psychological objectivism applies.

to assume that there can ever be categories in psychology that are "uncontaminated" by cultural forms and social forces, as those forms and forces influence both the metaphors that we use and the valued forms of behavior and experience that we attempt to promote.

The pragmatist, in contrast to the objectivist, would not conclude from the foregoing demonstration of psychoanalysis's genealogy that psychology need necessarily disabuse itself of the theodicy/*Bildung* trope, or of any other potentially useful metaphor. Instead, she would base her appraisal on what these metaphors yield in the way of more "effective" knowledge and (in the case of clinical applications) healing. What count are the results our metaphors buy us – clinically, educationally, and for social policy. The "pragmatic" child development researcher, for example, would be primarily concerned with whether invoking a particular generative metaphor to account for certain observations leads to practices that optimize desirable outcomes. And the pragmatist clinician would simply want to know whether using a certain model to make sense of a patient, and to interact with him or her, will lead to improvement and healing.

Surely these are worthy goals, and they are compatible with the mission of the healer to adopt and make use of what "works" and what "helps." Here I do not wish to enter into a detailed discussion of pragmatism's virtues and limitations, but only to highlight one such limitation. This is that such an orientation towards psychological knowledge and therapeutic practice begs the question of what constitute "desirable" outcomes, and the related question of how social, cultural, and political-economic forces and interests play a role in determining what is deemed desirable. Many leading pragmatist philosophers, from Dewey to Rorty, have tended to assume that, in a "healthy" society at least, the symbiosis between society and psychological science will by nature be a morally felicitous one – that the social purposes served by psychology can be of unproblematic benefit to all. Yet numerous social critics – from the Frankfurt School to feminist theorists to Foucault – have pointed out that various psychoanalytic and psychotherapeutic practices and goals (i.e., the promotion, whether explicit or implicit, of certain desired traits and characteristics) are neither so unambiguously benign, nor so uncontestable, as we often tend to think. My point here is not to disparage the promotion of enhanced comfort, "choice," flexibility, and some of the other standard goals of therapy. I merely call attention to the fact that an unself-consciously pragmatic attitude can work against some types of sustained critical reflection on our society and on the ambiguities inherent in the role psychology plays in it.

There is a variant of the pragmatic approach that also has been posed as a way of gauging the value of psychological theories. I call this second version "generative pragmatism." This approach grows out of the position that the metaphors used in social and psychological theories strongly influence how we perceive ourselves and the social world. Thus, according to this view, psychologists and other social scientists have a social and moral obligation to utilize metaphors that will promote constructive and socially felicitous forms of activity. In the words of David Leary, our metaphors must be selected so as to help us "'figure out' ... the contours and relations of a future world that would be more worthy and supportive of habitation."[6]

It is unlikely, however (as most "generativists" surely recognize), that a change of vocabulary alone can accomplish all that we might hope it would do. As a general principle, it is true that we do live and act in the world on the basis of received collective ways of making sense of our selves and the world. But those constructions go beyond mere articulated vocabularies – rather, they are our practices, what Wittgenstein called our forms of life. Thus, some aspects of these shared practices and the values that inform them are not, in fact, inscribed in our formal theories.[7]

A social theorist who adopts an interpretive or hermeneutic perspective would no doubt warm to this admonition that changing the discourse alone would be a superficial and ultimately useless move. This is so, the interpretivist would contend, because not all vocabularies are equally adequate to address the way things are. But "the way things are,"[8] here, is not meant in the way the objectivist would use such a phrase. Rather, the truths interpretivists strive for are those that facilitate greater integration of the self into the community via the invocation of shared cultural traditions of understanding.

For the interpretivist, it is meaningless to attempt to conceive of a

---

[6] David E. Leary, *Metaphors in the History of Psychology* (Cambridge: Cambridge University Press, 1990), p. 361.

[7] As the social philosopher Jane Flax has written: "[l]ike the use of language, interpretation of meaning is not a purely private or unbounded process, but the rules may be so much a part of the game that it is hard to bring them to consciousness. Nor can the rules be understood solely within or as generated by language because language and discursive rules both reflect and are located within complex contexts of social relations and power" (*Thinking Fragments: Psychoanalysis, Feminism, and Postmodernism in the Contemporary West* [Berkeley: University of California Press, 1990], p. 222). One implication of Flax's insight is that in addition to studying the rhetoric of psychology and psychotherapy, we must study their pragmatics as well – the "complex contexts" in which our language is deployed.

[8] Charles Taylor, "Language and Human Nature," in *Philosophical Papers,* vol. I (Cambridge: Cambridge University Press, 1985), p. 239.

"reality" that is independent of our interpretations of it. And since persons are fundamentally self-interpreting entities – since we are interpretation "all the way down" – what psychologists should seek for their theories are narratives that correspond to the narratives that their patients, as members of this society, live by. For the interpretivist, those narratives are not to be understood as simply disembodied and arbitrary, albeit shared, accounts. Rather, they are (or at any rate they should be) expressions of the practical sociohistorical situations and predicaments in which communities of humans are immersed, predicaments that are grasped in terms of shared interpretive traditions. Thus, on this view, there is nothing inherently specious or invalid about psychoanalytic developmental psychology because it is a cultural narrative; we must appraise it in terms of how adequately it seems to capture the situation of those it purports to explain and to help.[9]

Interpretive approaches are laudable in that they recognize and celebrate the inescapably evaluative and cultural character of the social and psychological studies – and of human life in general. They are powerful, too, in their attempt to steer a middle ground between the scylla of objectivist reification and the charybdis of some of the shallower and more ethically problematic forms of relativism. But as in the case of pragmatism, what often is underthematized in interpretive approaches is their tendency to abet a certain "conservative" orientation to social life (critical as interpretivists may be of our current sociocultural system for its hyperindividualism). Pragmatic and interpretivist stances, different as they are, both evince a rather sanguine attitude regarding the social role

[9] There is no single interpretive "line" on whether psychoanalytic or developmental theories are adequate and truthful. The hermeneuticist psychologist Mark Freeman, for example, defends psychoanalytic narratives, suggesting that in many instances they embody not a "defensive retreat from real life," but rather "a desire to encounter it head-on, toward the end of understanding and explaining both one's past and present self better than had previously been possible" (*Rewriting the Self: History, Memory, Narrative* [New York: Routledge, 1993], p. 108). Two other psychologists with interpretivist leanings, Louis Sass and Philip Cushman, are more critical, at least when it comes to post-Freudian psychoanalysis. Sass, in several publications, has suggested inadequacies in at least some psychoanalytic theories. He decries their overly inward and "self"-preoccupied cast ("The Self and its Vicissitudes: An 'Archaeological' Study of the Psychoanalytic Avant-Garde," *Social Research* vol. 55, no. 4, Winter 1988, pp. 551–607), as well as their inadequacy in capturing the phenomenology, and the sociohistorical situatedness, of schizophrenic illness (*Madness and Modernism: Schizophrenia in the light of Modern Thought and Art* [New York: Basic Books, 1992]). Cushman voices concern that Kohut's theory does not sufficiently admit of its own historicity and embeddedness in a problematic political system; he calls it "an artifact that both illuminates and distorts the social world it purports to describe," and asserts that "psychological discourse [including psychoanalytic theories and practices] not only describes but also actively prescribes the empty self" ("Why the Self is Empty: Toward a Historically Situated Psychology," *American Psychologist*, vol. 45, no. 5, May 1990, pp. 599–611, p. 605).

of our metaphors or inherited traditions of discourse. For the pragmatist, metaphorical language can be put in the service of a social betterment that ultimately also promotes individual betterment and fulfillment. For the interpretivist, language and other symbolic forms should be vehicles for social integration, forming the self in terms of culturally constituted moral visions that give meaning and good order to communal and physical life.

What such orientations are in danger of underplaying is the way in which our languages of psychological understanding and classification (including those models that strive to include the self's social surround) may promote distortion and domination as well as harmony and fulfillment. Those who adopt an alternative, poststructuralist stance (a line of thinking associated with Nietszche and Foucault) are less willing to gloss over or fully accept the fact that any discourse, any tradition, imposes as it integrates and constrains as it attunes. In the discussion that follows, I draw not only on the work of Foucault[10] but also on the ideas of political theorist William Connolly, who blends Foucaultian poststructuralism (which Connolly calls "genealogy"[11]) with older structuralist ideas and a commitment to democratic pluralism.

Genealogists are acutely sensitive to the ways in which all systems of knowledge are also systems of social order; they emphasize that in modern liberal democratic societies, psychology and psychiatry play a special and central role in maintaining that order. This is because such societies aim to ensure their legitimacy not through the external forms of constraint that characterized premodern societies but rather, most often, by ensuring that the will of the people does indeed come to be more closely harmonized with the social order. It is a hallmark of modernity that citizens are incited and taught to police themselves through the creation and strengthening of their "subjectivity" (a capacity for self-monitoring and self-management). The intrusion of this modern social discipline into the self's very core is seen by genealogists to be effected in great measure by a process called "normalization."[12] In order to ensure that subjects not only will act in accord with, but also will experience themselves as endorsing, the social order, "others" (repudiated forms of behavior and experience) must be identified both within and outside the self. These

---

[10] See *Discipline and Punish: The Birth of the Prison,* trans. Alan Sheridan (New York: Random House, 1977); *The History of Sexuality, Vol. I: An Introduction* (New York: Vintage Press, 1980). See also Nikolas Rose, *Governing the Soul: The Shaping of the Private Self* (London: Routledge, 1990).

[11] His use of the term is different from the use I make of it in the rest of this book, beginning with the definition offered in Chapter 1 (see pp. 24–5).

[12] Foucault also posits related processes including "individualization" and "confession."

others serve to more sharply delineate the character and boundaries of the positive "normal" self. They are then marginalized and excluded, or contained, rehabilitated, or "cured," so that the self comes to experience itself and to be perceived as more closely harmonized with the "normal" order. As was noted above, these normalizing pressures are seen by genealogists to be enacted mainly through the human sciences and helping professions, and through the ever-widening diffusion of these disciplinary forces throughout popular culture and everyday discourse.

The genealogist (at least as exemplified in the writings of democratic theorist Connolly) recognizes that any social order requires limitations and boundaries, and that concomitant to the endorsement of certain standards there will be a demarcation and devaluation of apparently anti- thetical forms of behavior, experience, and selfhood. Thus, as Connolly suggests, "some forms of otherness" are "the unavoidable effect of social- ly engendered harmonies."[13] What the genealogist finds problematic is that the proliferation of normalizing strategies in modern life, the naming of more and more segments of the populace and aspects of the self as "others," has resulted in the marginalization, and in some cases the exclusion, of these groups and aspects of self in a manner that runs counter to those democratic ideals which (at least in principle) affirm tolerance and inclusion of difference. To some degree this tension is inherent in the nature of democratic society: Liberal democracies valorize and create "free" citizens who expect, and accord to others, respect and dignity; yet the legitimacy of such regimes is grounded in a form of self- policing that must inevitably constrict and distort some forms of experience and personhood simply by virtue of their not being that which is "required" by current social and economic institutions. But while "othering" is inevitable in any social order, and normalization may be indispensable in modern society, Connolly suggests that it might be pos- sible to develop a democratic system in which the pressure to normalize difference is not so great or so inescapable as is currently the case, and that in any case, it behooves us to adopt a more self-conscious and ironic stance towards the standards of selfhood we endorse and enforce.[14]

The genealogist's imperative, then, is that we do not wholly embrace any shared discourse, "science," or interpretive tradition, no matter how "natural," "effective," moral, or profound it appears. He would have us be more attuned to the differences and forms of being that are

---

[13] William Connolly, "Democracy and Normalization," in *Politics and Ambiguity* (Baltimore: Johns Hopkins University Press, 1985), p. 11.

[14] See, e.g., "The Dilemma of Legitimacy," and "Discipline, Politics, Ambiguity," in *Politics and Ambiguity*.

"deflected, ignored, subordinated, excluded or destroyed"[15] by a given discursive formation, and to how "the norms which bind a populace into a coherent whole can also sustain the bondage of one segment of a populace within a social whole."[16] He would ask that we become more alert to the ambiguous, tragic, and in some instances arbitrary and non-rational effects of "othering" and normalization as these are enacted in psychoanalytic,[17] developmental, or any other "helping" discourse.

While the genealogical stance offers greater critical leverage than do the other perspectives, questions can be raised regarding its viability. Some would suggest that no social order can thrive with so much affir-mation of difference and inclusion of its "others" – that having that much "slack" or laxity in the order can only be the mark of a disintegrating society, not an improving one. Others might wonder whether one can be a healer if one takes such an ironic view of the beliefs and values that underlie one's healing system. Finally, it could be argued that, in this age of the biologization of psychiatry and bureaucratized medicine, the genealogist's concerns run so against the normalizing and bureau-cratizing tide as to be impractical or irrelevant. (Of course, it could be countered that it is precisely this naturalizing and normalizing swell that makes it all the more urgent that such concerns be raised.)

As I have implied, I find value, as well as limitations, in three of these positions – the pragmatic, the interpretive, and the genealogical. A fuller

[15] Connolly, *Politics and Ambiguity*, "Where the Word Breaks Off," p. 155.
[16] Ibid., pp. 62–3.
[17] Ironically, psychoanalysis would seem to have the potential to be less "normalizing" than most other psychiatric discourses. Specifically, there are elements in psychoanalysis that mitigate or at least complicate the difference-excluding tendencies of normalization. For there are some strains in psychoanalysis that tend to give a somewhat ironic cast to the norms it endorses; and if these strains are not always evident in the practices and theories of analysts, nevertheless they have been present from the beginning. Put most generally, Freud as well as many of the post-Freudians at times have tended to blur the boundaries between normal and abnormal, natural and civilized, and even rational and irrational. All forms of psychic organization are to be understood as different solutions to the same tragic situation (the vicissitudes of Oedipus, and/or of separation-individuation and disillusionment). Analytic perspectives stress the inescap-ability of that situation, and the imperfect and compromised nature of all possible solutions. Certainly few who call themselves "analytic" would assert that there is any absolute or ideal "normality." Of course, analytic theories do tend to rank the compro-mises in terms of "sicker" and "less sick." But alongside such bifurcation and hierarchi-calization, there also is evident a kind of perceived continuity between "normal" self and "different" other, and among the varieties of others, that makes of difference – even that which is designated eccentric, odd, or maladaptive – something that is neither so sharply other, nor so unequivocally in need of a particular set of prescribed interventions (in need of being remade in a particular way) as the "normalizing" scenario would suggest. If psychoanalytic theories and practices, particularly in the United States, do not always give evidence of this more ironizing stance, it is not because the psychoanalytic system is, in principle, devoid of it.

treatment of their respective merits and defects must be left to future work. But whichever stance, or combination of stances, one chooses to appraise the validity and legitimacy of psychoanalytic developmental theory, it will need to be informed by an underlying theme that I have sought to exemplify and to extend in the foregoing study. This is that analyses in terms of the familiar, modernist oppositions – between tradition and reason, culture and science, even the spiritual and the secular – scarcely seem adequate to account for how social knowledge is constructed and deployed in contemporary life. It has become increasingly evident that such bifurcations need to be reconsidered and refined. With such refinement will come a deeper understanding of the complex interplay between the healing and social-ordering functions of human science, and of the consequences that follow from our practices as contemporary knowers and healers.

Bibliography

Abrams, M.H. *Natural Supernaturalism.* New York: W.W. Norton, 1973.
"Rationality and Imagination in Cultural History: A Reply to Wayne Booth," *Critical Inquiry*, Spring 1976, pp. 447–64.

Abu-Lughod, Lila. "Writing Against Culture," in Richard G. Fox (ed.), *Recapturing Anthropology: Working in the Present.* Santa Fe: School of American Research Press, 1991, pp. 137–62.

Adler, Gerald. "Psychotherapy of the Narcissistic Personality Disorder Patient: Two Contrary Approaches," *American Journal of Psychiatry,* vol. 143, no. 4, April 1986, pp. 430–6.

Armstrong, A.H. "Plotinus," *Cambridge History of Later Greek and Early Medieval Philosophy*, part III. London: Cambridge University Press, 1967, pp. 195–268.
Plotinus. London: Allen and Unwin. Ethical and Religious Classics of East and West no. 10, 1953.

Arnou, René. *Le Désir de Dieu dans la philosophie de Plotin.* Rome: Presses de L'Université Gregorienne, 1967.

Ayrault, Roger. *La Genèse du romantisme allemand.* 2 vols. Paris: Aubier, 1961.

Bakan, David. *Sigmund Freud and the Jewish Mystical Tradition.* London: Free Association Books, 1990.

Balint, Michael. *The Basic Fault: Therapeutic Aspects of Regression.* New York: Brunner/Mazel, 1979.

Bate, Walter Jackson. *From Classic to Romantic.* Cambridge, MA: Harvard University Press, 1946.

Becker, Carl. "Progress," in *The Encyclopedia of the Social Sciences*, 1934.

Bellah, Robert, et al. *Habits of the Heart.* Berkeley: University of California Press, 1985.

Benz, Ernst. *The Mystical Sources of German Romantic Philosophy* (trans. Blair R. Reynolds and Eunice M. Paul). Allison Park, PA: Pickwick Publications, 1983.

Bergmann, Martin S. "Psychoanalytic Observations on the Capacity to Love." In John B. McDevitt and Calvin Settlage (eds.), *Separation–Individuation: Essays in Honor of Margaret Mahler.* New York: International Universities Press, 1971, pp. 15–40.

"On the Intrapsychic Function of Falling in Love," *Psychoanalytic Quarterly*, vol. 49, 1980, pp. 56–77.

Bernstein, Richard. *The Restructuring of Social and Political Theory.* New York: Harcourt, Brace and Jovanovich, 1976.

Beyond Objectivism and Relativism. Philadelphia: University of Pennsylvania Press, 1983.

"The Question of Moral and Social Development," in Leonard Cirillo and Seymour Wapner (eds.), *Value Presuppositions in Theories of Human Development.* Hillsdale, NJ: Lawrence Erlbaum Associates, 1986, pp. 1–12.

Best, Steven. *The Politics of Historical Vision: Marx, Foucault, Habermas.* New York: The Guilford Press, 1995.

Black, Max. *Models and Metaphors.* Ithaca: Cornell University Press, 1962.

"More about Metaphor." In Andrew Ortony (ed.), *Metaphor and Thought.* Cambridge: Cambridge University Press, 1979, pp. 19–43.

Blake, William. *The Poetry and Prose of William Blake* (ed. David V. Erdman). Garden City, NY: Doubleday, 1970.

Blanck, Gertrude and Rubin Blanck. *Ego Psychology: Psychoanalytic Developmental Psychology.* New York: Columbia University Press, 1974.

Ego Psychology II: Psychoanalytic Developmental Psychology. New York: Columbia University Press, 1979.

Beyond Ego Psychology: Developmental Object Relations Theory. New York: Columbia University Press, 1986.

Bloom, Harold (ed.). *Romanticism and Consciousness: Essays in Criticism.* New York: W.W. Norton, 1970.

Blos, Peter. "The Second Individuation Process in Adolescence." In *The Psychoanalytic Study of the Child*, vol. XXII. New York: International Universities Press, 1967, pp. 162–86.

Blum, Herbert. "The Prototype of Preoedipal Reconstruction." In Mark Kanzer and Jules Glen (eds.), *Freud and his Self-Analysis.* New York: Jason Aronson, 1979, pp. 143–63.

Blumenberg, Hans. *The Legitimacy of the Modern Age* (trans. Robert M. Wallace). Cambridge, MA: The MIT Press, 1991.

Boehme, Jacob. *The Signature of All Things with other writings* (trans. William Law, intro. Clifford Bax). New York: E.P. Dutton, 1912.

  The Confessions of Jacob Boehme (ed. W. Scott Palmer, intro. Evelyn Underhill). New York: Alfred Knopf, 1920.

  The Way to Christ (trans. John Joseph Stoudt; foreword by Rufus M. Jones). New York: Harper and Brothers, 1947.

  The Way to Christ (trans. and intro. by Peter Erb). New York: Paulist Press, 1978.

Bollas, Christopher. *The Shadow of the Object*. New York: Columbia University Press, 1987.

Booth, Wayne. "M.H. Abrams: Historian as Critic, Critic as Pluralist," *Critical Inquiry,* Spring 1976, pp. 411–45.

Brinton, Howard H. *The Mystic Will: Based on a Study of Jacob Boehme.* New York: Macmillan, 1930.

Broughton, John M. (ed.) *Critical Theories of Psychological Development.* New York: Plenum Press, 1987.

Brown, Lyn Mikel and Carol Gilligan. *Meeting at the Crossroads.* Cambridge, MA: Harvard University Press, 1992.

Brown, Robert F. *The Later Philosophy of Schelling: The Influence of Boehme on the Works of 1809–1815.* Lewisburg, PA: Bucknell University Press, 1977.

Bruner, Jerome S. "Value Presuppositions of Developmental Theory." In Leonard Cirillo and Seymour Wapner (eds.), *Value Presuppositions in Theories of Human Development.* Hillsdale, NJ: Lawrence Erlbaum Associates, 1986, pp. 19–28.

Burnham, John C. *Psychoanalysis and American Medicine, 1894–1918: Medicine, Science and Culture.* New York: International Universities Press, 1967.

Bury, J.B. *The Idea of Progress: An Inquiry into its Origin and Growth.* New York: Dover, 1987.

Buss, Allan R. *Psychology in Social Context.* New York: Irvington Press, 1979.

Cocks, Geoffrey. *The Curve of Life: Correspondence of Heinz Kohut, 1923–1981.* Chicago and London: University of Chicago Press, 1994.

Cohn, Norman. *The Pursuit of the Millennium.* New York: Oxford University Press, 1970.

Cole, Michael. "Society, Mind and Development." In Frank S. Kessel and Alexander Siegel (eds.), *The Child and Other Cultural Inventions: Houston Symposium 4.* New York: Praeger, 1983, pp. 89–114.

Coleridge, Samuel Taylor. *Poetical Works* (ed. Ernest Hartley Coleridge). London: Oxford University Press, 1969.

Biographia Literaria. (ed. J. Shawcross). Oxford: Oxford University Press, 1973.

Connolly, William. *Politics and Ambiguity.* Baltimore: Johns Hopkins University Press, 1985.

Coveney, Peter. *The Image of Childhood: The Individual and Society – A Study of the Theme in English Literature.* Harmondsworth: Penguin, 1967.

Cragg, G.R. *From Puritanism to the Age of Reason.* Cambridge: Cambridge University Press, 1950.

Cuddihy, John Murray. *The Ordeal of Civility: Freud, Marx, Levi-Strauss and the Jewish Struggle with Modernity.* New York: Basic Books, 1974.

Cushman, Philip. "Why the Self is Empty: Toward a Historically Situated Psychology," *American Psychologist,* vol. 45, no. 5, May 1990, pp. 599–611.

"Ideology Obscured: Political Uses of Self in Daniel Stern's Infant," *American Psychologist,* vol. 46, no. 3, March 1991, pp. 206–19.

Damon, S. Foster. *A Blake Dictionary: The Ideas and Symbols of William Blake.* Hanover, New Haven: University Press of New England, 1988.

Damrosch, Leopold, Jr. *Symbol and Truth in Blake's Myth.* Princeton: Princeton University Press, 1980.

Danziger, Kurt. "Generative Metaphor in the History of Psychology." In David E. Leary (ed.), *Metaphors in the History of Psychology.* Cambridge: Cambridge University Press, 1990, pp. 331–56.

Davis, Madeleine and David Wallbridge. *Boundary and Space: An Introduction to the Work of D.W. Winnicott.* London: H. Karnac Ltd., 1981.

Derrida, Jacques. *Of Grammatology* (trans. G. Spivak). Baltimore: Johns Hopkins University Press, 1976.

Dixon, Roger A. and Richard M. Lerner. "Darwinism and the Emergence of Developmental Psychology." In Georg Eckhardt, Wolfgang G. Bringmann, and Lothar Sprung (eds.), *Contributions to a History of Developmental Psychology.* New York: Mouton, 1985.

Dodds, E.R. (trans.). *Select Passages Illustrating Neoplatonism.* New York: Macmillan, 1923.

The Greeks and the Irrational. Berkeley: University of California Press, 1959.

Pagan and Christian in an Age of Anxiety. New York: W.W. Norton, 1970.

The Ancient Concept of Progress and other Essays on Greek Literature and Belief. New York: Oxford University Press, 1985.

Doi, L. Takeo. "Some Thoughts on Helplessness and the Desire to Be Loved," *Psychiatry*, vol. 26, no. 3, 1963, pp. 266–72.
The Anatomy of Dependence (trans. John Bester). New York: Kodansha International, 1973.

Dumont, Louis. *Homo Hierarchichus: The Caste System and Its Implications.* Chicago: University of Chicago Press, 1980.
"A Modified View of our Origins: The Christian Beginnings of Modern Individualism." In Michael Carrithers, Steven Collins, and Steven Lukes (eds.), *The Category of the Person.* Cambridge: Cambridge University Press, 1985.
"The Christian Beginnings: From the Outworldly Individual to the Individual-in-the-World," in *Essays on Individualism: Modern Ideology in Anthropological Perspective.* Chicago: University of Chicago Press, 1986, pp. 23–59.

Dunbar, H. Flanders. *Symbolism in Medieval Thought.* New Haven: Yale University Press, 1929.

Durkheim, Emile. "Individualism and the Intellectuals," in *On Morality and Society: Selected Writings* (ed. Robert Bellah). Chicago: University of Chicago Press, 1973.

Eagle, Morris N. *Recent Developments in Psychoanalysis.* New York: McGraw-Hill, 1984.

Ellenberger, Henri. *The Discovery of the Unconscious: The History and Evolution of Dynamic Psychiatry.* New York: Basic Books, 1970.

Emerson, Ralph Waldo. "Self-Reliance," in *Selected Essays, Lectures and Poems.* New York: Bantam, 1990.

Erikson, Erik. *Childhood and Society.* New York: W.W. Norton, 1963.

Fairbairn, W.R.D. *An Object-Relations Theory of the Personality.* New York: Basic Books, 1952.

Fancher, Raymond. *Psychoanalytic Psychology: The Development of Freud's Thought.* New York: W.W. Norton, 1973.

Fenichel, Otto. *The Psychoanalytic Theory of Neurosis.* New York: W.W. Norton, 1945.

Ferenczi, Sandor. "Stages in the Development in the Sense of Reality," in *Sex in Psychoanalysis.* New York: Basic Books, 1950.

Feyerabend, Paul. *Against Method: Outline of an Anarchistic Theory of Knowledge.* London: NLB, 1975.

Field, Joanna (Marion Milner). *On Not Being Able to Paint.* Los Angeles: J.P. Tarcher, 1957.

Fischer, David Hackett. *Albion's Seed: Four British Folkways in America.* New York: Oxford University Press, 1989.

Flax, Jane. *Thinking Fragments: Psychoanalysis, Feminism, and*

Postmodernism in the Contemporary West. Berkeley, CA: University of California Press, 1990.

Fogelson, Raymond. "Person, Self and Identity: Some Anthropological Retrospects, Circumspects and Prospects." In Benjamin Lee (ed.), *Psychosocial Theories of the Self.* New York: Plenum Press, 1982.

Foucault, Michel. *The Order of Things: An Archaeology of the Human Sciences.* New York: Pantheon, 1971.

"What is an Author?" in *Language, Counter-Memory, Practice* (ed. Donald F. Buchard). Ithaca: Cornell University Press, 1971, pp. 113–38.

Discipline and Punish: The Birth of the Prison (trans. Alan Sheridan). New York: Random House, 1977.

The History of Sexuality, Vol. 1: An Introduction (trans. Robert Hurley). New York: Vintage Press, 1980.

Fraser, Nancy. *Unruly Practices: Power, Discourse and Gender in Contemporary Social Theory.* Minneapolis: University of Minnesota Press, 1989.

Freeman, Mark. *Rewriting the Self: History, Memory, Narrative.* New York: Routledge, 1993.

Fremantle, Anne (ed.). *The Protestant Mystics* (intro. by W.H. Auden). New York: New American Library, 1964.

Freud, Anna. *The Ego and the Mechanisms of Defense* (trans. Cecil Baines). London: The Hogarth Press, 1954.

Freud, Sigmund. *The Standard Edition of the Complete Psychological Works of Sigmund Freud.* 24 vols. (trans. and ed. James Strachey). London: The Hogarth Press, 1953–1974 (SE).

Beyond the Pleasure Principle, 1900. SE, XVIII.

Introductory Lectures on Psychoanalysis, 1900. SE, XV and XVI.

Mourning and Melancholia, 1917. SE, XIV.

Group Psychology and the Analysis of the Ego, 1921. SE, XVIII.

The Ego and the Id, 1923. SE, XIX.

The Future of an Illusion, 1927. SE, XX.

Civilization and Its Discontents, 1930. SE, XXI.

Fromm, Erich. Escape from Freedom. New York: Avon Books, 1969.

Gadamer, Hans-Georg. *Truth and Method* (trans. G. Burden and J. Cumming). New York: Seabury Press, 1975.

Gaines, Atwood D. "Cultural Definitions, Behavior, and the Person in American Psychiatry." In A.J. Marsella and G.M. White (eds.), *Cultural Conceptions of Mental Health and Therapy.* Dordrecht: D. Reidel, 1982.

"From DSM I to III-R: Voices of Self, Mastery and the Other: A

Cultural Constructivist Reading of U.S. Psychiatric Classification," *Social Science and Medicine,* vol. 35, no. 1, 1992, pp. 3–24.

"Ethnopsychiatry: The Cultural Construction of Psychiatries," in *Ethnopsychiatry: The Cultural Construction of Folk and Professional Psychiatries.* Albany: State University of New York Press, 1992, pp. 3–49.

Gay, Peter. *The Enlightenment: An Interpretation.* vol. 1: The Rise of Modern Paganism. London: Weidenfeld and Nicolson, 1966.

Freud, Jews and Other Germans. New York: Oxford University Press, 1978.

A Godless Jew: Freud, Atheism and the Making of Psychoanalysis. New Haven: Yale University Press, 1987.

Freud: A Life for our Time. New York: W.W. Norton, 1988.

Gedo, John. *Psychoanalysis and its Discontents.* New York: Guilford Press, 1984.

Gedo, John E. and Arnold Goldberg. *Models of the Mind.* Chicago: University of Chicago Press, 1973.

Gedo, John E. and George Pollock. *Freud, the Fusion of Science and Humanism: The Intellectual History of Psychoanalysis.* New York: International Universities Press, 1976.

Geertz, Clifford. "'From the Native's Point of View': On the Nature of Anthropological Understanding." In Richard A. Shweder and Robert A. LeVine (eds.), *Culture Theory: Essays on Mind, Self and Emotion.* Cambridge: Cambridge University Press, 1984.

George, Charles H. and Katherine. *The Protestant Mind of the English Reformation.* Princeton: Princeton University Press, 1961.

Gergen, Kenneth J. "The Social Constructionist Movement in Modern Psychology," *American Psychologist,* vol. 40, no. 3, March 1985, pp. 266–75.

"Introduction" and "The Language of Psychological Understanding." In Henderikus J. Stam, Timothy B. Rogers and Kenneth J. Gergen (eds.), *The Analysis of Psychological Theory: Metapsychological Perspectives.* Washington, DC: Hemisphere Publishing Corporation, 1987, pp. 1–24 and 115–28.

"If Persons are Texts." In Stanley B. Messer, Louis A. Sass and Robert L. Woolfolk (eds.), *Hermeneutics and Psychological Theory: Interpretive Perspectives on Personality, Psychotherapy and Psycho-pathology.* New Brunswick: Rutgers University Press, 1988, pp. 28–51.

"Social Understanding and the Inscription of Self." In James S. Stigler, Richard A. Shweder and Gilbert Herdt (eds.), *Cultural Psychology:*

Essays on Comparative Human Development. Cambridge: Cambridge University Press, 1990.

Gergen, Kenneth J. and Mary M. Gergen. "Narrative Form and the Construction of Psychological Science." In T.R. Sarbin (ed.), *Narrative Psychology: The Storied Nature of Human Conduct.* New York: Praeger, 1986.

Gifford, Sanford. "'Repression' or Sea-Change: Fenichel's *Rundbriefe* and the 'Political Analysts' of the 1930's," *International Journal of Psycho-Analysis*, vol. 66, 1985, pp. 265–71.

Gilligan, Carol. *In a Different Voice.* Cambridge, MA: Harvard University Press, 1982.

"Remapping Development: The Power of Divergent Data." In Leonard Cirillo and Seymour Wapner (eds.), *Value Presuppositions in Theories of Human Development.* Hillsdale, NJ: Lawrence Erlbaum Associates, 1986, pp. 37–53.

Goldberg, Arnold (ed.). *The Future of Psychoanalysis: Essays in Honor of Heinz Kohut.* New York: International Universities Press, 1983.

Goodwin, Barbara. *Social Science and Utopia.* Sussex: Harvester Press, 1978.

Gorer, Geoffrey. *The American People: A Study in National Character.* New York: W.W. Norton, 1948.

Exploring English Character. New York: Criterion, 1955.

Greenacre, Phyllis. "The Childhood of the Artist," in *Emotional Growth: Psychoanalytic Studies of the Gifted and a Great Variety of Other Individuals.* New York: International Universities Press, 1971.

Greenberg, Jay and Stephen Mitchell. *Object Relations in Psychoanalytic Theory.* Cambridge, MA: Harvard University Press, 1984.

Grolnick, Simon. *The Work and Play of Winnicott.* Northvale, NJ: Jason Aronson, 1990.

Guntrip, Harry. *Psychoanalytic Theory, Therapy, and the Self.* New York: Basic Books, 1973.

Gupta, Akhil and James Ferguson. "Beyond Culture: Space, Identity and the Politics of Difference," *Cultural Anthropology*, vol. 7, no. 1, 1992, pp. 6–23.

Guthrie, W.K.C. *In the Beginning: Some Greek Views on the Origins of Life and the Early State of Man.* Ithaca: Cornell University Press, 1957.

Haldane, E.S. "Jacob Boehme in his Relation to Hegel," *Philosophical Review*, vol. 6, 1897, pp. 1446–61.

Hale, Nathan G. Jr. *Freud and the Americans.* New York: Oxford University Press, 1971.

"From Berggasse XIX to Central Park West: The Americanization of Psychoanalysis, 1919–1940," *Journal of the History of the Behavioral Sciences*, vol. 14, 1978, pp. 299–315.

The Rise and Crisis of Psychoanalysis in the United States: Freud and the Americans 1917–1985. New York: Oxford University Press, 1995.

Harrington, Mona. *The Dream of Deliverance in American Politics.* New York: Alfred A. Knopf, 1986.

Hartmann, Heinz. *Ego Psychology and the Problem of Adaptation* (trans. David Rapaport). New York: International Universities Press, 1958.

Essays on Ego Psychology. New York: International Universities Press, 1964.

Heelas, Paul. "Emotion Talk Across Cultures." In Rom Harré (ed.), *The Social Construction of Emotion.* Oxford: Basil Blackwell, 1986, pp. 234–66.

Heelas, P. and A. Lock. *Indigenous Psychologies: The Anthropology of the Self.* New York: Academic Press, 1981.

Heidegger, Martin. *Being and Time* (trans. J. Macquarrie and E. Robinson). New York: Harper and Row, 1962.

Heller, Thomas C., Morton Sosna, and David E. Wellbery (eds.). *Reconstructing Individualism: Autonomy, Individuality and Self in Western Thought.* Stanford: Stanford University Press, 1986.

Henriques, Julian, Wendy Hollway, Kathy Urwin, Couze Venn, and Valerie Walkerdine. *Changing the Subject: Psychology, Social Regulation and Subjectivity.* New York: Methuen, 1984.

Hesse, Mary. *Revolutions and Reconstructions in the Philosophy of Science.* Brighton, England: Harvester Press, 1980.

Hill, Christopher. *Reformation to Industrial Revolution.* New York: Pantheon, 1967.

Hirsch, E.D., Jr. *Wordsworth and Schelling: A Typological Study of Romanticism.* New Haven: Archon Books, 1971.

Hofstader, Richard. *Social Darwinism in American Thought.* Boston: Beacon Press, 1955.

Holt, Robert R. "Ideological and Thematic Conflicts in the Structure of Freud's Thought." In Sydney Smith (ed.), *The Human Mind Revisited: Essays In Honor of Karl A. Menninger.* New York: International Universities Press, 1978, pp. 51–98.

Freud Reappraised: A Fresh Look at Psychoanalytic Theory. New York: Guilford Press, 1989.

Horney, Karen. *The Neurotic Personality of Our Time.* New York: W.W. Norton, 1937.

New Ways in Psychoanalysis. New York: W.W. Norton, 1939.

House, Humphrey. "Kublai Khan, Christabel and Dejection." In Harold Bloom (ed.), *Romanticism and Consciousness: Essays in Criticism.* New York: W.W. Norton, 1970.

Hughes, H. Stuart. *Consciousness and Society: The Reorientation of European Social Thought.* New York: Alfred A. Knopf, 1958.

"The Sea Change," in *Beyond Commitment and Disillusion: The Obstructed Path and the Sea Change 1930–1965.* Middletown, CT: Wesleyan University Press, 1987.

Hughes, Judith. *Reshaping the Psychoanalytic Domain.* Berkeley: University of California Press, 1989.

Inge, William Ralph. *Christian Mysticism.* London: Methuen, 1948.

Ingleby, David. *Critical Psychiatry: The Politics of Mental Health.* New York: Pantheon, 1980.

Jacobson, Edith. *The Self and the Object World.* New York: International Universities Press, 1964.

Jacoby, Russell. *Social Amnesia: A Critique of Conformist Psychology from Adler to Laing.* Boston: Beacon Press, 1975.

The Repression of Psychoanalysis: Otto Fenichel and the Political Freudians. New York: Basic Books, 1983.

Jones, Rufus M. *Mysticism and Democracy in the English Commonwealth.* New York: Octagon, 1965.

Jordan, Frank, Jr. *The English Romantic Poets: A Review of Research and Criticism.* New York: Modern Languages Association of America, 1972.

Jung, Carl G. *The Collected Works of C.G. Jung.* London: Routledge and Kegan Paul, 1981.

Kagan, Jerome. "Presuppositions in Developmental Inquiry." In Leonard Cirillo and Seymour Wapner (eds.), *Value Presuppositions in Theories of Human Development.* Hillsdale, NJ: Lawrence Erlbaum Associates, 1986, pp. 63–78.

Unstable Ideas: Temperament, Cognition and the Self. Cambridge, MA: Harvard University Press, 1989.

Kaplan, Bernard. "A Trio of Trials." In Richard Lerner (ed.), *Developmental Psychology: Historical and Philosophical Perspectives.* Hillsdale, NJ: Lawrence Erlbaum Associates, 1983, pp. 185–228.

"Value Presuppositions in Theories of Human Development," in Leonard Cirillo and Seymour Wapner (eds.), *Value Presuppositions in Theories of Human Development.* Hillsdale, NJ: Lawrence Erlbaum Associates, 1986, pp. 89–103.

Kaplan, Louise. *Oneness and Separateness: From Infant to Individual.* New York: Simon and Schuster, 1979.

Kegan, Robert. *The Evolving Self.* Cambridge, MA: Harvard University Press, 1982.

Kernberg, Otto. *Borderline Conditions and Pathological Narcissism.* New York: Jason Aronson, 1975.

Internal World and External Reality. New York: Jason Aronson, 1980.

Kessen, William. "The American Child and Other Cultural Inventions," *American Psychologist,* vol. 34, no. 10, Oct. 1979, pp. 815–20.

"The Child and Other Cultural Inventions." In Frank S. Kessel and Alexander W. Siegel (eds.), *The Child and Other Cultural Inventions.* New York: Praeger, 1983, pp. 26–39.

Talk on "The Idea of Development" before the Wellesley Colloquium on the History of Psychology, Wesleyan University, May 1985.

Talk on "The Idea of Development" at Harvard University, March 1986.

The Rise and Fall of Development. Worcester, MA: Clark University Press, 1990.

Kirschner, Suzanne R. "Judaeo-Christian Mystical Themes in Psychoanalytic Developmental Psychology: From Cosmology to Personality." Unpublished doctoral dissertation. Harvard University, 1991.

Klein, Dennis. *Jewish Origins of the Psychoanalytic Movement.* New York: Praeger, 1981.

Klein, Milton. "On Mahler's Autistic and Symbiotic Phases: An Exposition and Evaluation," *Psychoanalysis and Contemporary Thought,* vol. 4, 1981, pp. 69–105.

Kohon, Gregorio (ed.). *The British School of Psychoanalysis: The Independent Tradition.* New Haven: Yale University Press, 1986.

Kohut, Heinz. *The Analysis of the Self: A Systematic Approach to the Psychoanalytic Treatment of Narcissistic Personality Disorders.* New York: International Universities Press, 1971.

The Restoration of the Self. New York: International Universities Press, 1977.

"Summarizing Reflections." In A. Goldberg (ed.), *Advances in Self Psychology.* New York: International Universities Press, 1980.

Kondo, Dorinne K. *Crafting Selves: Power, Gender and Discourses of Identity in a Japanese Workplace.* Chicago: University of Chicago Press, 1990.

Koyré, Alexandre. *Mystiques, Spirituels, Alchimistes.* Paris: A. Colin, 1955.

La Philosophie de Jacob Boehme. New York: Franklin, 1968.

Kris, Ernst. *Psychoanalytic Explorations in Art.* New York: International Universities Press, 1952.

"On Some Vicissitudes of Insight in Psychoanalysis," *International Journal of Psycho-Analysis*, vol. 37, 1956, pp. 445–55.

Kuhn, Thomas. *The Structure of Scientific Revolutions* (2nd edn. enl.). Chicago: University of Chicago Press, 1970.

Kurtz, Stanley. *All the Mothers Are One*. New York: Columbia University Press, 1992.

Kurzweil, Edith. *The Age of Structuralism: Levi-Strauss to Foucault*. New York: Columbia University Press, 1980.

The Freudians: A Comparative Perspective. New Haven: Yale University Press, 1989.

Lakoff, George. *Women, Fire and Dangerous Things*. Chicago: University of Chicago Press, 1987.

Lakoff, George and Mark Johnson. *Metaphors We Live By*. Chicago: University of Chicago Press, 1980.

Laplanche, J. and J.-B. Pontalis. *The Language of Psychoanalysis* (trans. Donald Nicholson-Smith). New York: W.W. Norton, 1973.

Lasch, Christopher. *The Culture of Narcissism: American Life in an Age of Diminishing Expectations*. New York: W.W. Norton, 1979.

Lasky, Melvin J. *Utopia and Revolution: On the Origins of a Metaphor*. Chicago: University of Chicago Press, 1976.

Leary, David E. "Psyche's Muse: The Role of Metaphor in the History of Psychology," and "Metaphor, Theory and Practice in the History of Psychology," in *Metaphors in the History of Psychology*. Cambridge: Cambridge University Press, 1990, pp. 1–78 and 357–67.

Lebra, Takie. *Japanese Patterns of Behavior*. Honolulu: University of Hawaii Press, 1976.

Lepenies, Wolf. *Between Literature and Science: The Rise of Sociology* (trans. R. J. Hollingdale). New York: Cambridge University Press, 1988.

Lerner, Richard. "The History of Philosophy and the Philosophy of History in Developmental Psychology: A View of the Issues," in Lerner (ed.), *Developmental Psychology: Historical and Philosophical Perspectives*. Hillsdale, NJ: Lawrence Erlbaum Associates, 1983, pp. 3–26.

LeVine, Robert. "The Self and its Development in an African Society: A Preliminary Analysis." In Benjamin Lee (ed.), *Psychosocial Theories of the Self*. New York: Plenum Press, 1982, pp. 43–65.

"Infant Environments in Psychoanalysis: A Cross-Cultural View." In James W. Stigler, Richard A. Shweder, and Gilbert Herdt (eds.), *Cultural Psychology: Essays on Comparative Human Development*. Cambridge: Cambridge University Press, 1990, pp. 454–74.

"Properties of Culture: An Ethnographic View." In Richard A. Shweder and Robert A. LeVine (eds.), *Culture Theory: Essays on Mind, Self and Emotion*. Cambridge: Cambridge University Press, 1984, pp. 67–87.

LeVine, Robert A. and Merry I. White. *Human Conditions: The Cultural Basis of Educational Development*. New York: Routledge and Kegan Paul, 1986.

Levinson, Daniel. *Seasons of a Man's Life*. New York: Ballantine, 1979.

Levy, Robert. *Tahitians: Mind and Self in the Society Islands*. Chicago: University of Chicago Press, 1973.

"Emotion, Knowing and Culture." In Richard A. Shweder and Robert A. LeVine, *Culture Theory: Essays on Mind, Self and Emotion*. Cambridge: Cambridge University Press, 1984.

Lieberman, E. James. *Acts of Will: The Life and Work of Otto Rank*. New York: Free Press, 1985.

Lipset, Seymour Martin. "Anglo-American Society." *International Encyclopedia of the Social Sciences*. New York: Macmillan Co./The Free Press, 1968, pp. 289–301.

Loewald, Hans. *Papers on Psychoanalysis*. New Haven: Yale University Press, 1980.

Louth, Andrew. *The Origins of the Christian Mystical Tradition: From Plato to Denys*. Oxford: Clarendon Press, 1981.

Lovejoy, A.O. "Schiller and the Genesis of German Romanticism," in *Essays in the History of Ideas*. Baltimore: Johns Hopkins Press, 1948, pp. 207–27.

"On the Discrimination of Romanticisms," in *Essays in the History of Ideas*. Baltimore: Johns Hopkins Press, 1948, pp. 228–53.

"Milton and the Paradox of the Fortunate Fall," in *Essays in the History of Ideas*. Baltimore: Johns Hopkins Press, 1948, pp. 277–95.

Lovejoy, A.O. and George Boas. *Primitivism and Related Ideas in Antiquity*. New York: Octagon Books, 1965.

Lowith, Karl. *Meaning in History: The Theological Implications of the Philosophy of History*. Chicago: University of Chicago Press, 1949.

Lukes, Steven. *Individualism*. Oxford: Basil Blackwell, 1973.

Lutz, Catherine. "Ethnopsychology Compared to What? Explaining Behavior and Consciousness Among the Ifaluk." In Geoffrey M. White and John Kirkpatrick (eds.), *Person, Self and Experience: Exploring Pacific Ethnopsychologies*. Berkeley: University of California Press, 1985, pp. 35–79.

Unnatural Emotions: Everyday Sentiments on a Micronesian Atoll and their Challenge to Western Theory. Chicago: University of Chicago Press, 1988.

Lyotard, Jean-François. *The Postmodern Condition: A Report on Knowledge* (trans. Geoff Bennington and Brian Massouri). Minneapolis: University of Minnesota Press, 1984.

McDevitt, John and Calvin Settlage (eds.). *Separation-Individuation: Essays in Honor of Margaret S. Mahler.* New York: International Universities Press, 1971.

MacFarlane, Alan. *The Origins of English Individualism.* Oxford: Basil Blackwell, 1978.

McGill, David and John K. Pearce. "British-American Families." In Monica McGoldrick, John K. Pearce, and Joseph Giordano (eds.), *Ethnicity and Family Therapy.* New York: The Guilford Press, 1982, pp. 457–79.

McGoldrick, Monica, John K. Pearce, and Joseph Giordano (eds.). *Ethnicity and Family Therapy.* New York: The Guilford Press, 1982.

McGrath, William J. *Freud's Discovery of Psychoanalysis: The Politics of Hysteria.* Ithaca: Cornell University Press, 1985.

"Freud and the Force of History." In Toby Gelfand and John Kerr (eds.) *Freud and the History of Psychoanalysis.* Hillsdale, NJ: The Analytic Press, 1992.

MacIntyre, Alasdair. *After Virtue.* Notre Dame: University of Notre Dame Press, 1984.

Mahler, Margaret S. "On the Current Status of the Infantile Neurosis," in *The Selected Papers of Margaret S. Mahler.* New York: Jason Aronson, 1975.

The Memoirs of Margaret S. Mahler (ed. Paul Stepansky). New York: The Free Press, 1988.

Mahler, Margaret S., Fred Pine and Anni Bergman. *On Human Symbiosis and the Vicissitudes of Individuation.* New York: International Universities Press, 1968.

The Psychological Birth of the Human Infant. New York: Basic Books, 1975.

Mandelbaum, Maurice. *History, Man and Reason.* Baltimore: The Johns Hopkins Press, 1971.

Mann, Thomas. "Freud's Position in the History of Modern Thought," in *Past Masters and Other Papers* (trans. H.T. Lowe-Porter). New York: Alfred A. Knopf, 1933, pp. 167–200.

"Freud and the Future," in *Freud, Goethe, Wagner.* New York: Alfred A. Knopf, 1939.

Marecek, Jeanne and Rachel T. Hare-Mustin. "A Social History of the Future: Feminism and Clinical Psychology," *Psychology of Women Quarterly,* vol. 15, no. 4, December 1991, pp. 521–36.

Marcus, George and Michael M.J. Fischer. *Anthropology as Cultural Critique.* Chicago: University of Chicago Press, 1986.

Marsella, Anthony J., George Devos and Francis L.K. Hsu. *Culture and Self: Asian and Western Perspectives.* New York: Tavistock, 1985.

Martensen, Hans L. *Jacob Boehme: Studies in his Life and Teaching* (trans. T. Rhys Evans). New York: Harper and Brothers, 1949.

Mauss, Marcel. "A Category of the Human Mind: the Notion of Person; The Notion of Self" (trans. W. D. Halls). In Michael Carrithers, Steven Collins and Steven Lukes (eds.), *The Category of the Person: Anthropology, Philosophy, History.* Cambridge: Cambridge University Press, 1985, pp. 1–25.

Mazlish, Bruce. *Psychoanalysis and History.* Englewood Cliffs, NJ: Prentice-Hall, 1963.

  The Riddle of History: Great Speculators from Vico to Freud. New York: Harper and Row, 1966.

Mead, Margaret. *And Keep Your Powder Dry: An Anthropologist Looks at America.* New York: William Morrow and Company, 1942.

Meissner, William. *The Borderline Spectrum: Differential Diagnosis and Developmental Issues.* New York: Jason Aronson, 1984.

Menaker, Esther. *Otto Rank: A Rediscovered Legacy.* New York: Columbia University Press, 1982.

Messer, Stanley B., Louis A. Sass, and Robert L. Woolfolk (eds.). *Hermeneutics and Psychological Theory: Interpretive Perspectives on Personality, Psychotherapy and Psychopathology.* New Brunswick: Rutgers University Press, 1988.

Mills, C. Wright. "Situated Actions and Vocabularies of Motive," in *Power, Politics and People: The Collected Essays of C. Wright Mills.* New York: Oxford University Press, 1979.

Miller (Guinsberg), Arlene A. "Jacob Boehme: From Orthodoxy to Enlightenment," Ph.D. dissertation, Stanford University, 1971.

Miller, Perry. "The Marrow of Puritan Divinity," *Publications of the Puritan Society of Massachusetts*, vol. 32, 1937, pp. 245–300.

Modell, Arnold. *Object Love and Reality.* New York: International Universities Press, 1968.

  Psychoanalysis in a New Context. New York: International Universities Press, 1984.

Morsbach, H. and W.J. Tyler. "A Japanese Emotion: *Amae,*" in Rom Harré (ed.), *The Social Construction of Emotion.* Oxford: Basil Blackwell, 1986.

Mukerji, Chandra and Michael Schudsen (eds.). *Rethinking Popular Culture: Contemporary Perspectives in Cultural Studies.* Berkeley: University of California Press, 1991.

Murphy, Gardner and Lois B. Murphy. *Asian Psychology*. New York: Basic Books, 1968.

Nelson, Benjamin. "Self-Images and Systems of Spiritual Direction in the History of European Civilization." In S.Z. Klausner (ed.), *The Quest for Self-Control*. New York: The Free Press, 1965.

"Max Weber, Ernst Troeltsch, Georg Jellinek as Comparative Historical Sociologists," *Sociological Analysis*, vol. 36, no. 3, 1975, pp. 229–40.

On the Roads to Modernity: Conscience, Science and Civilization (ed. Toby E. Huff). Totowa, NJ: Rowman and Littlefield, 1981.

Nelson, John S., Allan Megill and Donald N. McCloskey (eds.). *The Rhetoric of the Human Sciences: Language and Argument in Scholarship and Public Affairs*. Madison: University of Wisconsin Press, 1987.

Nisbet, Robert. *History of the Idea of Progress*. New York: Basic Books, 1980.

Oberndorf, Clarence P. *A History of Psychoanalysis in America*. New York: Grune and Stratton, 1953.

Olinor, Marion Michel. *Cultivating Freud's Garden in France*. New York: Jason Aronson, 1988.

Otto, Rudolph. *The Idea of the Holy*. New York: Oxford University Press, 1958.

Mysticism East and West: A Comparative Analysis of the Nature of Mysticism. New York: Macmillan, 1960.

Pagliaro, Harold. *Selfhood and Redemption in Blake's Songs*. University Park, PA: The Pennsylvania State University Press, 1987.

Parker, Ian and John Shotter (eds.). *Deconstructing Social Psychology*. New York: Routledge, 1990.

Pepper, Stephen. *World Hypotheses: A Study in Evidence*. Berkeley: University of California Press, 1942.

Perry, Helen Swick. *Psychiatrist of America*. Cambridge, MA: Harvard University Press, 1983.

Perry, Ralph Barton. *Puritanism and Democracy*. New York: Vanguard Press, 1944.

Peterfreund, Emmanuel. "Some Critical Comments on Psychoanalytic Conceptions of Infancy," *International Journal of Psychoanalysis*, vol. 59, 1978, p. 427–41.

Peuckert, Will–Erich. *Das Leben Jacob Bohmes*. Stuttgart: Fr. Frommannes Verlag, 1961.

Phillips, Adam. *Winnicott*. Cambridge, MA: Harvard University Press, 1988.

Pine, Fred. *Developmental Theory and Clinical Process*. New Haven: Yale University Press, 1985.

Plotinus. *Enneads* (trans. Stephen MacKenna). London: Faber and Faber, 1962.

The Essential Plotinus (trans. Elmer O'Brien). New York: New American Library, 1964.

Enneads (trans. A.H. Armstrong). Cambridge, MA: Harvard University Press, 1988.

Pollock, George H. and John E. Gedo (eds.). *Psychoanalysis: The Vital Issues*. New York: International Universities Press, 1984.

Pontalis, J.-B. *Entre le rêve et la douleur*. Paris: Gallimard, 1977.

Prickett, Stephen. *Coleridge and Wordsworth: The Poetry of Growth*. Cambridge: Cambridge University Press, 1970.

Quinn, Susan. *A Mind of Her Own*. New York: Summit, 1987.

Ricoeur, Paul. *Freud and Philosophy*. New Haven: Yale University Press, 1970.

Rieff, Philip. *The Triumph of the Therapeutic: The Uses of Faith After Freud*. New York: Harper and Row, 1966.

The Feeling Intellect: Selected Writings. Chicago: University of Chicago Press, 1990.

Rist, J.M. *Plotinus: The Road to Reality*. Cambridge: Cambridge University Press, 1967.

Ritvo, Lucille. *Darwin's Influence on Freud*. New Haven: Yale University Press, 1990.

Roazen, Paul. *Freud and his Followers*. New York: New American Library, 1976.

(ed.). *Sigmund Freud*. Englewood Cliffs: Prentice-Hall, 1973.

Encountering Freud. New Brunswick: Transaction Publishers, 1990.

Robert, Marthe. *From Oedipus to Moses: Freud's Jewish Identity* (trans. Ralph Mannheim). Garden City: Anchor Press, 1976.

Robertson, Roland. "On the Analysis of Mysticism: Pre-Weberian, Weberian and Post-Weberian Perspectives," *Sociological Analysis*, vol. 36, no. 3, 1975, pp. 241–66.

Robinson, Paul. *The Freudian Left: William Reich, Geza Roheim, Herbert Marcuse*. New York: Harper and Row, 1969.

Roland, Alan. *In Search of Self in India and Japan: Towards A Cross-Cultural Psychology*. Princeton: Princeton University Press, 1988.

Rorty, Richard. *Philosophy and the Mirror of Nature*. Princeton: Princeton University Press, 1979.

Rosaldo, Michelle Z. *Knowledge and Passion: Ilongot Notions of Self and Social Life*. Cambridge: Cambridge University Press, 1980.

"Toward an Anthropology of Self and Feeling." In Richard Shweder and Robert A. LeVine (eds.), *Culture Theory.* Cambridge: Cambridge University Press, 1984, pp. 137–57.

Rose, Nikolas. *Governing the Soul: The Shaping of the Private Self.* London: Routledge, 1990.

Rudolph, Erwin Paul. *William Law.* Boston: Twayne Publishers, 1980.

Ruitenbeek, Hendrik M. *Freud and America.* New York: Macmillan, 1966.

Sampson, Edward, E. "Psychology and the American Ideal," *Journal of Personality and Social Psychology,* vol. 35 no. 1, Jan. 1977, pp. 767–82.

"The Decentralization of Identity: Towards a Revised Concept of Personal and Social Order," *American Psychologist,* vol. 40, no. 11, Nov. 1985, pp. 1203–11.

"The Debate on Individualism: Indigenous Psychologies of the Individual and their Role in Personal and Societal Functioning," *American Psychologist,* vol. 43, no. 1, Jan. 1988, pp. 15–22.

"The Deconstruction of the Self." In John Shotter and Kenneth J. Gergen (eds.), *Texts of Identity.* London: Sage, 1989, pp. 1–19.

Sass, Louis A. "The Self and its Vicissitudes: An 'Archaeological' Study of the Psychoanalytic Avant-Garde," *Social Research,* vol. 55, no. 4, 1988, pp. 551–607.

"Humanism, Hermeneutics and the Concept of the Subject." In Stanley B. Messer, Louis A. Sass and Robert L. Woolfolk (eds.), *Hermeneutics and Psychological Theory.* New Brunswick: Rutgers University Press, 1988, pp. 222–71.

"Humanism, Hermeneutics and Humanistic Psychoanalysis: Differing Conceptions of Subjectivity," *Psychoanalysis and Contemporary Thought,* vol. 12, no. 3, 1989, pp. 433–504.

Madness and Modernism: Schizophrenia in the Light of Modern Thought and Art. New York: Basic Books, 1992.

"Psychoanalysis, Romanticism, and the Nature of Aesthetic Consciousness – With Reflections on Modernism and Postmodernism," in Margery B. Franklin and Bernard Kaplan (eds.), *Development and the Arts: Critical Perspectives.* Hillsdale, NJ: Lawrence Erlbaum Associates, 1994.

Schafer, Roy. *Aspects of Internalization.* New York: International Universities Press, 1968.

A New Language for Psychoanalysis. New Haven: Yale University Press, 1976.

Scheper-Hughes, Nancy. *Death Without Weeping: The Violence of Everyday Life in Brazil.* Berkeley, CA: University of California Press, 1993.

Schiller, Friedrich. *Complete Works* (trans. and ed. by Charles J. Hempel). Philadelphia: I. Kohler, 1861.

On the Naive and Sentimental in Literature (trans. Helen Watanabe-O'Kelly). Manchester: Carcanet New Press, 1981.

On the Aesthetic Education of Man: In a Series of Letters (trans. and ed. by Elizabeth M. Wilkinson and L.A. Willoughby). Oxford: Oxford University Press, 1986.

Scholem, Gershom. *Major Trends in Jewish Mysticism*. New York: Schocken Books, 1954.

Zohar. New York: Schocken Books, 1963.

Kabbalah. New York: New American Library, 1974.

Schorske, Carl E. *Fin-de-Siècle Vienna: Politics and Culture*. New York: Alfred A. Knopf, 1980.

Shalin, Dmitri. "Romanticism and the Rise of Sociological Hermeneutics," *Social Research*, vol. 53, 1986, pp. 77–124.

Shapiro, David. *Autonomy and Rigid Character*. New York: Basic Books, 1981.

Shelley, Percy Bysshe. *Shelley's Poetry and Prose* (eds. Donald H. Reiman and Sharon B. Powers). New York: W.W. Norton, 1977.

Shotter, John. *Social Accountability and Selfhood*. Oxford: Basil Blackwell, 1984.

Shweder, Richard. "Cultural Psychology: What is it?" In James W. Stigler, Richard A. Shweder and Gilbert Herdt (eds.), *Cultural Psychology: Essays on Comparative Human Development*. Cambridge: Cambridge University Press, 1990, pp. 1–43.

Smalley, Beryl. *The Study of the Bible in the Middle Ages*. Oxford: Clarendon Press, 1941.

Spence, Donald P. *Narrative Truth and Historical Truth: Meaning and Interpretation in Psychoanalysis*. New York: W.W. Norton, 1982.

The Freudian Metaphor: Toward Paradigm Change in Psychoanalysis. New York: W.W. Norton, 1987.

"The Hermeneutic Turn: Soft Science or Loyal Opposition?" *Psychoanalytic Dialogues*, vol. 3, no. 1, 1993, pp. 1–10.

The Rhetorical Voice of Psychoanalysis. Cambridge, MA: Harvard University Press, 1994.

Spitz, Réné. *A Genetic Field Theory of Ego Formation*. New York: International Universities Press, 1959.

The First Year of Life: A Psychoanalytic Study of Normal and Deviant Object Relations. New York: International Universities Press, 1965.

Stace, W.T. *Mysticism and Philosophy*. London: Macmillan, 1961.

Stallknecht, Newton P. *Strange Seas of Thought: Studies in William*

Wordsworth's Philosophy of Man and Nature. Durham: Duke University Press, 1945.

Stam, Henderikus J. "Is There Anything Beyond the Ideological Critique of Individualism?" In Henderikus J. Stam, Warren Thorngate, Leendert P. Mos, and Bernie Kaplan (eds.), *Recent Trends in Theoretical Psychology Volume III.* New York: Springer-Verlag, 1993, pp. 143–51.

Stephenson, Peter. "Going to McDonald's in Leiden: Reflections on the Conception of Self and Society in the Netherlands," *Ethos,* vol. 17, no. 2, 1989, pp. 226–47.

Stern, Daniel. *The Interpersonal World of the Infant: A View from Psychoanalysis and Developmental Psychology.* New York: Basic Books, 1985.

Stone, Lawrence. *The Family, Sex and Marriage in England 1500–1800.* New York: Harper, 1979.

Stoudt, John Joseph. *From Sunrise to Eternity: A Study in Jacob Boehme's Life and Thought.* Philadelphia: University of Pennsylvania Press, 1957.

Sulloway, Frank. *Freud: Biologist of the Mind: Beyond the Psychoanalytic Legend.* New York: Basic Books, 1979.

Tawney, R.H. *Religion and the Rise of Capitalism.* New York: Penguin, 1984.

Taylor, Charles. "Interpretation and the Sciences of Man." In Paul Rabinow and William S. Sullivan (eds.), *Interpretive Social Science: A Reader.* Berkeley, CA: University of California Press, 1979, pp. 25–71.

"Language and Human Nature," *Philosophical Papers,* vol. I. Cambridge: Cambridge University Press, 1985.

Sources of the Self. Cambridge, MA: Harvard University Press, 1989.

Tillich, Paul. *A History of Christian Thought from its Judaic and Hellenistic Origins to Existentialism* (ed. Carl E. Braten). New York: Touchstone, 1968.

Tobin, Joseph, David Y.H. Wu, and Dana Davidson. *Preschool in Three Cultures: Japan, China and the United States.* New Haven: Yale University Press, 1989.

Tolpin, Marian. "Discussion of *Psychoanalytic Developmental Theories of the Self: An Integration* by Morton Shane and Estelle Shane." In Arnold Goldberg (ed.), *Advances in Self Psychology.* New York: International Universities Press, 1980, pp. 47–68.

Tomasic, Thomas Michael. "Neoplatonism and the Mysticism of William of St. Thierry." In Paul Szarmach (ed.), *An Introduction to the Medieval Mystics of Europe.* Albany: State University of New York Press, 1984, pp. 53–76.

Trilling, Lionel. *Freud and the Crisis of Our Culture.* Boston: Beacon Press, 1955.

Troeltsch, Ernst. *The Social Teaching of the Christian Churches,* vol. I. New York: Macmillan, 1931.

Protestantism and Progress: A Historical Study of the Relation of Protestantism to the Modern World. Boston: Beacon Press, 1958.

Trosman, Harry. "Freud's Cultural Background," in *The Annual of Psychoanalysis,* vol. I. New York: Quadrangle, 1973.

Tseng, Wen-Shing and John F. McDermott. *Culture, Mind and Therapy: An Introduction to Cultural Psychiatry.* New York: Brunner/Mazel, 1981.

Turkle, Sherry. *Psychoanalytic Politics: Freud's French Revolution.* Cambridge, MA: MIT Press, 1981.

Tuveson, Ernest Lee. *Millennium and Utopia: A Study in the Background of the Idea of Progress.* Berkeley: University of California Press, 1949.

Underhill, Evelyn. *Mysticism: A Study in the Nature and Development of Man's Spiritual Consciousness.* New York: New American Library, 1974.

Van den Berg, J.H. *The Changing Nature of Man: Introduction to a Historical Psychology.* New York: W.W. Norton, 1983.

Vermorel, Madeleine and Henri Vermorel. "Was Freud a Romantic?" *International Review of Psycho-analysis,* vol. 13, 1986, pp. 15–37.

Vidich, Arthur and Stanford Lyman. *American Sociology: Worldly Rejections of Religion and Their Directions.* New Haven: Yale University Press, 1985.

Viorst, Judith. *Necessary Losses.* New York: Simon and Schuster, 1986.

Wallace, Robert. "Progress, Secularization and Modernity: The Lowith–Blumenberg Debate," *New German Critique,* no. 22, Winter 1981, pp. 63–79.

Wallis, R.T. *Neoplatonism.* New York: Charles Scribner's Sons, 1972.

Walsh, David. "Revising the Renaissance: New Light on the Origins of Modern Political Thought," *Political Science Review,* vol. 1, 1981, pp. 27–52.

"The Historical Dialectic of Spirit: Jacob Boehme's Influence on Hegel," in *Hegel's Philosophy of History: Proceedings of the Hegel Society of America,* 1982.

The Mysticism of Innerworldly Fulfillment: A Study of Jacob Boehme. Gainesville, FL: University Presses of Florida, 1983.

Walzer, Michael. *The Revolution of the Saints: A Study in the Origin of Radical Politics.* Cambridge, MA: Harvard University Press, 1965.

Wartofsky, Marx. "The Child's Construction of the World and the World's Construction of the Child." In Frank S. Kessel and Alexander W. Siegel (eds.), *The Child and Other Cultural Inventions.* New York: Praeger, 1983, pp. 188–215.

"On the Creation and Transformation of Norms of Human Development." In Leonard Cirillo and Seymour Wapner (eds.), *Value Presuppositions in Theories of Human Development.* Hillsdale, NJ: Lawrence Erlbaum Associates, 1986, pp. 113–32.

Weber, Max. *The Protestant Ethic and the Spirit of Capitalism.* New York: Scribners, 1958.

From Max Weber: Essays in Sociology (eds. Hans Gerth and C. Wright Mills). New York: Oxford University Press, 1958.

Weeks, Andrew. *Boehme: An Intellectual Biography of the Seventeenth-Century Philosopher and Mystic.* Albany, NY: State University of New York Press, 1991.

Weintraub, Karl Joachim. *The Value of the Individual: Self and Circumstance in Autobiography.* Chicago: University of Chicago Press, 1978.

Wellek, Réné. "The Concept of 'Romanticism' in Literary History," *Comparative Literature*, vol. 1, nos. 1–2, 1949, pp. 1–23, 147–72.

Wexler, Philip. *Critical Social Psychology.* Boston: Routledge and Kegan Paul, 1983.

White, Geoffrey. "The Self: A Brief Commentary," *Anthropology and Humanism Quarterly,* vol. 16, no. 1, March 1991, pp. 33–5.

"What is Ethnopsychology?" In Theodore Schwartz, Geoffrey M. White and Catherine A. Lutz (eds.), *New Directions in Psychological Anthropology.* Cambridge: Cambridge University Press, 1992, pp. 21–46.

White, Sheldon. "The Idea of Development in Developmental Psychology." In Richard Lerner (ed.), *Developmental Psychology: Historical and Philosophical Perspectives.* Hillsdale, NJ: Lawrence Erlbaum Associates, 1983, pp. 55–77.

"Psychology as a Moral Science." In Frank S. Kessel and Alexander W. Siegel (eds.), *The Child and Other Cultural Inventions.* New York: Praeger, 1983, pp. 1–25.

Williams, George. *The Radical Reformation.* Philadelphia: Westminster Press, 1962.

"Popularized German Mysticism as a Factor in the Rise of Anabaptist Communism." In Hrsg von G. Muller and W. Zeller (eds.), *Glaube,*

Geist, Geschichte: Festschrift für Ernst Benz. Leiden: E.J. Brill, 1967.

Winnicott, D.W. *The Family and Individual Development.* London: Tavistock, 1964.

The Child, the Family and the Outside World. Harmondsworth: Penguin Books, 1978.

Collected Papers: Through Paediatrics to Psycho-analysis. New York: Tavistock, 1958.

The Maturational Processes and the Facilitating Environment. New York: International Universities Press, 1965.

Playing and Reality. New York: Routledge, 1989.

Home is Where We Start From: Essays by a Psychoanalyst. New York: W.W. Norton, 1986.

Wishy, Bernard. *The Child and the Republic.* Philadelphia: University of Pennsylvania Press, 1968.

Wittgenstein, Ludwig. *Philosophical Investigations* (trans. G. Anscombe). Oxford: Basil Blackwell, 1953.

Wolf, Ernest. "On the Developmental Line of Selfobject Relations." In A. Goldberg (ed.), *Advances in Self Psychology.* New York: International Universities Press, 1980, pp. 117–30.

Wordsworth, William. *The Prelude* (ed. J.C. Maxwell). London: Penguin Classics, 1988.

Wyss, Dieter. *Depth Psychology: A Critical History* (trans. Gerald Onn). London: George Allen and Unwin Ltd., 1966.

Yates, Frances. *Giordano Bruno and the Hermetic Tradition.* Chicago: University of Chicago Press, 1964.

Yerushalmi, Yosef Hayim. *Freud's Moses: Judaism Terminable and Interminable.* New Haven: Yale University Press, 1991.

Zaehner, Robert C. *Mysticism: Sacred and Profane.* Oxford: Clarendon Press, 1969.

"Conclusion." In R.C. Zaehner (ed.), *The Concise Encyclopedia of Living Faiths.* Boston: Beacon Press, 1967, pp. 413–17.

Index